ARCHAEOLOGY AND THE WORLD OF JESUS

ARCHAEOLOGY AND THE NEW TESTAMENT

Archaeology and the Ministry of Paul

Archaeology and the World of Jesus

ARCHAEOLOGY AND THE WORLD OF JESUS

A VISUAL GUIDE

David A. deSilva

Published by Baker Academic
a division of Baker Publishing Group
Grand Rapids, Michigan
BakerAcademic.com

Printed in the United States of America

Library of Congress Cataloging-in-Publication Data
Names: deSilva, David A., 1967– author.
Title: Archaeology and the world of Jesus : a visual guide / David A. deSilva.
Description: Grand Rapids, Michigan : Baker Academic, a division of Baker Publishing Group, [2025] | Series: Archaeology and the New Testament | Includes bibliographical references and index.
Identifiers: LCCN 2025005421 | ISBN 9781540960962 (paperback) | ISBN 9781493451661 (ebook) | ISBN 9781493451678 (pdf)
Subjects: LCSH: Bible. Gospels—Antiquities | Israel—Antiquities | Excavations (Archaeology)—Israel | Jesus Christ
Classification: LCC BS621 .D475 2025 | DDC 225.9/3—dc23/eng/20250411
LC record available at https://lccn.loc.gov/2025005421

Unless otherwise credited, photos are the author's.

Cover design by Paula Gibson.

Baker Publishing Group publications use paper produced from sustainable forestry practices and postconsumer waste whenever possible.

25 26 27 28 29 30 31 7 6 5 4 3 2 1

To Bob and Jan Archer,
with gratitude for their devotion
to the mission of Ashland University
and Ashland Theological Seminary

CONTENTS

PART 3 THE REALMS OF THE ROMAN PREFECTS

INTRODUCTION

It has long been a tradition at my church to have short "hymn sings" before our services during the summers when our choirs and other musical groups are on hiatus. Two hymns that members of the congregation request with some regularity are "Tell Me the Stories of Jesus I Love to Hear" and "I Love to Tell the Story." Those who request these songs are, in my experience, in no danger of thinking of these stories as *just* stories—pleasant tales often with good morals attached to them. But there is still the danger that we will engage these stories as words on a page in black and white (or black, red, and white) to be fleshed out in our minds however our own imaginations fancy. Those who have undertaken to travel to Israel and the Palestinian Territories with a view to visiting the sites associated with "the stories of Jesus" return to those stories with two important advantages over those who have not—a deeper sense of the rootedness of the Christian faith in a particular historical and geographical context and a far-better-equipped historical imagination with which to engage those stories.

It is my hope that this present volume will provide readers with the fruits of what such travel might be expected to supply in terms of immersing them in the archaeological and material remains of a broad selection of sites. These sites offer windows into the lived spaces and practices of the Galileans, Samaritans, and Judeans of the first century AD—which are also the lived spaces that Jesus inhabited and the practices in which he participated or, in some instances, which he critiqued.

The book opens with a historical overview of Judea and its surrounding regions from the time of Alexander the Great's conquest of Syria and Palestine (334–332 BC) through the First Jewish Revolt (AD 70), which will provide the reader with the larger story—with its various periods and important personalities—with which the discussion of the archaeological remnants of each site intersects. The remainder of the book falls, then, into three parts. The first focuses on sites in Galilee and Peraea, the territories under the authority of Antipas during the period of Jesus's active ministry, and Gaulanitis, one of the territories in the domain of Philip during the same period. The second part focuses more briefly on a number of sites representing the cities of the Decapolis, a region that figures in several episodes in Jesus's ministry. The third and largest part focuses on sites in Samaria and Judea, two of the territories under the direct oversight of a Roman prefect during Jesus's ministry. The focus in each section is limited to what each site offers to visitors in terms of opening up windows into the early first-century environment of Jesus, his opponents, and the first generation or two of his followers. It is not the goal of each section to give a comprehensive survey of any given site, such as a general tour book would be expected to provide. Material remains from the late Roman, Byzantine, and early Islamic periods are almost entirely ignored, except when these can reasonably still shed light on typical first-century structures and practices. These material remains are generally discussed only in the absence of well-preserved, earlier material remains.

Most of the sites selected have a clear connection with episodes in the life and ministry of Jesus. These include Bethlehem, Nazareth, Cana, Capernaum, Bethsaida, Chorazin, Caesarea Philippi, Jericho, Emmaus, and, of course, Jerusalem. They also include Gadara's (alternatively, Gerasa's) hinterlands as the location of the exorcism of "Legion" and Mount Gerizim as a topic of discussion in Jesus's celebrated dialogue with the woman of Samaria in the village of Sychar at the base of that mountain. Even though the place is not mentioned by name, Machaerus also belongs in this category as the likeliest site for the imprisonment and execution of John the Baptist. The remaining sites have been selected because of what they reveal concerning the larger environment in which Jesus's ministry took place and his teachings were heard. These include sites that represent administrative centers under Herodian and Roman rule (Sepphoris, Tiberias, Herodium, and Masada); sites that broaden our understanding of the residential, industrial, and civic life of Galilee (Magdala), the Decapolis (Scythopolis [Beit Shean], Hippos), and Samaria (Sebaste); and finally a site that, along with its library, opens up important vistas into the religious and literary environment of first-century Judea (Qumran).

Readers will learn about the varied nature of residences in the region: simple homes in villages throughout Galilee, such as the house in Nazareth in which Jesus grew up or the one in Capernaum that became a kind of base for his Galilean ministry; the elite, spacious, priestly courtyard mansions in

Jerusalem, such as Caiaphas owned, in which a portion of the Sanhedrin could be convened for the purpose of dealing with a teacher deemed dangerous; and the stunning opulence and expansiveness of the multiple palace complexes of Herod the Great and his successors (and the advanced degree to which these brought Roman styles and structures into his realm). They will discover what can be known about the appearance, layout, and functions of first-century synagogues, such as Jesus frequented for the purpose of disseminating his teaching and such as were frequent settings for healings and exorcisms. They will explore the fortresses that ensured the safety of Herodian rule and the administrative centers that ensured the efficiency with which taxes and other resources were extracted from Herod's subjects. And, of course, they will tour the archaeological and other material remains that illumine the temple that stood at the heart of Judean and Galilean religious observance and that was the setting for so much of Jesus's teaching and activity during the climactic week in the Gospel narratives.

A great deal of the material culture from the century around the turn of the era informs us about the means by which the populations of Galilee and Judea, in particular, sustained their lives and families. Thus we will encounter artifacts and facets of archaeological sites that put us in touch with the practice of fishing and the broader fishing industry that was so important to the villages surrounding the Sea of Galilee. We will see artifacts that illumine the manner in which the staple agricultural products of Galilee, Samaria, and Judea—grain, olives, and grapes—were processed. We will explore the provisions that were made for other essentials, like maintaining a regular supply of water so as to sustain populations in a land with limited periods and amounts of rainfall. We will consider the material evidence for the pervasive interest in ritual purity and purificatory rites, whether represented by chalk or limestone vessels of varying types and sizes for different uses or by ritual immersion pools (mikvaoth) that appear in a wide variety of settings, including in priestly houses, near agricultural installations (for safeguarding the purity of olive oil and wine during production), beside synagogues, and, of course, surrounding the temple precincts. We will also see many examples of first-century tomb complexes, such as those that provided the setting for the raising of Lazarus and the resurrection of Jesus.

Along the way, we will examine what settlement patterns and distribution of artifacts tell us about the ethnicity of particular sites and whole regions, and thus the degree to which people would be exposed to "the other" and their practices. We will also explore the degree to which, and the manner in which, Greek and Roman styles, entertainment, *and* religion were being introduced into the regions under Herodian and Roman rule in the generations before and after the turn of the era—and the ways in which the religious purity of Judean territories was respected even as other facets of Romanization advanced. We will also evaluate the probability of the genuineness of particular sites—for example, the house of Peter in Capernaum and the Church of the Holy Sepulchre.

In sum, we will plumb as fully as possible in the space of one volume how the archaeology of sites throughout the regions with which Jesus's travels and ministry intersected can inform our understanding and our visualization of the world in which his travels and ministry occurred.

This book would have been significantly poorer were it not for the splendid opportunity afforded me by the Catholic Biblical Association to spend several months in Jerusalem as a visiting professor at the École biblique et archéologique française de Jérusalem. I cannot speak highly enough of the library resources that were available to me there and of the generous hospitality and fraternity of the resident members of the Dominican order and the camaraderie of those who study with them. I remain grateful as well to Mr. James Ridgway of Educational Opportunities Tours, based in Lakeland, Florida, for several occasions to visit sites in Israel and the Palestinian Territories in connection with "Lands of the Bible" cruises. Some of the material in this book first took shape as presentations I gave to groups traveling under the auspices of this company. Finally, I wish to thank the trustees and administration of Ashland Theological Seminary for study leaves and for professional development funds that gave me the freedom and resources to travel multiple times to Israel and the Palestinian Territories since 2013.

ABBREVIATIONS

GENERAL

AT	author translation	Heb.	Hebrew
cf.	*confer*, compare	i.e.	*id est*, that is
e.g.	*exempli gratia*, for example	Lat.	Latin
Grk.	Greek	//	parallel(s)

OLD TESTAMENT

Gen.	Genesis	Eccles.	Ecclesiastes
Exod.	Exodus	Song	Song of Songs
Lev.	Leviticus	Isa.	Isaiah
Num.	Numbers	Jer.	Jeremiah
Deut.	Deuteronomy	Lam.	Lamentations
Josh.	Joshua	Ezek.	Ezekiel
Judg.	Judges	Dan.	Daniel
Ruth	Ruth	Hosea	Hosea
1 Sam.	1 Samuel	Joel	Joel
2 Sam.	2 Samuel	Amos	Amos
1 Kings	1 Kings	Obad.	Obadiah
2 Kings	2 Kings	Jon.	Jonah
1 Chron.	1 Chronicles	Mic.	Micah
2 Chron.	2 Chronicles	Nah.	Nahum
Ezra	Ezra	Hab.	Habakkuk
Neh.	Nehemiah	Zeph.	Zephaniah
Esther	Esther	Hag.	Haggai
Job	Job	Zech.	Zechariah
Ps(s).	Psalm(s)	Mal.	Malachi
Prov.	Proverbs		

NEW TESTAMENT

Matt.	Matthew	1 Tim.	1 Timothy
Mark	Mark	2 Tim.	2 Timothy
Luke	Luke	Titus	Titus
John	John	Philem.	Philemon
Acts	Acts	Heb.	Hebrews
Rom.	Romans	James	James
1 Cor.	1 Corinthians	1 Pet.	1 Peter
2 Cor.	2 Corinthians	2 Pet.	2 Peter
Gal.	Galatians	1 John	1 John
Eph.	Ephesians	2 John	2 John
Phil.	Philippians	3 John	3 John
Col.	Colossians	Jude	Jude
1 Thess.	1 Thessalonians	Rev.	Revelation
2 Thess.	2 Thessalonians		

OLD TESTAMENT APOCRYPHA

1 Macc.	1 Maccabees	Sir.	Sirach
4 Macc.	4 Maccabees		

DEAD SEA SCROLLS

CD	Damascus Document	1QSa	Rule of the Congregation
1QS	Rule of the Community	4QMMT	Some Works of the Law

PHILO

Hypoth.	*Hypothetica*	*Prob.*	*Quod omnis probus liber sit (That Every Good Person Is Free)*
Legat.	*Legatio ad Gaium (On the Embassy to Gaius)*		
Mos. 2	*De vita Mosis* II *(On the Life of Moses 2)*		

JOSEPHUS

Ag. Ap.	*Against Apion*	*J.W.*	*Jewish War*
Ant.	*Jewish Antiquities*	*Life*	*The Life*

RABBINIC LITERATURE

b.	Babylonian Talmud	Mid.	Middot
B. Bat.	Baba Batra	'Ohal.	'Ohalot
m.	Mishnah	Pesaḥ.	Pesaḥim
Meg.	Megillah	Sanh.	Sanhedrin

CLASSICAL AUTHORS

Dio Cassius

Hist. rom. *Historiae romanae* (*Roman History*)

Eusebius

Vit. Const. *Vita Constantini* (*Life of Constantine*)

Jerome

Hom. *Homily*

Origen

Cels. *Contra Celsum* (*Against Celsum*)
Comm. Jo. *Commentarii in evangelium Joannis* (*Commentary on John*)

Pliny the Elder

Nat. *Natural History*

Polybius

Hist. *The Histories*

Ptolemy

Geogr. *Geography*

Socrates Scholasticus

Ch. Hist. *Church History*

Suetonius

Aug. *Divus Augustus*
Claud. *Divus Claudius*
Tib. *Tiberius*

Tacitus

Ann. *Annales* (*Annals*)

Velleius Paterculus

Hist. Rom. *History of Rome*

THE HISTORICAL BACKGROUND OF JESUS'S WORLD

The discussions of archaeological sites and artifacts throughout this book will refer to the Ptolemaic, Seleucid, Hasmonean, and other periods. The names of a good number of historical figures will populate these pages as well. It seems therefore useful—not to mention considerate—to begin with an overview of the history of the territories relevant to Jesus and his ministry that will place all these terms and names in a coherent narrative.[1]

Alexander and the Ptolemaic Period

The story told in the historical books of the Old Testament extends into the Persian period with the waves of Judeans returning from exile in Babylon, resettling Jerusalem and its environs, and rebuilding the temple and the city walls (see Ezra and Nehemiah). Between 334 and 332 BC, Alexander the Great seized control of the regions of Syria, Palestine, and Egypt. (I use the term "Palestine" to conveniently capture the multiple regions concerned: Idumea, Judea, Samaria, and Galilee since, by the Hellenistic period, "Israel" had ceased to be a meaningful geographical term.) By 323 BC, he had conquered the remaining

1. The treatment here will be necessarily brief. Those interested in a fuller account of the period may wish to consult deSilva, *Judea Under Greek and Roman Rule*, or Schäfer, *History of the Jews in the Greco-Roman World*.

territories of the Persians and lands further east but succumbed to a fever in Babylon. His ambitious generals tore his empire apart and were enmeshed in wars against one another as each tried to win a larger share for himself.

Ptolemy I had secured Egypt, Cyprus, and Palestine by 302 BC, founding a dynasty that would endure until the suicide of Cleopatra VII in 31 BC. The Ptolemies would retain control of Judea, Samaria, and Galilee through 200 BC. They invested substantially in rebuilding the cities of the coastal plain, which had suffered a great deal since Alexander's initial invasion, because of their military and commercial importance. They also planted military colonies in Galilee and the Decapolis as a safeguard against invasion by their rivals to the north, the kings of the Seleucid Empire (so named after its founder, Seleucus I, once a general in Ptolemy's employ). Their primary interest was in the agricultural resources and other wealth that could be extracted from Palestine, allowing a substantial degree of autonomy under the high priest and the senate (a council of elders drawn from the Judean elite) as long as the tribute flowed in the assigned amounts.

The Seleucid Period

Antiochus III, ruler of the Seleucid Empire from 226 to 187 BC, brought Ptolemaic rule over Palestine to an end. After a failed attempt to wrest this territory from Ptolemy IV in 217 BC, Antiochus succeeded in capturing it in 200 BC when Egypt was under less effective leadership and was less able to mobilize its resources. The Judean leadership in Jerusalem appears to have been ready for a regime change, as they were remembered to have welcomed Antiochus III into their city and provided local military support for his siege of the Ptolemaic garrison there (Josephus, *Ant.* 12.133–34). Antiochus reciprocated with formal decrees granting Jews throughout his realm the right to follow their ancestral laws (which they had enjoyed anyway) and granting the people of Jerusalem three years' exemption from tribute for the sake of the city's economic recovery (12.138–44).

Antiochus III's ambitions brought him into conflict with Rome as he sought to extend his empire further west. After a decisive defeat at the Battle of Apamea in 188 BC, Antiochus was forced to pay an enormous war indemnity to Rome in order to avoid giving them a pretext for military action against him and his heartland. His son Seleucus IV (ruled 187–175 BC) would spend his whole reign under the shadow of this ongoing debt, which was fully paid off only in 173 BC.

Seleucus IV was succeeded by his younger brother, Antiochus IV (ruled 175–164 BC), under whom some truly watershed events took place in Judea.

First, a party of Judean elites, eager to advance a more cosmopolitan agenda for Jerusalem, appealed to the new king to replace the high priest Onias III with his pro-Hellenizing younger brother, Jason. Further, they appealed to him to allow Jerusalem to shift its internal polity from one based on the law of Moses to one based on a Greek constitution. Thus Jerusalem was essentially refounded as "Antioch-at-Jerusalem," and a gymnasium was built for the education of Jerusalem's elite youth in Greek language and culture and the introduction of Greek forms of exercise and athletics. Jason's party pledged an enormous increase in annual tribute to Antiochus, so confident were they of the economic growth these changes would invite.

In 172 BC, however, an even more progressive party within Jerusalem secured Antiochus's consent—with promises of still higher tribute—to replace Jason with an even more radically Hellenizing high priest named Menelaus. Menelaus proved unable to make good on these unrealistic pledges and fell back on appropriating the sacred vessels of gold and silver in the temple to use as bribes to secure reprieves, resulting in open rioting against him in Jerusalem. Antiochus was busy himself during this time (169–168 BC) defending his southern border against an incursion by Egypt, which he followed up with an attempt to gain a foothold for himself in Egypt. A rumor that he had been killed in these efforts led Jason to attempt to regain his office. He brought an army of mercenaries against Menelaus but fled upon hearing that Antiochus was alive and marching toward Jerusalem. Whether Jason had help within the city—or whether more conservative parties in the city used his attack as an opportunity to try to repel both Hellenizing high priests—Antiochus interpreted the situation as Jerusalem revolting against his duly appointed deputy and thus against his rule. He engaged in a shock-and-awe campaign of massacres and home invasions against its people and restored control of the city to Menelaus. Menelaus himself conducted Antiochus into the temple's inner chambers and treasury to confiscate whatever he felt was his due in back tribute.

Antiochus went further, however. He left a garrison of his own soldiers in Jerusalem as a peacekeeping force, who fortified their position in a structure known as the Akra, probably south of the temple and north of the City of David—thus in a position to oversee and exercise control over both. In the face of continued resistance, Antiochus pursued a program of forced assimilation. He made continued observance of the law of Moses—including circumcision, Sabbath observance, and keeping kosher—a capital criminal offense. In 167 BC, in keeping with the multiethnic population of Jerusalem (made so particularly by his garrison), he rededicated the temple itself to other deities alongside the God of Israel, apparently going out of his way to shock Jerusalem's residents into acknowledging the new order of things (for example, ordering swine to be sacrificed on the altar). This would be remembered as "the abomination of desolation" (so NASB, among other translations) or "desolating sacrilege" (NRSVue) of Daniel 11:31 and 12:11 (cf. 1 Macc. 1:54). Judeans were forced to participate in Greco-Syrian rites and in the civic feasts that followed—thus to eat food that had been sacrificed to idols, even the meat of swine.

These measures only served to galvanize resistance further. It emerged in its most effective form in the town of Modein, about 20 miles west of Jerusalem, under the leadership of a disaffected priest named Mattathias and his five sons, the most famous of which was Judas Maccabaeus. Antiochus had taken the greater part of his army into Babylonia to reassert control over the eastern provinces of his empire. This allowed the guerrilla band that formed first around Mattathias and, after his death, around his son Judas to wreak havoc on apostate Judeans and detachments of the local Seleucid peacekeeping force. As Antiochus's deputy, Lysias, continued to send insufficient forces against Judas's band of insurgents, the latter grew better armed, gained greater confidence, and increased in number till they were a formidable force themselves. By 164 BC, first Antiochus (before his death that year) and then Lysias (who was made regent of the young Antiochus V) were more inclined to negotiate with Judas than continue hostilities.

Judas and his forces continued the fight until they regained control of the temple in Jerusalem, removed all the defiling and offensive paraphernalia, and saw to its ritual cleansing, putting it back in the service of the one God. Lysias essentially made peace with the situation, even executing Menelaus for his part in the deteriorating relations between the province and the empire, and turned his own attention to internal threats to himself and the young Antiochus V. This marked the beginning of the civil strife that would thoroughly weaken and, a century later, eventually end the Seleucid Empire. Indeed, at this point the son of Seleucus IV, Demetrius I—the person who *ought* to have succeeded his father but was preempted by Antiochus IV—established himself on the throne. He killed Lysias and the young Antiochus V and installed a new high priest in Jerusalem—Alcimus, who seemed to have an acceptable pedigree. Judas nevertheless continued his revolution, perhaps already believing that national independence was possible. He was, however, killed on the battlefield in 160 BC.

Judas's allies and armies latched onto his brother Jonathan as their new leader, who surprisingly led them to several further victories against the forces Demetrius I had sent. Demetrius's general came to terms with Jonathan, who essentially set up a rival government at Michmash to the one in Jerusalem.

When Alexander Balas, alleged to be another son of Antiochus IV, arose as a rival to Demetrius I for the Seleucid throne, both figures vied with one another for Jonathan's support. Jonathan sided with Alexander and was made high priest and deputy over Judea as a result. Further intrigues led to Jonathan's capture and death, and his last surviving brother, Simon, emerged as the leader of the cause of Judean independence. He sided with Demetrius II against the pretender who had caused Jonathan's death and was rewarded with the high priesthood, the lifting of tribute from Judea (acknowledging Judea to be an allied state rather than a vassal one), and the removal of the Seleucid garrison from Jerusalem. Thus Jewish sources remember 141 BC as the year Judea regained its independence after 456 years of foreign domination.

The Hasmonean Period

With Simon, the Hasmonean dynasty—"the family of those men through whom deliverance was given to Israel" (1 Macc. 5:62)—was firmly established. Power transferred seamlessly to his (last surviving) son, John Hyrcanus I, after Simon's murder by an ambitious son-in-law in 134 BC. The opening years of Hyrcanus's reign show that Judeans and Seleucids had different ideas concerning just how independent Judea had become. Antiochus VII, who succeeded Demetrius II after the latter had been captured by the Parthian Empire to the east, besieged Hyrcanus in Jerusalem for almost a year to reassert his sovereignty. Hyrcanus eventually acquiesced and, a good vassal once again, marshaled his army to accompany Antiochus VII on a punitive expedition against Parthia. The latter's death on this campaign in 129 BC, however, freed Hyrcanus to reassert Judean independence and to engage in a decades-long campaign of Judean expansion into Samaria, western Galilee, and the Golan through conquest and settler colonization.

Hyrcanus was succeeded first by his oldest son, Judah Aristobulus I (104–103 BC), and then by his third son, Alexander Jannaeus (103–76 BC). Both continued their father's expansionist policies, pushing further into Upper Galilee, the Golan, the Transjordan, the Decapolis cities, and the cities of the coastal plains. By this time, the Hasmoneans' realm equaled or exceeded that of the kingdoms of Israel and Judah at their height. Both Hyrcanus I and Jannaeus invested in constructing several fortresses at strategic positions, chiefly near borders, which would remain important features of the landscape through the early Roman period. There was a great deal of internal opposition to Jannaeus, led largely by the faction of the Pharisees who had been alienated from positions of influence by his father, Hyrcanus I. Jannaeus's cruelty in suppressing such resistance brought the dynasty to a new moral low.

Jannaeus entrusted the kingdom to his widow, Salome Alexandra (76–67 BC), and the high priesthood to his eldest son, John Hyrcanus II. Salome maintained the kingdom's borders but engaged in no attempts to expand it. She reconciled her government with the members of the Pharisaic party, who used their newfound power to persecute their Sadducean rivals. As a result, Salome entrusted her border fortresses to the Sadducees, in large measure to safeguard their lives. As she was declining, she shared the powers of government with Hyrcanus II, who was to succeed to the kingship as well. His younger brother Judah Aristobulus II, however, was not content to be passed over. He rallied his supporters—which included the many Sadducees who had been entrusted with the border fortresses—and set about initiating a coup before his mother had even died.

Hyrcanus II's position was weaker, with the result that he abdicated in favor of Aristobulus II after a military defeat near Jericho in 67 BC. An Idumean named Antipater, however, the son of the man whom Alexander Jannaeus had made his governor in Idumea, came alongside Hyrcanus II and urged him to claim his birthright. Antipater brokered the military support of the Nabatean king to the southeast, who led his army against Aristobulus II in Jerusalem. It is precisely here that Rome poked its nose under the tent. Pompey the Great had been engaged in reorganizing the client kingdoms and other territories in the buffer zone between the Roman and Parthian Empires and sent a deputy south into Palestine to reconnoiter the region. He found Judea erupting into civil war and interposed himself. Both Hyrcanus II and Aristobulus II presented him with their claim to the throne, and he decided in favor of Aristobulus, probably because he was in a stronger position to make good on his promises of bribes and because it was easier to drive away the Nabatean army than to besiege Aristobulus in Jerusalem.

Antipater would not allow Hyrcanus to give up, and so they presented their case to Pompey himself when he came as far as Damascus. Aristobulus, of course, was on hand as well to assert his rights—as was a delegation from Judea asking Pompey to end the dynasty of priest-kings entirely and return to rule by a high priest and council of elders. Pompey ordered both parties to keep the peace until he could investigate the situation more thoroughly. Aristobulus took this as a sign that Pompey might unseat him and prepared his forces for a siege. Pompey regarded this as an act of aggression (if not also a personal affront) and besieged Aristobulus in Jerusalem, eventually gaining access, placing Aristobulus under arrest, and planting Hyrcanus as the more reliable person to rule. As Aristobulus's soldiers had taken up their position in the temple, Pompey thoroughly inspected it for stragglers—including the holy of holies itself—an act that was hardly auspicious for the beginning of Rome's oversight of Judea.

Pompey appears to have heeded the delegation of the citizenry: Hyrcanus was not allowed the title of king but allowed only the titles of ethnarch and high priest, while the authority of the Judean senate was increased. Pompey detached from Hyrcanus's domain many of the territories that his ancestors had conquered, placing them under the Roman governor of the newly created province of Syria, to whom Judea would also pay an annual tribute. Hyrcanus and Antipater proved reliable allies in terms of upholding Rome's interests in the region. Even though Aristobulus and his sons were taken to Rome as prisoners of war, they would not cease from finding opportunities to escape, rally support back home, and instigate a series of civil wars against Hyrcanus and Antipater. In regard to these uprisings, Rome would also generally prove a reliable ally in terms of lending military aid to its duly appointed ethnarch.

Antipater's rise to power as Hyrcanus's right-hand man allowed two of Antipater's sons—Phasael and Herod—also to become prominent generals and deputy governors in Judea and Galilee. Herod (who would later be called "Herod the Great") was quick to learn that the path to long-term success was to distinguish himself as someone who could make Rome's regional interests his own interests. He, like his father and Hyrcanus, was also marvelously adept at adapting his loyalties to whoever emerged as Rome's representative in the east. This was no easy matter, as Rome's leading citizens were enmeshed in civil wars from about 49 BC through 31 BC. First it was the clients and armies of Julius Caesar against those of Pompey the Great; then the armies of Caesar's partisans—Marc Antony and Octavian (who would later become the emperor Augustus)—against those of Caesar's assassins, Brutus and Cassius; finally those of Octavian against those of Marc Antony and Cleopatra VII of Egypt. Each successive victor, however, recognized in Herod a willingness to serve Rome's interests unwaveringly.

The aging Hyrcanus recognized Herod's potential and sought to secure him as an ally for his family rather than see him emerge as a competitor. He therefore arranged for Herod's betrothal to his granddaughter Mariamne, thus bringing him into the Hasmonean fold. The union, promised in 42 BC, would not be consecrated until five years later, however. The Parthian Empire had been pushing against Rome's eastern frontier for some time and was also intent on creating its own proxies in the region. They made such an arrangement with Mattathias Antigonus, the last surviving son of Aristobulus II, and advanced on Jerusalem. Hyrcanus II was taken prisoner, and his ears were cut off to disqualify him from holding the office of high priest ever again; Herod's brother Phasael killed himself to avoid a prolonged and degrading execution. Herod himself was forced to flee with several members of his family and supporters, whom he left at the fortress of Masada, traveling himself to Rome to seek aid.

The Herodian Period

Marc Antony and Octavian, Rome's chief representatives in 40 BC, knew that they could not allow Parthia to call the shots in Judea, so they threw their whole weight behind Herod as someone Rome could trust to protect their interests in the region. Herod was proclaimed "king of the Judeans" (Josephus, *Ant.* 14.384–85; *J.W.* 1.284) by the Senate in the same year. It would take three more years, however, for Rome's forces to be in sufficient command of the border with Parthia to turn their attention to dislodging Mattathias Antigonus and installing Herod in Jerusalem, which they did in 37 BC (though Herod had been active during this time with the forces entrusted to him, both fighting for Rome's interests on the border and harrying Antigonus's forces in Judea). Herod was initially entrusted with Judea, Idumea, Peraea, and Galilee, but his competence won him several additional grants of territory from Octavian—better known as Augustus after the Senate awarded him that honorific in 27 BC. These included Samaria, the cities of the coastal plain, several of the Decapolis cities, and the largely Gentile districts northeast of Galilee (Gaulanitis, Trachonitis, Batanea, and Auranitis). As a layperson, Herod had to delegate the office of high priest to others—generally to the member of a priestly family whom Herod most trusted to support his own rule and agenda.

As a client king, Herod could not engage in campaigns against neighboring regions in an effort to gain territory. Rome's firm control of the region, however, also meant that Herod would not waste his resources in defensive wars or civil wars against rivals for his throne. His ambitions were, as a result, channeled almost entirely toward the improvement of the territory that Augustus had allotted to him, which he did magnificently. Herod left hardly a corner of his realm untouched by his ambitions as a builder. Many of the archaeological sites throughout Israel are testimonies to the more constructive and often inspired side of this complicated figure of history. These include Caesarea-by-the-Sea (Caesarea Maritima);[2] Sebaste in Samaria; improvements to the fortress-palaces throughout his realm (Masada, Machaerus, Cypros)

2. Caesarea Maritima plays no discernible part in the ministry of Jesus, though it certainly looms large in the narrative of Paul's ministry in Acts (see, e.g., chaps. 23–25) as well as Peter's earlier apostolic ministry (see Acts 10). This site is treated, therefore, in deSilva, *Archaeology and the Ministry of Paul.*

Map 1.1. The territories of Herod's kingdom and the Decapolis.

and the creation of new ones (Herodium, the citadel at Jerusalem); new palaces outside of Jericho; and, most famously, the temple complex at the heart of Jerusalem. Herod changed the architectural landscape of the historic territory of Israel more than any other previous ruler, including David, Solomon, and Hezekiah.

Herod also aspired to achieve the international status and recognition of a generous Hellenistic ruler. He subsidized the costs of building a gymnasium and theater in Damascus; porticoes, temples, and marketplaces in Tyre and Berytus; and a colonnaded street in Antioch-on-the-Orontes. His gifts reached Pergamum, Delos, Rhodes, even Athens.[3]

Herod was able to finance all of this activity and beneficence because of the vast and varied resources at his disposal. First, he enjoyed significant income

3. See the full catalog in Richardson, *Herod*, 201–2.

from the private estates he inherited in Idumea from his father, Antipater.[4] Second, he had the income from the "royal lands" throughout his territory at his disposal. These included large portions of the Jezreel Valley and the oases of Ein Gedi and Jericho—fertile land that had been claimed for the imperial power since the Persian period and that had been exploited in turn by Ptolemies, Seleucids, and Hasmoneans. Third, he collected a variety of taxes, including a poll tax levied on each adult person (adulthood being initiated at fourteen for males and twelve for females), a tax on land, and taxes on goods that crossed his borders in any direction. The latter were particularly profitable, sometimes levied at 25 percent of the value of the goods themselves.[5] Herod's control of sizable stretches of land routes and his new maritime port of Caesarea gave him substantial opportunity for revenue from such taxes.[6] At the same time, Herod's building projects certainly gave a boost to certain sectors of the population. Well after the major work was finished, his temple project still kept eighteen thousand people employed.

Herod's family life, however, was a disaster. A good deal of the dysfunction came from the fact that his royal Hasmonean relatives (however short-lived their dynasty) never accepted the Idumean commoner as one of them. As a result of the distrust and the bedroom conspiracies, Herod would execute his old patron, Hyrcanus II; his young brother-in-law, Aristobulus III; his second wife and love of his life, Mariamne; Mariamne's mother; and two of his own sons by Mariamne. His oldest son, Antipater—the fruit of his first marriage to the commoner Doris, whom Herod divorced as a precondition of marrying into the royal line—also fell afoul of his father and was executed days before Herod himself expired of a wretched and wasting disease.

The Early Roman Period

Days before his death in 4 BC, Herod drafted a will naming his eldest surviving son, Archelaus, as ruler of Idumea, Judea, Samaria, and the coastal cities—the lion's share of his kingdom. Antipas, his next oldest, was to be given oversight of Galilee and Peraea, and Philip the diverse northeastern territories. (More will be said about Antipas and Philip in chapters to come.) In AD 6, however, Archelaus was removed for incompetence and banished to Gaul. At this point, his territories came under the direct oversight of a series of Roman prefects. These officials were drawn from the second tier of Roman

4. Levine, *Jerusalem*, 188.
5. Schäfer, *History of the Jews in the Greco-Roman World*, 90–91.
6. Levine, *Jerusalem*, 189.

Map 1.2. The division of Herod's kingdom in 4 BC.

society (the equestrian class rather than the senatorial). They enjoyed broad judicial and military (policing) powers and were entrusted with the collection of taxes and protection of Rome's interests in the region. They also inherited Herod's right to appoint and depose high priests, a fact that no doubt continued to degrade the authority of the office in the eyes of many Judeans. The prefect was answerable to the governor of the Roman province of Syria, to whom their subjects would occasionally appeal for judicial redress, and to whom the prefect might appeal for additional military support.

Table 1. Basic Periods and Their Date Ranges

Ptolemaic period[a]	323–200 BC
Seleucid period	200–141 BC
Hasmonean period	141–40 BC
Herodian period	40 BC–AD 6
Early Roman period	AD 6–70

a. The Ptolemies, Seleucids, and Hasmoneans all belong within the "Hellenistic Period" (another term readers will frequently encounter in this volume).

The most famous of these prefects was, of course, Pontius Pilate, whom Tiberius assigned to this post from AD 26 to 36—an unusually long time, though in keeping with Tiberius's personal preference for longer terms. He appropriately quipped that it was kinder to allow the same fleas to live on a particular dog, since once they were full they would suck lesser amounts of blood, than to change out the fleas too often (Josephus, *Ant.* 18.172–78). Caesarea Maritima was chosen as the new administrative center when rule passed from Herod's son Archelaus to the Roman prefect in AD 6. Its location on the seacoast made for faster communication with the governor of Syria, whose capital was Antioch-on-the-Orontes, and with Rome itself. Founded by Herod as a *Greek* city, complete with temples to the Greco-Roman gods

Figure 1.1. A partial inscription from Caesarea Maritima recording Pontius Pilate's name and his subvention of some monument or shrine in honor of Tiberius. The inscription also provides his proper title: "prefect."

Figure 1.2. The remains of Herod's promontory palace in Caesarea Maritima, featuring the mosaic that once adorned the triclinium, or formal dining room, and the outline of the swimming pool that was the centerpiece of this courtyard palace. The Roman prefects and, later, procurators would use this palace as their principal base of operations.

and facilities for Greco-Roman entertainment (like a theater, hippodrome, and baths), it was also culturally and religiously more appropriate to the administrative staff and military cohorts that would be stationed there.

Judea and its surrounding territories experienced a brief return to Herodian rule between AD 41 and 44, when the emperor Claudius awarded these territories to Herod's grandson, Agrippa I, who had previously been granted the territories of his uncles Philip and Antipas. Agrippa's early death meant a return of all those territories, now including Galilee, to direct Roman rule, now under officials bearing the title "procurator." From AD 44 through 66, these Roman appointees showed increasing ineptitude and venality.

The period was marked by a variety of simmering tensions that frequently reached a boiling point. These tensions were not all directed against *Roman* figures, though the procurators seemed largely incapable of or uninterested in resolving them. Tensions between Samaritans and Judeans flared, erupting into significant exchanges of violence on one occasion. Gangs of bandits became more numerous, largely as a result of people being forced off their lands and deprived of any reliable means of sustaining themselves and their families. Tensions between the Jewish and Gentile residents of Caesarea Maritima reached the breaking point several times in the 60s, often with the Jews getting the worst of it. Finally, Gessius Florus, procurator from 64 to 66, acted with such a high hand that explicitly anti-Roman actions became inevitable. He sent his auxiliaries into the temple complex to appropriate massive funds deposited there (probably in compliance with Nero's orders to his deputies everywhere to raise money by any means for the restoration of Rome after the great fire of 64). He let the same auxiliaries loose on the citizenry when they dared to protest, going so far as to crucify Judeans who were Roman citizens (and thus supposed to enjoy legal protection from such treatment).

When the governor of Syria failed to respond to the Judeans' appeal for redress in 66, they took matters into their own hands. Sacrifices on behalf of the emperor were suspended. The bridges connecting the Antonia fortress to the temple were destroyed. A band of insurgents captured Masada and raided its substantial stockpile of arms to equip themselves and others. Judeans overwhelmed and killed the cohorts stationed in the Antonia and in the praetorium (Herod's former palace in Jerusalem). The governor of Syria, hearing of the unrest, mobilized his troops, gained the upper hand against any resistance he met in Galilee and Judea, and initiated a siege of Jerusalem. The revolt could have been ended then and there with far less bloodshed and devastation if he had but pressed the siege. He lifted it, however, and began to move his troops to Caesarea, presumably to winter there. As he retreated, the insurgents inflicted such casualties upon his rear guard that Rome was honor bound to strike back with all its might.

A provisional revolutionary government was established in Jerusalem, led by its priestly elite, and generals were appointed to make preparations for the inevitable onslaught. They had a year before Nero's appointee for the task of suppressing the revolt, a seasoned general named Vespasian, arrived at the head of three legions as well as the auxiliary armies of regional client kings—a strike force of sixty thousand. Within a year they had eradicated all active resistance in Galilee, Idumea, and Judea save for the city of Jerusalem itself. Only Nero's death by suicide in AD 68 halted the campaign, as a Roman general's mandate ended with the death of the emperor who issued it. The power vacuum in Rome led to a year of civil war as the generals of the legions in Spain (Galba) and Germany (Vitellius), a senator supported by the aristocracy and Praetorian guard (Otho), and Vespasian himself with the support of the legions from the east fought one another with a view to establishing themselves. In the end, it was Vespasian who prevailed.

The Year of the Four Emperors proved to be disastrous also for Judea. Rather than use the reprieve to develop a unified front and invest fully in the fortification of Jerusalem, rival revolutionary parties made war on one another in the city—and all of them preyed on the common folk. They burned one another's stores of grain and other supplies in an attempt to weaken their rivals' positions. It was not until early summer of AD 70, when Vespasian's son Titus encircled Jerusalem with four legions, that the remaining revolutionary leaders came to terms and focused on the real problem. With the siege initiated, starvation began to set in, followed by disease as the bodies of the dead were too numerous to contain. Titus finally mobilized his forces to breach the walls, making their way to the Antonia fortress and thence forcing their way into the temple, a principal stronghold of one of the revolutionary parties. In the process, the temple itself was set ablaze and destroyed. By September, Titus's forces had gained control of the whole city. Jerusalem was largely destroyed; tens of thousands of Jews were sold as slaves; thousands more were earmarked to die in gladiatorial shows throughout the province of Syria and back in Rome itself; perhaps hundreds of thousands had perished in the siege.

As a consequence of the revolt, the province was reorganized. Judea, Samaria, Galilee, and Peraea were broken off from the province of Syria and made an independent senatorial province with a full resident legion of about six thousand soldiers (rather than five or six cohorts of five hundred soldiers each, as under the procurators). The remaining pockets of resistance in the fortresses of Machaerus, Herodium, and Masada were efficiently dislodged and neutralized. Several new Roman colonies were created to provide the veterans of the army with their hard-earned reward, including Neapolis in Samaria (modern Nablus). For all the devastation, economic recovery appears to have been quick. Vespasian had already set many of his soldiers to work rebuilding Galilee in 68, and Judea itself sustained little damage outside of the capital city. By AD 120, Judea became a consular province with a second resident legion, more likely with a view to strengthening its defensive capacity against the Parthians than to fending off further revolutionary activity, though that would come in the form of a Second Jewish Revolt (AD 132–136)—with disastrous consequences for the population of Judea.

PART I

THE REALMS OF ANTIPAS AND PHILIP

2

THE GALILEE OF JESUS

When we think of Galilee, we will most likely think first about the Sea of Galilee and the villages that line its coasts. So many of the episodes of the Gospels that take place in Galilee occur around or *on* this large lake. The region of Galilee itself was much bigger. It stretched at least 15 miles to the north, 15 to the south, and about 25 to the west of the center of the Sea of Galilee. The village of Nazareth is a full day's journey—an 18-mile walk—from the

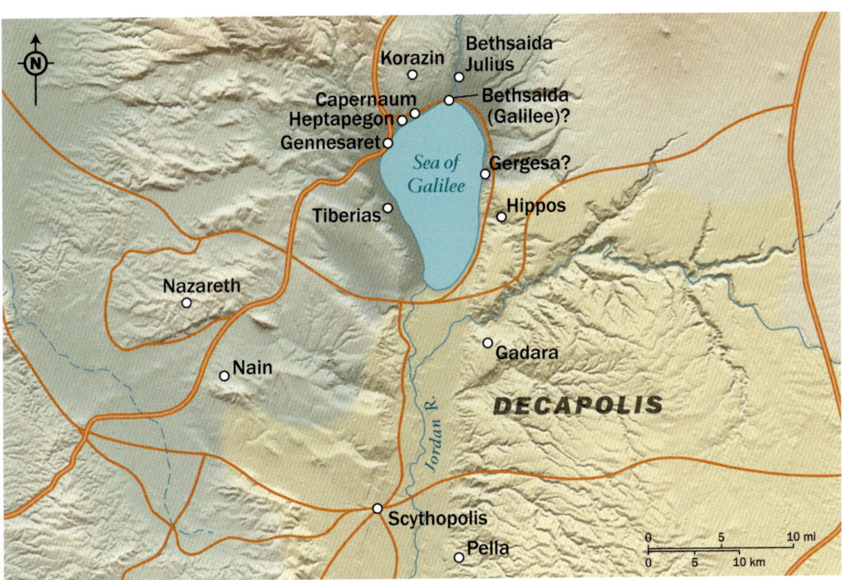

Map 2.1. The region around the Sea of Galilee.

western shore of the Sea of Galilee. But apart from the villages of Nazareth and Cana, it is really the Sea of Galilee and its surrounding settlements that dominate the set, as it were, of Jesus's activity in this region.

Well before the birth of Jesus, Galilee was no longer the "Galilee of the Gentiles" in any sense (Matt. 4:15, quoting Isa. 9:1). It was surrounded by the Greek cities of the Decapolis on its eastern and southern sides and the hinterlands of the Greek coastal cities of Ptolemais (modern Haifa) and Tyre on its northwest. Any Gentile colonies that had taken root within Galilee itself, however, were reduced by the many battles fought there between the Ptolemaic and Seleucid armies (or between rival Seleucid armies) that destroyed both villages and farmland. Most remaining Gentile villages were co-opted or destroyed and their residents driven out by aggressive colonization by Judeans under the Hasmonean dynasty. By the time of Herod the Great, the population of Galilee was overwhelmingly Jewish.[1]

Excavations have uncovered the same telltale signs of renewed Jewish occupation that one finds in Judea to the south. Two of these reflect increasing and widespread concern with the purity regulations of the law of Moses: the use of household vessels made of chalk or limestone—which, unlike pottery vessels, were considered incapable of being rendered impure (cf. John 2:6; m. 'Ohal. 5.5)—and the appearance of ritual immersion pools (mikvaoth) in the wealthier homes, beside synagogues, and in the vicinity of many agricultural installations like olive and wine presses. Three other kinds of artifacts reflect an interest in obtaining and using wares that were produced locally by fellow Jews: pottery storage jars, many of which were produced in the village of Shikhin; pottery table and cooking wares, many of which were produced in Kefar Hananya or resemble that type; and oil lamps made from Jerusalem clay, a sign of a widespread desire for a sense of connection with the mother city of Jews, interestingly focused on the vessels that provided light in the houses. Finally, we find an overwhelming increase in Hasmonean coinage throughout the region in the late second and early first centuries BC, and the emergence of burial practices in Galilee that tend to reflect those in Judea, notably including the use of ossuaries for the collection and permanent storage of the deceased's bones after the flesh had decayed, just as one finds throughout Judea's first-century BC (and AD) tombs. The ethnicity of the population is also supported by what is *not* found in the occupation layers of the Hasmonean, Herodian, and early Roman periods. One is hard-pressed to find pig bones anywhere, suggesting adherence to the dietary laws laid down

1. Freyne, *Galilee from Alexander the Great to Hadrian*, 259–304; Reed, *Archaeology and the Galilean Jesus*, 9–10; Chancey, *Greco-Roman Culture and the Galilee of Jesus*, 19.

in the law of Moses. There is also an almost total absence of pagan cultic sites and artifacts.[2]

The fact that Galileans were surrounded by Greek cities and their populations—and the fact that some of these cities, like Scythopolis (Beth Shean), Hippos, and Gadara, lay in very close proximity—suggests that many Galileans would have had some familiarity with pagan practice and civic life.[3] Evidence for the use of the Greek language or the spread of Greek culture among the towns and villages of Galilee in the first centuries BC and AD, however, is quite sparse.[4] This was likely limited to major centers like Sepphoris, Tiberias, and Magdala.

During the chaos that surrounded the civil war between Hyrcanus II and his brother Aristobulus II (67–63 BC) and the decades that followed, Galilee suffered more than its share because a good portion of its population kept lending active support to Aristobulus and his heirs. Many battles in the course of these uprisings were fought in Galilee, resulting in a good deal of destruction and large-scale interruptions of the fragile, agricultural economy. One lost growing season could make a huge difference in the financial stability, even the survival, of a family. Alongside this, Galilee was subjected to some heavy-handed shakedowns and suppression of revolutionary activity on the part of the Romans, who continued to act as watchdogs for Hyrcanus II and, then, Herod the Great—their approved client rulers over Judea and Galilee.

For all that, it would be a mistake to think of Galilee's population as particularly "revolutionary." The majority of its inhabitants were farmers whose concerns only occasionally rose above planting and harvesting the next cycle of crops. Subsistence-level living does not give much leisure for dissent and resistance. And however secure most Galileans were on their land at the beginning of Roman oversight of the region, many were well positioned to have lost it or to be on the precipice of losing it—becoming tenant farmers on land that used to be their own or relocating to farm the state lands or the farms of larger landholders—by the time Herod the Great died. These were some of the economic realities of both Galilee and Judea reflected in Jesus's parables—for example, the parable of the laborers in the vineyard, who are hired throughout the day as the landowner returns to the city square (Matt. 20:1–16), or the parable of the wicked tenants (Mark 12:1–9; Matt. 21:33–41). When the landowner in the first parable pays a full day's wage to those who

2. Berlin, "Jewish Life Before the Revolt," 425, 467; Reed, *Archaeology and the Galilean Jesus*, 21.

3. Chancey, *Greco-Roman Culture and the Galilee of Jesus*, 222.

4. Freyne, *Galilee from Alexander the Great to Hadrian*, 138–45; Chancey, *Greco-Roman Culture and the Galilee of Jesus*, 122–65.

worked only a few hours, he is doing what few if any landowners in Galilee or Judea would actually do. But Jesus knows what happens to the families of those laborers if they do not get hired that day and if they don't go home with a full day's wage, and he challenges both landowners *and* those who enjoy more stable work to show greater compassion and generosity. The sting of the second parable is that the chief priests and the elders to whom Jesus addresses it are almost all likely in the position of the owner of vineyards and lands who rents out the lands to tenants and sits back waiting for his share of their labor. This is why, in Mark's version of the parable at least, the chief priests and elders are so eager to see the vineyard owner take vengeance on the tenants—and are so put off when Jesus casts *them* in the role of the murderous tenants of *God's* vineyard.

After Herod's death, when his kingdom was divided among his three eldest surviving sons, Galilee, together with the district of Peraea east of the Jordan River, was given to Antipas—the "Herod" associated with the imprisonment and execution of John the Baptist (Matt. 14:1–12; Mark 6:14–29; Luke 9:7–9) and the trial of Jesus (Luke 23:6–12). None of Herod the Great's successors received the title of "king" (as Mark 6:14 suggests). Antipas was given the lower title of "tetrarch" (Matt. 14:1; Luke 3:1), as coins minted in Galilee attest. It might well have changed the dynamics of the region to have its Roman-backed rulers in the immediate vicinity—with Antipas making his capital first in Sepphoris and then in Tiberias—rather than at some distance in Jerusalem.[5] Rule by a member of the family of Herod, however, could still mask the bitter reality that would break through the facade of Jewish independence in full force with the death of Agrippa I and the assumption of direct rule of Galilee by the Roman procurator in AD 44.

5. Horsley, *Archaeology, History, and Society in Galilee*, 11.

3

NAZARETH

Given Nazareth's importance in the life of Jesus *of Nazareth* (Matt. 2:23; Luke 1:26; 2:39; John 1:45; 18:5–8; 19:19), the extent to which first-century AD remains of Jesus's village have been uncovered beneath the thriving modern city is bound to disappoint. Burials tended to take place outside the occupied area of a village, town, or city. Thus the discovery of over twenty tombs to the north, west, and south of the Basilica of the Annunciation provides some indication of the perimeter of the Roman-period village.[1] Nazareth might have covered less than 16 acres in the early Roman period, constituting a village of a mere fifty houses.[2]

The modern Basilica of the Annunciation and its courtyard shelter the "nucleus of the small Roman-period village."[3] Almost nothing remains of the built structures of the Roman period, though one can spot in the exposed rock the contours of some of the carved foundations of the houses that once stood here. Rather, the remains consist of the carved spaces and natural (or adapted) caves that existed *below* the Roman-period residential area. To maximize the space available to them, the residents of Nazareth carved storage silos, cellars, wells, and cisterns into the bedrock beneath them (see figs. 3.1, 3.2).[4] Some of these underground structures were extensive. Under Saint Joseph's Church, for example, a four-level silo or storage complex had been carved out deep into the relatively soft, and therefore easily workable, limestone. Several

1. McRay, *Archaeology and the New Testament*, 158.
2. Strange, "Nazareth," 2:168; Magness, *Archaeology of the Holy Land*, 201.
3. Alexandre, *Mary's Well, Nazareth*, 7.
4. Wright, "Size and Makeup of Nazareth," 36.

Figure 3.1. A subterranean cave with workspaces and in-ground storage silos beneath the Basilica of the Annunciation. Holes were bored into the rocky column (center), probably for tethering animals. This would likely have stood beneath a Roman-period house and served as an underground extension of its facilities.

Figure 3.2. A cistern with steps carved into the rock beneath the Roman village of Nazareth, presently beneath the Basilica of the Annunciation.

Figure 3.3. A stepped pool from the first through third centuries AD, found beneath Saint Joseph's Church in the Basilica of the Annunciation complex. It has been variously described as a mikveh (Strange, "Nazareth," 2:176), a pre-Constantinian baptistery (Murphy-O'Connor, *Holy Land*, 426), and a winepress (Alexandre, *Mary's Well, Nazareth*, 6–7; Alexandre, "Settlement History of Nazareth," 81), though it may also have served any two or all three of these functions in different periods.

Roman-period artifacts found at the site, including pottery vessels and lamps and glassware, confirm the date of occupation.

Further excavations in a very limited area beneath the Centre International Marie de Nazareth, located just across the street to the northwest of the Basilica of the Annunciation, revealed the remains of a house inhabited during the late Hellenistic and early Roman periods. As in the rest of the residential area uncovered so far, the basement-level rooms had been partially carved into the rock, into which cisterns and silos were also cut (see fig. 3.4). One of the storage pits led down to storage areas on two further sublevels. Above

Figure 3.4. Remains of the silos and foundation structures beneath a Roman-period residence in the Centre International Marie de Nazareth.

Figure 3.5. Traces of both Iron Age and early Roman-period residential structures beneath the Centre International Marie de Nazareth.

these were found the foundations and lower courses of walls delineating small rooms arranged around an inner courtyard, as is typical for the period (see fig. 3.5). One pit was found to contain a large amount of broken pottery, which, together with the discovery of some chalk vessels, suggests that the residents were scrupulous concerning ritual purity. Purity regulations required, for example, the breaking and discarding of all clay vessels present in a house at the time someone died, since clay vessels were susceptible to corpse pollution.[5] As with many sites in Lower Galilee, there was evidence of an earlier occupation period during the late Iron Age (the centuries leading up to the Assyrian invasion of the Northern Kingdom of Israel and final conquest of the same in 722 BC) followed by a long period of desertion until the late Hellenistic period and the period of Hasmonean expansion.[6] The evidence in Nazareth aligns, therefore, with evidence elsewhere suggesting that Galilee was largely resettled by Judeans during the Hasmonean period.

Just 80 yards west of the excavated area beneath the Basilica of the Annunciation sits the entrance to the Sisters of Nazareth Convent. Excavations in the cellar of the convent revealed a potpourri of Roman, Byzantine, and

5. Alexandre, "Settlement History of Nazareth," 35–46.
6. Alexandre, "Settlement History of Nazareth," 78, 86; Strange, "Nazareth," 2:175.

Figure 3.6. The well-carved threshold and doorway separating an outer courtyard from an inner room in what is believed to have been a largely rock-carved Roman-period house beneath the Sisters of Nazareth Convent.

Figure 3.7. A beautiful example of a "rolling stone" tomb with loculi was found beneath the Roman-period house in the Sisters of Nazareth Convent. The tomb appears to date from the middle to the late first century AD—and its very presence here suggests that the house above had ceased to be occupied before this date.

Crusader-era structures. A find of potential importance is a rock-cut room with a carefully cut door and threshold with what looks like part of another room fronting it, partially surrounded by rock-carved walls, from the Roman period (see fig. 3.6). A Crusader-era staircase appears to have been built over a more ancient one to the left of the structure, possibly suggesting that the earlier structure once had a second story. It is unclear whether this was part of a larger courtyard house, some of which had been created by carving into the rocky side of the hill, or a smaller dwelling, perhaps even a temporary dwelling for quarry workers.[7] In either event, it offers one more, small piece in the puzzle of first-century Nazareth. If a residence, it appears to have been abandoned during the first half of the first century, as a tomb with four loculi and an entrance that could be sealed with a large, round stone was carved out of the space below and slightly to the south (see fig. 3.7). The presence of the tomb raises questions: Was this site ever part of the village of Nazareth proper? Was the population shrinking during the first century, such that space for tombs opened up closer to the residential center of the village?

7. Dark, *Archaeology of Jesus' Nazareth*, 122–25.

Figure 3.8. The remains of the early first-century AD synagogue at Gamala.

Excavations on the grounds of the Nazareth Hospital, which lies well outside the perimeter of the Roman-period village, unearthed several agricultural installations, including a watchtower, a winepress, and a rock quarry.[8] Such installations would be appropriately found surrounding a primarily agricultural village like Nazareth.

One structure that the Gospels might lead us to expect to see, but which the very limited archaeological excavations in Nazareth have failed to uncover, is a synagogue (Matt. 13:54–58; Mark 6:1–6; Luke 4:14–30). The Greek word that gives us our English "synagogue" simply means "gathering," not requiring a dedicated structure as long as *some* structure (for example, a large courtyard house) was available for regular meetings. Nevertheless, the growing number of first-century synagogues that have been excavated in Galilee and Judea strongly suggest that Nazareth might have had one as well.[9] To visualize such a building, we might first consider the remains of the synagogue at Gamala in Gaulanitis (the modern Golan Heights), a few miles east of the Sea of Galilee (see fig. 3.8). Gamala (or Gamla) is a perfect time capsule from AD 68, the

8. Alexandre, *Mary's Well, Nazareth*, 7.

9. Other early Roman-period synagogues have been found at Magdala, Modein, Shikhin, Qiryat Sepher, Tel Rekhesh, and Beth Shemesh (Ben David, "On the Number of Synagogues," 182). Literary evidence for the presence of synagogues includes Mark 1:21–29; Luke 4:16–30; Acts 6:9; Josephus, *J.W.* 2.285–89; *Ant.* 19.300–305; *Life* 277–80 (Sharon, *Judea Under Roman Domination*, 321; Bonnie et al., *Synagogue in Ancient Palestine*, 7).

Figure 3.9. Ritual immersion pools (mikvaoth), like this one at Gamala, are frequently found in close proximity to synagogues. This might reflect a concern on the part of those who gathered for safeguarding the ritual purity of others, though it might also indicate that those assembled in the synagogues for prayer and study were aware that they were preparing for an encounter with the holy God, even as they made use of the mikvaoth in the vicinity of the temple to fit themselves for entering the temple precincts. (On the Gamala synagogue and mikveh compound, see Yavor, "Architecture and Stratigraphy of the Eastern and Western Quarters," 41–61.)

year the Romans besieged the town, breached its walls, and killed most of its inhabitants. The site was never resettled, though it was stripped of a good deal of its building materials over the centuries. The remnants of the synagogue here display a footprint similar to that of other structures identified as synagogues from the period before AD 70—a large, central space with multiple rows of bench seating surrounding the perimeter. There was also a "study room" (Heb., *beit ha-midrash*) attached to this synagogue (a smaller room provided with perimeter benches) as well as several storage rooms. The whole would have been under a roof, partially supported by the pillars whose bases are still visible.[10] Since Gamala was a fortified city with a significantly larger population, we would expect its synagogue to be proportionately larger and better endowed than any such structure that stood in Nazareth at this time.

10. Yavor, "Architecture and Stratigraphy of the Eastern and Western Quarters," 60–61; Syon and Yavor, "Gamala," 5:1739.

By the turn of the era, the synagogue had become an important and pervasive institution in Judea and Galilee. It originated in diaspora Jewish communities far removed from Judea, where the need to create structures that would nurture social and religious cohesion among Jews was greater since the temple in Jerusalem could not regularly serve such purposes. Inscriptions from late third-century BC Egypt bear witness to the existence of "houses of prayer" (Grk., *proseuchai*) as places Jews would gather to express their common devotion as well as attend to a wide variety of community needs: the hearing of judicial cases in matters internal to the Jewish community; the drafting of contracts, wills, and marriage documents; mourning and funerary rites for the deceased; and the discussion of any other matters of community concern.[11] The shift in terminology from "house of prayer" to the more familiar "synagogue" (Grk., *synagōgai*, places of "gathering") may reflect this growing range of purposes served by these structures.[12]

On the Sabbath, at the very least, synagogues provided places for reading and studying the Torah and other Scriptures, as reflected in Gospel narratives of Jesus's teaching ministry in Galilee (e.g., Mark 1:21–29; 6:1–6; Luke 4:16–37, 44; 6:6; 7:5). This was where most Jews would have gained the level of knowledge about their ancestral law that the first-century Jewish authors Josephus (*Ag. Ap.* 2.175) and Philo (*Mos.* 2.211–16) boasted about.[13]

We cannot be sure what a service of prayer and study in the synagogue would have looked like in the first century. The earliest, complete description comes from the Mishnah (m. Meg. 4.1–5), a codification of Jewish legal opinions and practices committed to writing only around AD 200. There we read about the liturgy starting with a recitation of the *Shema*, the fundamental faith statement of Jews that begins with the declaration: "Hear, O Israel: The Lord is our God, the Lord alone. You shall love the Lord your God with all your heart, and with all your soul, and with all your might" (Deut. 6:4–5).[14] Josephus (*Ant.* 4.212) claims that this was recited by pious Jews twice daily, making it no surprise, then, that Jesus would recite this as the first and greatest commandment (Mark 12:28–31).

11. Grabbe, "Synagogues in Pre-70 Palestine," 402–3; Bloedhorn and Hüttenmeister, "The Synagogue," 3:269.

12. Josephus (*Life* 277–79), however, still uses the term "prayer house" to refer to a large building in Tiberias of Galilee that also served as a community center where common concerns could be discussed. Williams, "Contribution of Jewish Inscriptions," 3:77.

13. Cohen, "The Temple and the Synagogue," 3:305.

14. The extent of the *Shema* in the first century is a matter of debate. It would eventually come to incorporate all of Deut. 6:4–9; 11:13–21; Num. 15:37–41. Reif, "The Early Liturgy of the Synagogue," 3:350.

This was followed by a series of prayers known as the "Eighteen Benedictions" (*Shemoneh Esreh*), though some number of these petitions postdate the destruction of Jerusalem in AD 70.[15] The petitions likely to predate that event cultivate an awareness that God is merciful toward his people's iniquities (pardoning them) and toward their infirmities (healing them). God also provides for them in life (through the provision of food and safety) and in death (through the hope of the resurrection). The prayers reinforce the conviction that the God of the universe is also in some special sense the God of Abraham, Isaac, and Jacob, and the defender of their descendants, "Israel." The prayers orient the worshipers' hopes in a decidedly nationalistic direction, nurturing a longing for the land of Israel, the glorification of Jerusalem, the restoration of native leadership (as opposed to foreign domination), and the regathering of Jews living outside the land.

The largest part of the service was given to the reading and discussion of the Torah (and other scriptural texts), perhaps on the basis of an initial "word of exhortation."[16] The service closed with a recitation of the priestly benediction (if a quorum of at least ten was gathered).[17] There is no archaeological or ancient literary evidence to support the idea that women were seated in a separate section in Roman-period synagogues, despite the frequency with which one encounters this assertion.[18]

THE "NAZARETH INSCRIPTION"

A controversial artifact associated with Nazareth—and long thought to have some bearing on the Easter story—is the so-called Nazareth Inscription. This is a Greek inscription of twenty-two lines recording, in rather informal and summary language, a more official decree on the part of the Roman emperor (referred to here merely as "Caesar") to the effect that graves, tombs, and the bodies therein laid to rest should not be disturbed. A line that has caught particular attention concerns the relocation of bodies "with malicious deception."[a] Was this an imperial response to the disappearance of the body of Nazareth's most illustrious (or notorious) son?

Franz Cumont, who is generally credited with publishing the inscription, suggested two possible contexts for the decree: (1) Augustus and his revival

15. Reif, "The Early Liturgy of the Synagogue," 3:350.

16. As in Mark 6:2; Luke 4:16–21; Acts 13:15–16; Philo, *Legat*. 156. This is corroborated by the Theodotus inscription (see discussion in chap. 26, under "A Synagogue for Diaspora Jews"), which lists among the purposes of a particular synagogue for Greek-speaking Jews in Jerusalem "the reading of the law and the study of the commandments."

17. Horbury, "Women in the Synagogue," 3:363.

18. Ilan, "Gender Issues," 61.

of traditional Roman religious values and laws, here specifically treating the disturbance of the buried dead as equivalent to sacrilege; and (2) Tiberius responding to a report from Pilate concerning the probable theft of the body of the crucified revolutionary, Jesus.[b] Mary Smallwood essentially adopted the second option, but postponed its date to the reign of Claudius (and specifically after AD 44), when direct Roman rule was established over Galilee after the death of Agrippa I.[c] Since then, a third possibility has gained favor. The marble itself on which the inscription was carved has been found, by means of isotope analysis, to have originated on the island of Cos. The content, then, would enshrine a response on the part of Augustus to the disturbance of the tomb of Nikias, ruler of Cos, in 20 BC.

The inscription's connection to Nazareth is tenuous. It was likely purchased in Nazareth in the late nineteenth century, but Nazareth and Jerusalem were both thriving antiquities markets, and there is no actual record of the provenance of the inscription itself. Yet it would be odd for an inscription originally erected on the Greek island of Cos to end up in Nazareth. Moreover, since all marble in Palestine was imported marble, and since there was a *lot* of marble imported to Palestine, determining the origin of the material does not seem very promising for determining the origin of the actual inscription or the situation that called forth the inscription. It would not be odd, however, for an inscription originally erected in one of the cities of the Decapolis or the territory of Philip, or even the cities of the coastal plains, to make its way to the antiquities market in nearby Nazareth. Moreover, had the inscription actually been occasioned by the alleged theft of Jesus's body, it would have made far more sense for the decree to have been posted in Jerusalem (the location of the alleged crime) than in Nazareth (the place of reputed origin of the victim).

In the final analysis, the inscription hardly provides evidence for the resurrection. At best, it is evidence for an empty tomb—and the explanation for that empty tomb that it presumes is the theft of a body with intent to deceive. There is therefore nothing theologically at stake in regard to the historical question of the inscription's origins; though, as Metzger notes, if such penalties as the decree sets forth for making away with a corpse were in force in AD 29, this would diminish even further the likelihood that Jesus's fearful followers would have attempted the act themselves.[d]

a. Metzger, *New Testament Studies*, 77.
b. Cumont, "Un rescript impérial," 265–66.
c. Smallwood, *Jews Under Roman Rule*, 213.
d. Metzger, *New Testament Studies*, 90–91.

4

CANA IN GALILEE

"Jesus did this, the first of his signs, in Cana of Galilee, and revealed his glory; and his disciples believed in him" (John 2:11). Cana becomes a very important site in the Gospel of John as the location for the first of Jesus's miracles, which, in John's understanding, starts the timer counting down, as it were, to the arrival of Jesus's "hour"—the final and climactic revelation of the Son in his crucifixion. In John's Gospel, Cana is also where Jesus is accosted by a royal official from Capernaum seeking healing on behalf of his son (or servant) (John 4:46–54; cf. Luke 7:2–10). Cana is also the hometown of one of Jesus's disciples, Nathanael of Cana (John 21:2).

Archaeologists do not agree, however, on the location of the first-century village of Cana. The traditional site is Kafr Kanna, 4 miles northeast of Nazareth. Kafr Kanna enjoys a long history of Christian pilgrimage, and Jerome and Theodosius both identified this as the biblical Cana in the fifth and sixth centuries, respectively.[1] Excavations around the Catholic and Orthodox churches commemorating Jesus's miraculous transformation of water into wine, however, have been extremely limited and have not uncovered significant evidence of Roman-period occupation (see fig. 4.1).[2]

A number of salvage operations in a neighborhood within Kafr Kanna known as Karm er-Ras, however, have revealed the presence of an early Roman-period Jewish village. Like many other such sites, this village was likely established during the Hasmonean period as part of the Judean colonization

1. Luca, "Kafr Kanna," 2:159–60.
2. Luca, "Kafr Kanna," 2:166.

Figure 4.1. One of the few excavation areas visible in Kafr Kanna, here revealing remains of early Roman, Byzantine, and medieval structures.

of Galilee in the late second century BC.[3] Finds include terraced houses, courtyards, storage pits and tabun ovens (clay ovens built into the ground), grinding stones, and loom weights. There is plentiful evidence that this village was inhabited by Jews: three mikvaoth (two in private homes), storage jars manufactured in Shikhin, cooking vessels from Kefar Hananya, and locally made pottery wares from an early Roman pottery workshop together with chalk vessels from a local quarry (see figs. 4.2, 4.3). Animal bones found in these sites reflect a kosher diet.[4] It is possible that these finds mark the site of the Roman-period village that later expanded east into Kafr Kanna, with the latter growing and the former declining over the next few centuries.[5]

Excavations at a site 8 miles north of Nazareth have uncovered evidence of another Jewish settlement from the early Roman period that some archaeologists would identify as Cana (hence it is known as Khirbet Qana).[6] The settlement was located atop and along the sides of a fairly steep hill, covering an area of just 12 or 13 acres, to judge from location of tombs around the

3. Alexandre, "Karm er-Ras," 2:150. "Salvage excavations" occur as a building project or new development uncovers some traces of archaeological remains. Work stops on the new construction, and archaeologists come in to make as thorough an examination of the remains as possible in a limited amount of time. Generally, after the finds are documented, construction proceeds, and the site is lost; on some occasions the finds are deemed so significant that their proper excavation and preservation takes precedence over the new construction.

4. Alexandre, "Karm er-Ras," 2:150.

5. Alexandre, "Karm er-Ras," 2:155.

6. Coins from the Hasmonean period have been found on the site, but no clearly Hasmonean structures have yet been uncovered (McCullough, "Khirbet Qana," 2:134). Since Hasmonean bronze coins continued to be used well into the Roman period, it would be risky to date the founding of the settlement to the earlier period on this basis.

Figure 4.2. Cylindrical cores cut out from pieces of chalk in the process of making chalk vessels (in this case, cups), bearing witness to a local workshop for the production of such stone vessels.

Figure 4.3. One finished and several unfinished chalk cups.

Author photo, courtesy of the Terra Sancta Museum, Jerusalem

periphery. Sixty cisterns carved into the rock of the hill supplied the twelve hundred or so residents with water during the dry summer season.[7] It was surrounded by the fertile lands of the Beit Netofa Valley, which continue to be farmed extensively today. An elite home, recognized as such not only by its size but also by the presence of plastered surfaces and even molded, decorative plaster, was found on the top of the hill,[8] together with a large hall (about 15 by 20 yards) that has tentatively been identified as a synagogue. In favor of this identification is the fact that a smaller room (about 3 by 5 yards) is attached to one side, suggesting the typical "study room" (Heb., *beit ha-midrash*) often found incorporated into a synagogue complex.[9] On the steeper eastern and southern slopes, the houses were essentially piled on top of one another, with the roof of a lower house serving as a terrace for an upper house. The flatter, northern slope allowed houses to take on the more normal courtyard-style house pattern.[10] A number of mikvaoth, alongside the usual pottery and stone vessel finds, confirm the expected Jewish identity of the population. The site continued to be occupied and to expand throughout the Roman period into the Byzantine period.

A history of Christian pilgrimage to the site and the presence of a cave complex that was made a place of veneration strengthens Khirbet Qana's claim

7. McCullough, "Khirbet Qana," 2:137.
8. McCullough, "Khirbet Qana," 2:138.
9. McCullough, "Khirbet Qana," 2:141. The synagogue may postdate the First Jewish Revolt, however.
10. McCullough, "Khirbet Qana," 2:137–38.

to authenticity. Within the cave complex, one cave was plastered and bore graffiti of a clearly Christian nature (for example, "Lord have mercy [Grk., *Kyrie eleison*]" and "Lord . . . enter . . . deign to"). There was a bench along one wall, a sarcophagus lid turned on its side to serve as a kind of liturgical screen, and behind it, a carved shelf with two large stone vessels found in place and enough empty space for four more (see figs. 4.4, 4.5).[11] Uncertainty about whether Khirbet Qana or Kafr Kanna was the site of Jesus's first miracle thus reaches back to the post-Constantinian period.

Author photo, courtesy of the Israel Museum, Jerusalem

Figure 4.4. Five large stone vessels of a type similar to those envisioned in John 2:6. Vessels of such size were used as basins in which to immerse, and thus purify, other vessels that were, unlike stone, susceptible to becoming ritually polluted.

Author photo, courtesy of the Sisters of Zion Convent, Jerusalem

Figure 4.5. A large stone purification vessel of a decidedly more ordinary sort.

11. McCullough, "Khirbet Qana," 2:130–31.

5

SEPPHORIS AND TIBERIAS

Neither Sepphoris nor Tiberias appears in the Gospel narratives at any point. This is surprising, since Sepphoris and Tiberias were, alongside Magdala, the largest and most prominent settlements on the Galilean landscape. Herod the Great had done very little to advance the urbanization or stimulate the economy of Galilee, focusing his attentions on Judea, Samaria, and the coastal cities instead. Antipas, whose ambitions would be limited to Galilee and Peraea, took up the task of urbanization in these regions. Despite Antipas's efforts to improve his disappointingly small realm, it must be admitted that both Sepphoris and Tiberias were modest, even "backward," cities in comparison with the better-established cities of the Decapolis or his father Herod's projects at Sebaste or Caesarea Maritima (Caesarea-by-the-Sea).

Sepphoris

Antipas's first project was to rebuild and expand Sepphoris, a city located in the heart of Lower Galilee, halfway between the Sea of Galilee and the Mediterranean coast, and 4 miles north of Nazareth. As is the case with many other sites, there is evidence of Iron Age settlement followed by a long period of abandonment after the Assyrian invasion. Sepphoris was founded as a small, fortified city during the Hellenistic period under the Seleucids, only to be taken over under the Hasmonean dynasty in the late second or early first century BC (Josephus, *Ant.* 14.413–14; *J.W.* 1.303).[1] The remains

1. Weiss, "Sepphoris," 4:1324; Strange, "Sepphoris. A.," 2:25–26.

Figure 5.1. A portion of the remains of a Jewish residential area from the first century BC. Note the mikveh in the lower right.

of a residential area dating back to the Hasmonean era and persisting into the Roman period have been uncovered on the western side of the acropolis (see fig. 5.1). These are mostly medium-sized courtyard houses of around 2,000 square feet each.[2] Only one of these residences was constructed from finely carved ashlars. Some show modest use of mosaic flooring. One room had fragments of frescoed plaster.[3] The residents were sufficiently well-off, but not extravagantly so.

The excavation of these houses revealed the usual markers of a Jewish population—cookware from Kefar Hananya, storage vessels from Shikhin, and the chalk or limestone vessels that show a strong interest in purity in accordance with early Jewish practice. Some of these chalk vessels have been traced to the workshops at Reinah, a village immediately north of Nazareth. The houses yielded less in the way of imported wares, though one does find terra sigillata tableware of a variety of types (hence, from a diversity of Mediterranean sources) as well as a few lamps with erotic scenes and even metal figurines of pagan deities. The animal bones recovered from the site mostly represent

2. Meyers et al., "Sepphoris. B.," 2:45.
3. Meyers et al., "Sepphoris. B.," 2:45.

kosher species, though a small number of pig bones were also present.[4] This suggests a largely Jewish population, at least in this neighborhood, with an increasing Gentile presence during the Herodian and early Roman periods. Several of the residences are equipped not only with cisterns, necessary for keeping water available throughout the dry season, but also with mikvaoth, the latter suggesting that several priestly families numbered among the inhabitants. Members of the priestly caste appear to have needed to maintain a higher degree of purity, not merely in connection with their more sporadic periods of temple service (for which the many mikvaoth available for priestly use in close proximity to the Jerusalem temple would have largely sufficed), but also for the consumption of sacred foods distributed to the priests, which also required a state of ritual purity for those partaking.

Sepphoris served for a time as the administrative center of Galilee under Gabinius's short-lived division of the territory into five districts (57–55 BC).[5] It likely remained an important node in Herod's administration of his kingdom. Immediately following Herod's death in 4 BC, Sepphoris was taken over by Judas ben-Hezekiah and his sizable band of insurgents during a revolt that might well have been motivated by economic desperation.[6] In the course of suppressing this revolt, Varus allegedly destroyed Sepphoris and slaughtered many of its inhabitants, though excavations have not revealed a destruction layer from this period.[7] When Antipas was awarded Galilee and Peraea as his portion of his father's kingdom, he immediately undertook to rebuild Sepphoris with the goal of making it his capital and "the ornament of all Galilee" (Josephus, *Ant.* 18.27).

There is little evidence of Romanization in the first century AD, however. Prior to the First Jewish Revolt, Jewish sensibilities regarding representations of human beings and (most) animals appear to have been respected. The many mosaics that can be viewed on the site today depicting mythical scenes, as well as all the statuary from the city, date from the second century AD and later. The discovery of objects bearing the name and title of an *agoranomos*—an official in charge of the agora, or marketplace—tell us that there was, as would be expected, a commercial forum in the city. A small theater was built into the side of the acropolis, but its date remains a matter of debate (see fig. 5.2).[8]

4. Meyers et al., "Sepphoris. B.," 2:45–49.

5. Josephus, *Ant.* 14.41; *J.W.* 1.170.

6. Horsley, *Archaeology, History, and Society in Galilee*, 112.

7. Meyers et al., "Sepphoris. B.," 2:41. Contrast the literary record in Josephus, *Ant.* 17.271–72, 289; *J.W.* 2.56, 68.

8. Weiss ("Sepphoris," 5:2031; and "Sepphoris. C.," 2:67) and Meyers et al. ("Sepphoris. B.," 2:42) date the theater as a whole to the second century AD; Weiss had previously assigned it to the first century ("Sepphoris," 4:1325), as does Strange ("Sepphoris. A.," 2:28).

Figure 5.2. The theater at Sepphoris, in its present dimensions dating from the second century AD.

It is at least possible that it, or a smaller, earlier version of this theater, was part of Antipas's urban renewal plan for the city. With a diameter of about 75 yards, the present theater could accommodate an estimated 4,000 to 4,500 spectators—too large of a percentage of the city's estimated total population of between 6,000 and 15,000 persons during the first century.[9]

Antipas was likely responsible for an earlier version of the basilica at the intersection of the principal roads of the city (the Cardo Maximus and Decumanus Maximus), as a space designated for judicial functions would have been essential to the functioning of the city—all the more its functioning as a capital. He also constructed the first of the two aqueducts that would assure the water supply for the growing city.[10] Prior to Antipas, the residents of Sepphoris relied entirely on rainwater, collected carefully into cisterns throughout the residential and public spaces.[11] Antipas surely had constructed a palace

9. Weiss, "Sepphoris," 4:1325; Reed, *Archaeology and the Galilean Jesus*, 80.

10. Strange, "Sepphoris. A.," 2:28; Strange, "The Sepphoris Aqueducts," 2:77. Probes beneath the decumanus uncovered a coin from the reign of Trajan (AD 98–117) and early second-century pottery shards, dating the flagstones of the currently excavated decumanus to the second century AD (Weiss, "Sepphoris. C.," 2:62). These major roads, however, surely had precursors in Antipas's capital.

11. Weiss, "Sepphoris. C.," 2:58.

Figure 5.3. The triclinium, or dining room, from the House of Dionysus, so named for this elaborate mosaic depicting scenes related to Dionysus and viticulture.

for himself in his capital, but this structure has not yet been located with any assurance. Fill found beneath the third-century AD mansion known as the House of Dionysus contained numerous fragments of frescoes, suggestive of an older, elite structure at that location, but this remains only one possibility.[12]

Though this mansion dates from a later period, its dining room gives us a clear window into the standard arrangement of the triclinium. The areas where the floor is covered with a relatively plain mosaic reveal the arrangement of the three couches (the basic sense of "triclinium") on which the diners would recline around a central area where food would be placed and, in the case of more elaborate parties, entertainments provided. In elite houses such as the House of Dionysus, an elegant mosaic might be featured where the diners' gaze would naturally be directed—but not wasted on the space beneath the couches themselves (see fig. 5.3). The diners' heads would face this central area, while their feet were oriented toward the room's walls. Luke assumes such a dining arrangement in the episode in which a Pharisee named Simon hosts Jesus for a meal and in which a grateful woman comes and stands "behind [Jesus] at his feet" (Luke 7:38). John also appears to have such an arrangement in mind for the Last Supper, as it would very naturally explain how the Beloved Disciple would be "lying close to Jesus's breast" (John 13:23 AT). With Jesus and all the disciples leaning on their left arms, the Beloved

12. Weiss, "Sepphoris. C.," 2:57.

Disciple would have been next to Jesus, in a position to lean back toward Jesus's chest to ask the fateful question about the betrayer. There was also a traditional, and highly specific, order for the seating of guests around a triclinium, with each of the three couches reflecting different levels of honor and, in the case of larger triclinia, the seating order on each of the couches reflecting the respective honor of the guests. Here, too, is a contemporary and culturally appropriate setting for thinking about those who sought out "the place of honor" at banquets, concerning which Jesus raises cautions (Matt. 23:6; cf. Luke 14:7–8).

During the late twentieth century, it became popular for scholars to suggest that, as a craftsperson in the construction business in some form (whether as a carpenter, mason, or both), Joseph could have regularly walked the 4 miles to Sepphoris to participate in its many building projects under Antipas, taking Jesus along as his apprentice, with Jesus perhaps continuing the practice after Joseph's death.[13] Some have even suggested that Jesus attended shows in the theater (if it existed in the early first century!) and rubbed shoulders with Cynic philosophers and the like in Sepphoris's marketplace. On the basis of further archaeological investigation, however, it now appears that Sepphoris was far less impressive of an urban center than scholars like John Dominic Crossan had assumed (and capitalized on for his theories concerning Jesus's ministry).[14] Doubts have also been raised about the necessity of making the commute to Sepphoris on anything like a regular basis when adequate work might be found in Nazareth and its nearby villages like Cana.[15]

Tiberias

Sepphoris did not satisfy Antipas's ambitions for long. By AD 19 or 20, he founded an entirely new city, winsomely set on the southwest shore of the Sea of Galilee and just north of some hot springs. Antipas named it Tiberias in honor of Augustus's successor, Tiberius (ruled AD 14–37; see fig. 5.4). He must have regarded the physical site as particularly advantageous, perhaps in part because of the

Figure 5.4. A bronze coin of Herod Antipas with a palm leaf and the legend "of Herod the tetrarch" on the obverse and the city name "Tiberias" within a wreath on the reverse.
CNGCoins.com

13. Batey, *Jesus and the Forgotten City*, 76.
14. Reed, *Archaeology and the Galilean Jesus*, 134–36.
15. Miller, "Sepphoris," 77.

hot springs immediately to the south, because building his city required the demolition of a necropolis (a cemetery) and the bribing of a number of settlers with houses and lands to bring the city's population up to an adequate level (Josephus, *Ant.* 18.36–38).

As quite a few episodes in the *Jewish War* take place in Tiberias, Josephus provides several details concerning the city and its architectural features. He claims that the city was fortified with a wall and was accessed through gates on the north and south sides (Josephus, *J.W.* 3.449, 459–60). A gate on the southern end of the city has been excavated (see fig. 5.5), but it has been incorporated into later walls from the Byzantine period; Roman-period walls have not yet been definitively located.

According to Josephus (*Life* 277–93), Antipas also supplied Tiberias with a theater as well as a large synagogue or "prayer house" (Grk., *proseuchē*). Josephus's designation of the latter building as a prayer house speaks to its primary function, though in Josephus's narrative it also serves as a kind of community center for the discussion of matters of public concern. It probably served all the functions attributed to synagogues elsewhere in Galilee and Judea. Antipas constructed a second palace in Tiberias, and this time he went so far as to decorate it with images of animals in apparent violation of

Figure 5.5. The south gate of Tiberias. The two round towers flanked the entrance to Antipas's city, opening onto a plaza immediately to the north.

Figure 5.6. The remains of the theater at Tiberias.

the prohibition of images in the second commandment (Exod. 20:4; Deut. 5:8). This would later make it the target of vandalism by revolutionaries during the First Jewish Revolt, though Josephus claims that they were driven more by a desire to pillage than a zeal for the prohibition against images (*Life* 64–66; *Ant.* 18.38). Neither the palace nor the prayer house has been identified, though a theater with its origins in the early Roman period can be seen on the site today (see fig. 5.6).[16] The theater continued to be used and remodeled into the Byzantine period; its final dimensions—large enough to seat five thousand—reflect the need to accommodate a larger theater-going population than the city would have had in the early Roman period (with a total population of between eight thousand and twelve thousand).[17]

Evidence of a first-century elite residence was found beneath a late Roman basilica.[18] It is tempting to consider that Chuza—Antipas's steward and husband of Joanna, who came to be among Jesus's followers (Luke 8:3)—lived in such a mansion. It can hardly be doubted, given his position, that he and Joanna resided in Tiberias at the time of her connection with Jesus.[19] Similarly, a bathhouse built in the late first or early second century is believed to cover the space of the early Roman agora.[20] A great deal of ancient Tiberias remains to be excavated, but even many of the portions that have been excavated have stopped short of recovering the shape of Tiberias given to it by

16. Strange, "Sepphoris. A.," 2:27.
17. Cytryn-Silverman, "Tiberias," 2:193; Reed, *Archaeology and the Galilean Jesus*, 80.
18. Hirschfeld, *Excavations at Tiberias*, 10–11.
19. Reed, *Archaeology and the Galilean Jesus*, 137.
20. Cytryn-Silverman, "Tiberias," 2:195.

Antipas and his generation. The city was also supplied with a stadium in the early Roman period (Josephus, *Life* 90–92; *J.W.* 3.537–40), portions of which have been discovered beneath the Galei Kinneret Hotel and the Plaza Hotel.[21]

Sepphoris, Tiberias, and the Politics and Economy of Galilee

The building of these cities is likely to have had two contrasting effects on Galilee's economy. The hundreds of masons, artisans, and laborers working on the cities, along with those who would provide the service industries necessary to urban life, would have benefitted significantly. Conversely, Antipas would also have siphoned off a good deal of other Galileans' meager wealth and their local resources through ongoing—and potentially increased—taxation without their enjoying the benefit of additional income.[22]

The Gospels' silence about any activity on Jesus's part in Sepphoris or Tiberias seems quite reasonable. Given John the Baptist's fate, Jesus would indeed have been wise to avoid Antipas's administrative centers.[23] Antipas reportedly kept an eye on Jesus and an ear out for what he was up to (as Luke 23:8 suggests). His execution of John the Baptist is a stark reminder of the powerlessness even of popular figures in the face of Antipas's power over life and death. When the Pharisees warned Jesus, "Get away from here, for Herod [Antipas] wants to kill you" (Luke 13:31), the danger was likely quite real. And while Jesus might have been assured that he would die only in God's time in the appointed manner, it is noteworthy that there is no record of Jesus's revolutionary proclamation of the kingdom of God in Sepphoris or Tiberias.

While these cities do not appear in the pages of the Gospels, their presence was no doubt felt in the lives of many Galileans. In the ancient world, a city was normally granted hinterlands, the amount of territory necessary to provide for the agricultural needs of the city, often worked by tenant farmers to provide the food required by the city's inhabitants. Existing villages could also be assigned to serve as hinterlands for new or enlarged cities, as appears to have been the case for the fourteen villages that came to be considered part of the territory of Antipas's improved city of Julias (Betharamphtha) in Peraea (see Josephus, *Ant.* 20.159). Their agricultural production, beyond the subsistence of those working the land, would be directed toward feeding the

21. Cytryn-Silverman, "Tiberias," 2:196.

22. Horsley, *Archaeology, History, and Society in Galilee*, 82, 123; Reed, *Archaeology and the Galilean Jesus*, 22. It is not clear whether Antipas enjoyed income from any of the royal lands that his father had enjoyed (the Jezreel Valley would have been the most likely, if he did) or if he relied wholly upon the various taxes in place for his subjects.

23. Freyne, "Archaeology," 140; Miller, "Sepphoris," 78.

city. The elites and semi-elites of cities generally enjoyed that status by virtue of having increased their own landholdings as well, generally at the expense of small landowners who fell into debt and eventually had to sell their land after a series of inadequate crop yields rendered them otherwise unable to repay. Throughout the late Hasmonean and early Roman periods, increasing numbers might have found themselves renting and working the land they (or their parents or their grandparents) once owned. Tenant farmers kept a share of their produce but yielded a good deal of it up the food chain. Others would eke out a subsistence-level existence as day laborers or, when that proved inadequate or impossible, might fall into banditry.[24] Several of Jesus's parables feature scenarios that reflect these harsh economic realities, such as the parable of the laborers in the vineyard and the parable of the wicked tenants (see Matt. 20:1–16; 21:33–41).

24. Horsley, *Archaeology, History, and Society in Galilee*, 10–11; Hamel, "Poverty and Charity," 312; Oakman, "Was the Galilean Economy Oppressive or Prosperous?" Grabbe (*History of the Jews and Judaism*, 4:110) rightly points out that there could have been a good deal of overlap between these categories. A small landowner might well also have let himself out as a day laborer when the seasonal work was slow or, during the season, when his own work did not require six days per week.

6

CAPERNAUM

Among all the villages around the Sea of Galilee, Capernaum is the one most often singled out in the Gospels as the specific location of one of Jesus's teachings or actions. According to the Gospel of Matthew, Jesus "made his home in Capernaum by the sea, in the territory of Zebulun and Naphtali" after his baptism and temptation (Matt. 4:13; cf. Mark 1:21). It became "his own town" (Matt. 9:1; cf. Mark 2:1), at least to the extent that the itinerant preacher and exorcist had a home. This was the setting of the healing of a "centurion," or officer of Antipas (Matt. 8:5–13; Luke 7:1–10; John 4:46); the healing of Peter's mother-in-law and many others (Matt. 8:14–17; Mark 1:29–34; Luke 4:38–41); the question about the temple tax (Matt. 17:24–27); Jesus teaching on a Sabbath and exorcising a demon (Mark 1:21–27; Luke 4:31–37); Jesus teaching on another Sabbath and healing a paralytic (Mark 2:1–13); a particular teaching about discipleship (Mark 9:33–50); and the "Bread of Life" discourse and the dispute that ensues (John 6:24–71). Because of Jesus's personal investment in the people of this village, he singles out Capernaum alongside Bethsaida and Chorazin in a pronouncement of woe for their unbelief despite his many miracles (Matt. 11:23–24; Luke 10:15).[1]

The presence of a man sitting at a customs desk in Capernaum (Matt. 9:9; Mark 2:14) invites explanation. Capernaum was the easternmost village in Antipas's Galilee, close to the border of his brother Philip's (largely Gentile)

1. First-century literary references to Capernaum are otherwise sparse. Josephus refers to it as a village near Bethsaida in *Life* 72, but not again save to mention a spring in the region that is named after it (*J.W.* 3.519).

territory. One source of income for Antipas's realm was the collection of import and export taxes—hence a customs kiosk was established in Capernaum, as in other border towns and villages, alongside the road passing from Philip's territory into Antipas's. Such import and export taxes grossly inflated the cost of goods on either side, which is why imported goods were luxury items generally out of reach for the majority of the population and why being an exporter involved a good deal of capital, limiting the market for the goods one produced if one lacked the means to pay export taxes.

No evidence has been found to suggest that the site was occupied during the period of the Israelite monarchy, and there is minimal evidence of occupation during the Persian and early Hellenistic periods.[2] Some settlement existed in Capernaum during the period of Seleucid control, when it appears to have had trade connections with the Mediterranean coast, importing fine wares and products (including wine from Rhodes). When the Hasmonean dynasty established its dominance in the region, the material culture of Capernaum came to reflect the typical profile for Judean-colonized Galilee—local cooking wares from Kefar Hananya and similar sources, storage vessels from Shikhin, chalk or limestone vessels reflecting commitment to ritual purity, and a radical drop in imported wares and goods.[3]

By the early Roman period, Capernaum (Kefar Naḥum) appears to have covered an area of about 12 to 15 acres.[4] This estimate is based on the area across which pieces of early Roman pottery were found during excavations. Many of the villages throughout Galilee would have been quite small—for example, three hundred to four hundred people for a village like Nazareth. Capernaum was a large village, by comparison. Population estimates based on acreage of residential area and likely occupancy per acre suggest a figure somewhere between six hundred and fifteen hundred inhabitants.[5] Even though several Gospels use the Greek word *polis* ("city") in reference to Capernaum (Matt. 9:1; 11:20; Mark 1:33; Luke 4:31), it was not a *polis* in any proper sense, evidenced by the absence of public buildings besides the synagogue, and it certainly possessed none of the trappings of the typical Greek city (theater, stadium, gymnasium, colonnaded streets).[6] The town gives no indication of actual urban planning, developing organically as families settled and expanded. There are also no archaeological indications of the presence of an

2. Reed, *Archaeology and the Galilean Jesus*, 145.

3. Mattila, "Capernaum," 2:244; Reed, *Archaeology and the Galilean Jesus*, 145.

4. Loffreda, *Recovering Capharnaum*, 18. The settlement would expand to about 40 acres by the late Roman period. Reed, *Archaeology and the Galilean Jesus*, 151.

5. Reed, *Archaeology and the Galilean Jesus*, 150–52.

6. Reed, *Archaeology and the Galilean Jesus*, 167.

elite class—no fragments of frescoed plaster, mosaics, marble, or roof tiles such as one finds everywhere in true cities.[7] No evidence of a formal agora or market has been found. Buying and selling likely took place on market days with kiosks and tents set up ad hoc for the purpose.[8] Jesus's Capernaum is best thought of as a large village inhabited primarily by fishermen and agricultural workers and their families, along with a number of people attached to the administration of Antipas, given the town's location near the border.

The Synagogue

The most distinctive ancient structure on the archaeological site of Capernaum is its synagogue, though the synagogue visible today dates to the fourth or fifth century AD (see fig. 6.1). The structure stands out all the more because it is the only building made from bright, pinkish limestone in the midst of a

Figure 6.1. The Byzantine-period synagogue in Capernaum. Note the stone benches lining the aisles and the ornate columns that defined the central space and supported the roof.

7. Reed, *Archaeology and the Galilean Jesus*, 157.

8. Reed, *Archaeology and the Galilean Jesus*, 155. The informal market that springs up on market days would be an appropriate venue for the activity to which Jesus refers in Matt. 11:16 // Luke 7:31–32; the Jerusalem setting of the tirade that includes Matt. 23:7 suggests a formal agora.

Figure 6.2. The black basalt foundation wall of an intermediate (late Roman) synagogue that served also as the foundation wall for the later Byzantine structure (Loffreda, *Recovering Capharnaum*, 47–49; Loffreda and Tzaferis, "Capernaum," 1:294). The large, enclosed courtyard adjoining the synagogue to the east is a fifth-century AD innovation, with no counterparts in the earlier iterations of the synagogue.

sea of black basalt, the more readily available building material used for all of the residential and small industrial complexes uncovered in Capernaum. Limestone blocks on display near the synagogue provide views into Jewish iconography of the late Roman and early Byzantine periods, featuring geometric and floral patterns, clusters of grapes and other regional produce, and musical instrumental like harps. Some of the more celebrated reliefs served to keep the later synagogue and those who worshiped there connected with the Jerusalem temple, long since destroyed. One area of the frieze depicts the ark of the covenant, conceived of as a sort of miniature of the temple mounted on a cart. Another depicts the seven-branched candelabra that lit the holy place along with the incense shovel used on the altar of incense and the ram's horn blown in connection with high holy days such as Rosh Hashanah and Yom Kippur.

The synagogue of first-century Capernaum was significantly smaller and likely far less ornate, though it was still in all probability the most impressive structure in the village. Probes beneath the pavement of the Byzantine synagogue revealed the footprints of residential buildings under the two aisles and a large stone pavement dating back to the first century beneath the central nave area (a date that coincides with Luke's reminiscence that an officer of Antipas's military force subsidized the construction).[9] This pavement, too large for a private dwelling in the early Roman village, was likely the floor of the first-century synagogue.[10] It was indeed most common in antiquity for renovated or new structures to be built over the older structures they were meant to replace (see fig. 6.2). Besides, no other candidates for the location of the first-century synagogue have been unearthed. Everything therefore points to this as the authentic space where, in an earlier version of the present structure, Jesus is remembered to have preached and cast out a demon (Mark 1:21–28; Luke 4:31–36) and to have healed a man with a deformed hand (Mark 3:1–6).

In Luke 7:4–5, a "centurion" is credited with having underwritten the construction of the original basalt synagogue, clearly desiring to establish himself as a benefactor of the community and not merely as a military presence. Readers of Luke's Gospel tend to assume that this was a Roman centurion, but Galilee was under the jurisdiction first of Herod the Great and then of his second surviving son, Antipas, who ruled on Rome's behalf. Rome used client kings, ethnarchs, and tetrarchs to protect Rome's interests in a particular territory without Rome having to take direct responsibility (or assume direct expense) for doing so. Thus it is very unlikely that a *Roman* army officer would be stationed in Capernaum. Antipas maintained his own military force for the purpose of internal policing and protection of his territory from aggression from without. The "centurion" was therefore more likely an officer in Antipas's local military.[11] He would, nevertheless, probably still have been a Gentile, if Antipas followed his father's policy on recruiting.

Residences

Another prominent feature of the Capernaum site is the partially reconstructed residential blocks on three sides of the synagogue (see fig. 6.3). The walls are made of the ubiquitous basalt stone that was far more readily available than wood. Roof beams might be carved from wood or, in shorter lengths, from basalt supported on pillars to achieve the required span. The roofs would

9. De Luca, "Capernaum," 1:174–76.

10. Loffreda, *Recovering Capharnaum*, 45–47.

11. Horsley, *Archaeology, History, and Society in Galilee*, 115; Reed, *Archaeology and the Galilean Jesus*, 156, 161–62. Reed also observes that material evidence for *Roman* legionnaires in Capernaum dates only from the reign of Hadrian and later (156).

Figure 6.3. A residential block between the Capernaum synagogue and the house of Peter, seen from the synagogue. Note the entrance giving access to a courtyard from the street (far left) and the window walls (center and, perpendicular to the camera, right) separating an open courtyard from an inside room.

be finished with timbers and thatched fronds, coated with mud and pitch to weatherproof them—hence the ability to "dig through" a roof, as a paralyzed man's friends did in order to lower him through Peter's roof and set him in front of Jesus to be healed (Mark 2:4).[12]

As with the synagogue, the current layout of the residences reflects their latest stage of occupation, likely the fifth century AD, and not their first-century state. Two factors suggest that we are still *close* to the first-century shape of housing in Capernaum. First, the streets and walkways, though not near the quality of Roman civic streets, would tend to keep the perimeters of residential blocks consistent. Second, the conservative nature of village life and building techniques—where one was pretty much on one's own when it came to renovation and expansion projects—suggests less rather than more change over generations. What might change with some frequency is the layout of any particular block. As one family expands (for example, through the marriage of a son) and makes a successful bid to purchase some portion of a neighbor's house, little more is required than to open up a new door in a solid wall and fill in a former doorway to create a solid wall. This likely accounts for a good deal of the irregularity in layout that we see in Capernaum.

12. When Luke says that they lowered the man "through the tiles," presumably after prying up and removing several ceramic plates (5:19), he appears to be imposing his own greater familiarity with urban building techniques on the scene in Capernaum. The consensus of archaeologists would favor Mark's description.

That said, one can still see traces here of first-century dwellings typical throughout both Galilee and Judea. These tended to be small three- or four-room dwellings (perhaps 500 to 600 square feet total) opening onto an open courtyard, which is often a common courtyard shared by the residents of more than one dwelling. Thus multiple families or, more likely, multiple segments of extended families might end up sharing a common courtyard area. While the houses in Capernaum largely had stone floors by the fifth century, the first-century floors were made from beaten earth. The largest room was a multipurpose room for cooking, dining, and often sleeping; the smaller rooms were used to store grain, other dry goods, olive oil, and wine. The stairways visible in some units signal that there were once upper-story lofts, perhaps little more than landings made from planks, generally for sleeping, if this was not done in the multipurpose room, or perhaps opening onto rooftop lofts (see fig. 6.4). Most activities, including flour grinding, weaving, and other household crafts, would be pursued in the courtyard in fair weather, where livestock would also be kept at least during the night, small vegetable gardens planted, and chickens and doves raised for their eggs, meat, and fertilizer. Cooking might be done in indoor kitchens or in corners of courtyards.

Figure 6.4. Another view of the same residential block. Note, in the center, the remains of the base of a clay oven (a tabun oven) and a stairway that once led to a loft or roof.

Entrance to the complex was generally through a single door opening into the courtyard from the street. The exterior walls facing the streets and alleys were typically solid for the sake of security, though some reconfiguration would allow one room to function as a venue for business and open onto the street. Light and ventilation came into the dwellings from the courtyard and through the doorways and internal walls, which were often perforated with large openings (called window walls). Such were the conditions under which the majority of the population of both Galilee and Judea would have lived in the first century.[13] The absence of mikvaoth in the village is probably to be explained, first, by the availability of the Sea of Galilee and, second, by the modest circumstances in which the inhabitants of the town appear to have lived (compared, for example, to the wealth of some of the inhabitants of nearby first-century Magdala).[14]

The House of Peter

One residence in particular has captured attention from as early as the late first century AD. The house itself is now barely visible beneath and in between the ruins of an octagonal church built over the premises in the fifth century, which had itself been built over a smaller fourth-century church (see fig. 6.5). This house is believed to have belonged to Simon Peter and his family, thus making it the site of Jesus's healing of Peter's mother-in-law and of many of the teaching events in Capernaum (cf. Matt. 8:14–15; Mark 1:29–31; Luke 4:38–39). Jesus's healing of the paralyzed man let down through the roof could have taken place in any residence in Capernaum, but it makes the most sense to infer that this happened in Peter's house.

The so-called house of Peter and one or two other domestic units (perhaps inhabited by the extended kinship group of both Peter and his wife) were arranged around an L-shaped courtyard. Excavations revealed a Hellenistic-era layer as well as an early Roman layer.[15] Sometime in the later first century, the space appears to have become a house church. A central room of about 12 square yards was plastered (six layers of plaster would eventually accrete), and no artifacts of everyday life were found in that space, suggesting a more public use. This was, in fact, the only plastered room found in Capernaum.[16] Graffiti suggestive of Christian motifs—the name of Jesus, a monogram of

13. Loffreda and Tzaferis, "Capernaum," 1:292; Reed, *Archaeology and the Galilean Jesus*, 157–60; Killebrew, "Village and Countryside," 198–200.

14. Reed, *Archaeology and the Galilean Jesus*, 158.

15. Loffreda, *Recovering Capharnaum*, 52–55.

16. Loffreda, *Recovering Capharnaum*, 57.

Figure 6.5. The domestic block reputed to have contained the house of Peter and his extended family, now dominated by the remains of the fifth-century octagonal church (and the twentieth-century church erected overtop the ruins).

Jesus, liturgical elements like "Amen" and "Kyrie, eleison"—began to appear by the early third century. The graffiti began to appear in multiple languages (Greek, Aramaic, Syriac, Latin), suggesting that this had become a widely visited pilgrimage site by the fourth and fifth centuries.[17] In the early fourth century, the whole block of the house of Peter was set off from the rest of the village by a broad, square wall and transformed into a church. In her account of her pilgrimage to the Holy Land, Egeria recounted visiting a structure here that she describes as a house transformed into a church, with elements of the original house still visible.[18] Modern visitors to Capernaum can still attest to the same. It is impossible to affirm with certainty that this was, in fact, the house of Peter in which so many important episodes involving Jesus himself took place, but the early and consistent history of the veneration of the site suggests a strong local memory that this was so.

Agriculture and Industry

Galilee's economy was, like that of most of the Mediterranean world, primarily agricultural. The region was surprisingly fertile, evidenced still by the presence of lush vegetation around the basin and the ongoing planting

17. Loffreda, *Recovering Capharnaum*, 60.
18. Loffreda, *Recovering Capharnaum*, 51.

of large-scale crops on a number of the hillsides (many of which are now fruit crops protected from the sun and animals by acre-sized burlap canopies). In the first century, wheat, olive trees, and grape vines were the principal crops, as these also produced the three most basic staples of the diet not only here but throughout the Mediterranean.

Figure 6.6. An upper millstone seated on its conical lower millstone recovered at Capernaum.

Visitors to Capernaum can see several basalt grain mills, the standard tools for processing wheat into usable flour throughout the Eastern Mediterranean. The top piece had an hourglass design open to the top and bottom; the lower piece was a cone on which the top piece sat with maximum contact around all its sides (see fig. 6.6). The upper grinding stone was fitted with a wooden yoke and poles that allowed it to be turned against the lower stone (see fig. 6.7). The wheat was poured into the top and ground by the turning stones, with flour falling out along the bottom seam. The flour would be mixed with olive oil and salt to make dough for baking; leaven (more like our sourdough starter than dried yeast) would often be added to ordinary dough to make it rise, though this was forbidden for bread in all ritual contexts and during certain seasons, most famously Passover. It is easy to imagine how tying the upper millstone about one's neck would accelerate one's descent to the bottom of a sea (Luke 17:2).

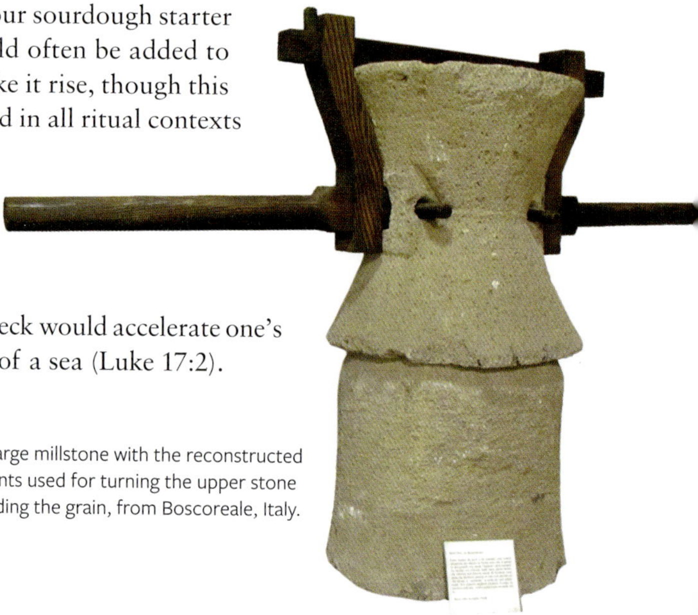

Figure 6.7. A large millstone with the reconstructed wooden elements used for turning the upper stone and, thus, grinding the grain, from Boscoreale, Italy.

Figure 6.8. The stone elements of several kinds of olive presses found at Capernaum. (On the process of olive oil production in first-century Galilee and Judea, see chap. 7 under the heading "Chorazin.") On the left is the apparatus for grinding olives and their pits into a pulp. On the right is the base of a screw press and the collection vat into which the expressed oil would flow.

There were, of course, other crops like dates, figs, lentils, chickpeas, and other protein-rich legumes. Families would often keep small gardens for vegetables and fruit. They also kept small livestock—chickens for eggs and, occasionally, meat; goats for milk and cheese. Of course, families in Capernaum also had ready access to fish.

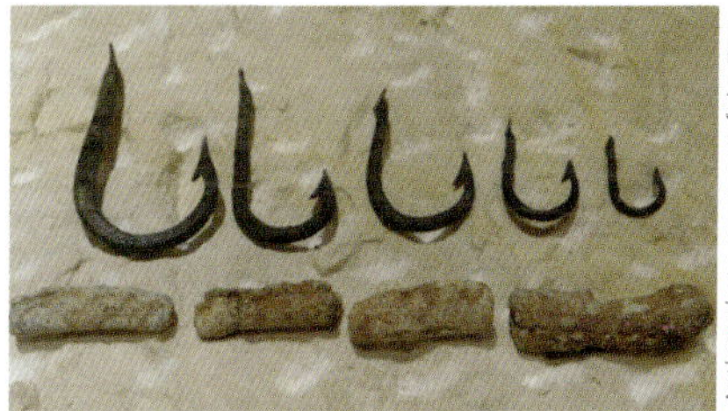

Author photo, courtesy of the Terra Sancta Museum, Jerusalem

Figure 6.9. An assortment of fishhooks and lead weights, the latter placed around the edges of nets cast into the sea from boats or the shoreline to trap fish (cf. Matt. 4:18–21; Luke 5:2). These weights were found in the residential areas of Capernaum.

Fishing was an important facet of the economy of the villages and towns surrounding the Sea of Galilee—and people from the regions of Galilee, Peraea, and the Decapolis all had a piece of it, as it were. Capernaum is celebrated as the home of four apostles who came from two fishing families, though there is little evidence of the industry there aside from fishhooks found in the courtyards of some of the houses (see fig. 6.9). The presence of hired hands in Mark 1:20 is less an indication of the wealth of the family of Zebedee and more an indication of the means by which dispossessed Galileans sustained themselves by hiring themselves out (or, if they were still small landholders, remained productive in the off seasons).[19]

19. Reed, *Archaeology and the Galilean Jesus*, 165.

7

BETHSAIDA AND CHORAZIN

Alongside Capernaum, Bethsaida and Chorazin are both remembered as important centers of Jesus's Galilean ministry. This is underscored in a most unflattering manner in one of Jesus's more exasperated pronouncements:

> Woe to you, Chorazin! Woe to you, Bethsaida! For if the deeds of power done in you had been done in Tyre and Sidon, they would have repented long ago in sackcloth and ashes. But I tell you, on the day of judgment it will be more tolerable for Tyre and Sidon than for you. And you, Capernaum,
>
> will you be exalted to heaven?
> No, you will be brought down to Hades.
>
> For if the deeds of power done in you had been done in Sodom, it would have remained until this day. But I tell you that on the day of judgment it will be more tolerable for the land of Sodom than for you. (Matt. 11:21–24; cf. Luke 10:13–15)

This saying presumes that Jesus invested himself rather heavily in these two cities—and that to an extent far greater than the Gospels indicate at the level of individual stories. Chorazin, 2 miles north of Capernaum and the shoreline, is named in the Gospels *only* here, a reminder that the Gospels are indeed only a selective witness to Jesus's teachings and deeds (John 20:30). Bethsaida, on the other hand, provides the setting for the healing of a blind person in a two-stage process (Mark 8:22–26) and the feeding of the five thousand, according to Luke (9:10–15), or its aftermath, according to Mark

(6:45–52).[1] According to the author of the Fourth Gospel, Philip, Simon Peter, and Andrew were originally from Bethsaida (John 1:44), which would not preclude Peter and Andrew putting down new roots in nearby Capernaum by the time they met Jesus.[2]

Bethsaida

The location of Bethsaida is the subject of a strenuous and ongoing debate.[3] As the city fell within the jurisdiction of Philip after the division of Herod's kingdom, it must have been located somewhere between twelve o'clock and two o'clock on the Sea of Galilee, since the area west of that belonged to Antipas and the area to the east and south to the cities of the Decapolis. Josephus further narrows this down to a location near the Sea of Galilee east of the Jordan River (*J.W.* 2.168; *Ant.* 18.28).

The two principal candidates that have emerged are Et-Tell, in the Beit Tsaida Nature Reserve, less than 2 miles northeast of the Sea of Galilee and under a half mile east of the Jordan River, and El-Araj, on the delta where the Jordan enters the Sea of Galilee. A Byzantine monastery has been excavated at El-Araj, which might suggest an ancient connection with a site of importance in the New Testament story.[4] The excavators believe that they have found earlier, Roman-period structures beneath and around the monastery, including what appears to have been a bath complex.[5] Some Roman pottery and architectural fragments have also been found in the vicinity.[6] The site has, however, not yet yielded any evidence of a first-century settlement.

While future seasons of archaeological work may require a reassessment of El-Araj, at present Et-Tell seems the more promising option, even though it, too, has yielded fewer Roman-period remains than one would have hoped, segments of a Roman-period wall and the renovation of a Hellenistic temple being the major finds. It has, however, reportedly yielded more numerous

1. Mark locates the feeding of the five thousand on a shore across the lake from Bethsaida (6:31–45).

2. John 12:21 appears to use the designation "Galilee" loosely when its author speaks of the disciple Philip coming "from Bethsaida in Galilee." Foreman, "Jesus Heals a Blind Man," 271.

3. See the discussions in Savage, *Biblical Bethsaida*, 159–63; Arav, "Bethsaida—A Response"; Arav, "Response"; Arav, "Searching for Bethsaida"; Notley and Aviam, "Et-Tell Is *Not* Bethsaida"; Notley and Aviam, "Searching for Bethsaida."

4. Notley and Aviam, "Searching for Bethsaida," 35–36, 38.

5. Notley and Aviam, "Searching for Bethsaida," 36, 38. The availability of a defunct bath complex, however, might also account for the choice of a location for a new monastery. Monasteries took root at two of Herod's fortress-palaces—Masada and Herodium—precisely for this practical reason.

6. Foreman, "Jesus Heals a Blind Man," 274–75.

early Roman-period artifacts than Capernaum, Nazareth, and Khirbet Qana combined.[7] Broader soundings and excavations need to be undertaken; at present, the excavated area within the nature reserve is quite limited.

Champions of El-Araj object that Et-Tell is too far removed from the Sea of Galilee to be the location of a town many of whose residents were involved in the fishing industry, such as the Gospels represent Bethsaida.[8] The fishhooks, net weights, sinkers, and anchors discovered in one Hellenistic-period dwelling, however, demonstrate that at least a number of the town's residents would have disagreed.[9] Geological studies also point to evidence for significant changes to the landscape in connection with a major earthquake, likely the one that rocked Palestine in AD 363.[10] A fair portion of the marshes and the plain between Et-Tell and the Sea of Galilee may have emerged as a consequence of this geological event and the deposit of large quantities of silt released into the Jordan upriver and coming to rest at its mouth.[11] Thus, in the first century, either the Jordan River or the Sea of Galilee—or both—might have been much more accessible for those living at the site of Et-Tell and its surrounding area.

During the Iron Age, Bethsaida was an important city of the kingdom of Geshur, a kingdom that formed an alliance with King David, sealing it by sending the princess Maacah to be his wife (from whom would be born Absalom, to David's eventual grief). Geshur remained independent of Israel (Josh. 13:13). The most impressive finds at Bethsaida (Et-Tell) date to this period, including city walls and a ninth-century BC city gate complex, notably featuring a shrine or "high place" dedicated to a local Canaanite deity just inside the gate (see fig. 7.1). The gate complex was destroyed in the Assyrian invasions of the late eighth century BC, invasions that left the city devastated and largely uninhabited for centuries.

7. Arav, "Bethsaida—A Response," 92–93, in response to Notley and Aviam, "Et-Tell Is *Not* Bethsaida," 224–26.

8. Notley and Aviam, "Et-Tell Is *Not* Bethsaida," 223–24. The objection that Josephus (*Life* 406) claims to have sailed to Bethsaida, and thus that the site had to be accessible by boat (Foreman, "Jesus Heals a Blind Man," 272–73), which the elevated portion of Et-Tell would surely not have been in any event, does not take into account the fact that Josephus elsewhere uses this language rather loosely. He also writes of sailing to Hippos (*Life* 153), a city soaring 1,000 feet above the Sea of Galilee, and even sailing to Rome (*Life* 422), when the ship in question actually landed at Ostia (Arav, "Searching for Bethsaida," 43–44).

9. Arav, "Searching for Bethsaida," 46; Arav, "Bethsaida—A Response," 94, 96.

10. Shroder and Inbar, "Geologic and Geographic Background"; Shroder et al., "Catastrophic Geomorphic Processes." These same studies suggest that El-Araj would have been a swamp for much of the Hellenistic and early Roman periods.

11. Excavations at Magdala on the west coast of the Sea of Galilee incidentally give clear evidence that the first-century shoreline was higher than it is today, having receded 200 feet away from the Hellenistic- and Roman-period quay and dock at that site.

Figure 7.1. The excavated remains of the Iron Age gate system and the ancient "high place" inside the gate of Bethsaida (Et-Tell).

Following the pattern of many Galilean sites, Bethsaida (Et-Tell) appears to have remained uninhabited until the Hellenistic period, when it was resettled during the reign of Ptolemy II or III, perhaps as a colony for veterans (who were given the usual rewards of farmland), perhaps even with a view to placing "reservists" close to the disputed northern border between the Ptolemaic and Seleucid Empires. The discovery of Rhodian amphora handles attests to the far-reaching trade relations of Hellenistic-era Bethsaida. This indirectly supports the hypothesis of Bethsaida being resettled by soldiers, active or otherwise, as Rhodian wine was a favorite with Greek-bred soldiers. The colony passed into Seleucid hands after Antiochus III established control over Coele-Syria with his victory at the battle of Panion (later known as Caesarea Philippi) in 200 BC.[12] Coins found throughout the excavations of Bethsaida show continuous occupation of the site from the late Ptolemaic through the late Roman periods. It was likely during the Hellenistic period that a templelike structure was built above the filled-in, defunct city gate. This was a smallish temple of about 5 by 20 yards.[13] Clay figurines of pregnant women

12. Savage, *Biblical Bethsaida*, 148; Arav and Savage, "Bethsaida," 2:260–62.
13. Strickert, *Philip's City*, 183.

Figure 7.2. A view of the kitchen (right) of the house of the vintner (Bethsaida/Et-Tell) with a portion of its courtyard (left) and the first of three adjacent smaller rooms (top left).

found in the vicinity have led some to speculate that the temple was originally dedicated to the Phoenician fertility goddess, Astarte.[14]

The remains of two houses from the Hellenistic period put us in touch with the domestic life of the well-off, but not well-to-do. Both are courtyard-style houses such as one finds at many sites during this period, though considerably larger than the courtyard houses found at Capernaum, Nazareth, or Jotapata. They do not, however, show the typical signs of elite homes (for example, plastered walls and floors, mosaic and fresco decorations). Access to each house was through a door opening onto the courtyard, the main workspace for the members of the household, from the street. The living areas and kitchen were accessed from the courtyard. The first of these houses is dubbed the "house of the fisherman," as over one hundred implements associated with fishing were found in the complex. It had four small rooms north of the courtyard, two kitchens east, and a large room south of the courtyard. The second house is dubbed the "house of the vintner" because of a wine cellar found in the far rear of the house beyond the kitchen area, containing four amphorae typically used for wine (see fig. 7.2). Excavators also found pruning hooks associated with viticulture, suggesting that the residents were indeed involved in the processing of grapes and making of wine,

14. Savage, *Biblical Bethsaida*, 149; Arav and Savage, "Bethsaida," 2:263.

a major staple of the Mediterranean economy.[15] While no treading floor was found on the premises, such an apparatus would have been necessary for the family's business. The kitchen in this house, which lay east of the courtyard, had a clearly marked oven area. Three smaller rooms were found north of the courtyard.[16] It is likely that each of these homes had at least a partial second floor for the families' bedrooms.

Under the Hasmonean rulers Aristobulus I (104–103 BC) and Alexander Jannaeus (103–77 BC), who pursued aggressive expansion of the Judean state, the Gentile presence in Bethsaida sharply declined and was replaced by Judean colonists. The house of the fisherman and house of the vintner appear to have been deserted by this period, likely in response to Hasmonean conquest.[17] Excavations have revealed here the shift in material culture typical for Galilee during this period—vessels made from limestone or basalt, both impervious to ritual pollution; locally produced clay vessels replacing imported (Gentile) ware; and, during the Herodian period, an increase in oil lamps produced in the Jerusalem area.[18] The Bethsaida that Jesus knew was thus largely, if not wholly, Jewish.

Though Philip received Bethsaida along with the northeastern regions of his father's kingdom in 4 BC, he appears not to have taken much of an interest in the town until AD 30, when he elevated Bethsaida to the status of a city and renamed it Julias in honor of Julia Augusta Livia, wife of Augustus and mother of the reigning emperor, Tiberius.[19] Josephus (*Ant.* 18.28) tells us that this increase in civic status involved increasing its population and strengthening its fortifications, and some evidence of repairing the Iron Age fortifications during the early Roman period has been identified.[20] Excavators

15. Appold, "Bethsaida and a First-Century House Church?," 2:381.

16. For a sense of scale, the courtyard in the house of the vintner measured about 11 yards squared, the kitchen about 10 by 5 yards, and the three rooms on the north side an average of about 4 by 3 yards. Appold, "Bethsaida and a First-Century House Church?," 2:379.

17. Arav and Savage, "Bethsaida," 2:264.

18. Savage, *Biblical Bethsaida*, 149; Arav and Savage, "Bethsaida," 2:275.

19. Josephus (*Ant.* 18.28) describes this Julia as "the emperor's daughter," which, taken at face value, would be highly problematic, given the fact that Augustus's biological daughter by that name was exiled to the island of Pandateria for multiple adulteries in 2 BC, just two years after Philip succeeded to his territory. Most scholars resolve this by assuming Josephus to be in error and the city named for Augustus's wife, Julia Augusta Livia. Strickert (*Philip's City*, 177–81) has cogently argued, however, that Josephus was not mistaken *and* that he was, in fact, referring to Augustus's widow, Livia, in terms that would have been proper for him in the last decades of the first century. After Augustus's death in AD 14, Livia was adopted posthumously as Augustus's daughter and, thus, inducted into the Julian line. The Senate also granted her the title/name of Augusta, the feminine form of the honorific they had bestowed on her now-deceased husband in 27 BC (Velleius Paterculus, *Hist. Rom.* 2.75.3). It would have been proper for Philip to honor Livia by naming a city Julias (rather than Livias) after AD 14.

20. Arav, "Searching for Bethsaida," 46–47.

Figure 7.3. The scant excavated outline of the vestibule and sanctuary of the early Roman-period temple in Bethsaida.

believe that Philip also remodeled the Hellenistic temple and dedicated it to Julia Livia, which would no doubt have scandalized the largely Jewish population of the city.[21] Again, this is a very small temple with a sanctuary of about 18 by 35 feet, a vestibule of 18 by 15 feet with two central pillars, and a rear antechamber of 18 by 12 feet, possibly surrounded by a small, plastered area functioning as its sacred precincts (see fig. 7.3).[22]

The identification of this building as a temple specifically dedicated to Julia Livia, however, has been contested. For one thing, Tiberius prevented the Senate from elevating his deceased mother to the status of a goddess (technically a *diva*, a divinized woman), a status she would attain only under Claudius.[23] The provinces, however, tended to run ahead of Rome in the worship of its

21. Strickert, "Renaming of Bethsaida"; Arav and Savage, "Bethsaida," 2:266. It seems unlikely that this temple, however, was celebrated on coins found at the site, as Arav ("Searching for Bethsaida," 46–47) claims. The temple on these coins reflects the tetrastyle temple to Augustus and Rome in or near Caesarea Philippi, not the two-pillared structure in Bethsaida.

22. Savage, *Biblical Bethsaida*, 146–47. The remains were further damaged by the Syrian army's construction of an outpost on the site in the Six Day War of 1967.

23. This is amply attested in Suetonius, *Tib.* 51; Tacitus, *Ann.* 5.1; Dio Cassius, *Hist. rom.* 58.2.1. On Claudius's action, see Suetonius, *Claud.* 11; Dio Cassius, *Hist. rom.* 60.5.2.

rulers.[24] Josephus himself makes no mention of such a temple in his description of Philip's improvements to Bethsaida, and there is very little in the way of physical evidence to suggest who might have been worshiped in the temple found on the site. The identification of that building, which does resemble a cult site of some kind, must remain tentative.

Bethsaida-Julias appears not to have risen to significant heights as a Roman city. It lacks many of the typical signs of urbanization that the nearby Decapolis cities of Hippos or Gadara exhibited—a theater, an odeon, mosaic floors, Greek capitals for columns, colonnaded streets.[25] Philip died in AD 34, and neither Agrippa I nor the interregnum Roman overseers appear to have cared to invest further in the site.[26] The city was abandoned after an earthquake in the fourth century, likely the earthquake of 363, which may have shifted the topography sufficiently to cause the shoreline of the Sea of Galilee to recede significantly from this early Roman fishing town.[27]

Chorazin

The excavated remains of the village of Chorazin likely all postdate the ministry of Jesus by several centuries. The basalt synagogue, the centerpiece of the site, dates from the late Roman or Byzantine period, roughly contemporaneous with the limestone synagogue at Capernaum. A number of the houses, also constructed from basalt, appear to reflect the design of an even later period.

Discoveries at Chorazin do put us in touch, however, with the manner of production of one of the most important staples of the ancient Mediterranean—olive oil. The olives were processed in two stages. First, the olives were ground into a pulp in stone mills (see fig. 7.4), which also produced oil runoff (what we might call "extra virgin olive oil" today). The olive pulp was then placed into woven baskets for pressing. In the first century, a beam press was used (see fig. 7.5). A horizontal wooden beam was fixed into a wall. The baskets or burlap sacks of olive pulp were, in turn, stacked on a large stone under the beam near the wall (that is, near the fulcrum of the lever). Stone weights were then attached to the free end of the horizontal beam, applying the pressure needed to express the oil from the olive pulp. The flow of the oil was directed into carved channels and into a stone basin reservoir. Olive oil was used

24. So also Arav, "Response," 104, who points out that Athens and Aphrodisias also appear to have dedicated cultic sites to Livia in spite of Tiberius's vetoing her formal divinization.

25. Arav and Savage, "Bethsaida," 2:276–77.

26. Smallwood, *Jews Under Roman Rule*, 116; Arav, "Bethsaida—A Response," 93.

27. Arav, "Searching for Bethsaida," 47.

Figure 7.4. Left: A first-stage olive press from Chorazin. The upright wheel comes from a different installation; a smaller wheel would have been required for use with this particular base. Right: A reconstruction of a similar olive press at Maresha (in Idumea) showing the wooden apparatus that would allow the grinding stone to be turned (often by a pack animal).

Figure 7.5. Left: An assortment of stone weights used with a beam press in Jotapata, a first-century city 9 miles north of Nazareth. Below: A reconstruction of the second-stage beam press from Maresha.

extensively in the preparation of food *and* as a staple food itself. For example, breakfast might consist of a piece of bread and olive oil for dipping. Oil was also the primary fuel used for artificial light in the lamps found throughout the Eastern Mediterranean from this period.

Figure 7.6. The stone elements of a screw press, an agricultural development from the second century AD. A wooden frame was anchored into the stone base. In the center of the horizontal beam atop the frame was inserted a pole that had been carved into a screw. As this central screw was turned by means of a short handle, it applied the necessary pressure to crush the bags of olive pulp and express the oil.

8

MAGDALA

The thriving Galilean town of Magdala is closely linked with one of Jesus's best-known disciples, Mary Magdalene, or Mary of Magdala.[1] Mary Magdalene is often identified with the former prostitute whom Jesus forgave in the house of Simon the Pharisee (Luke 7:36–50), but Luke makes no such connection. Rather, Luke speaks of Mary simply as a woman whom Jesus had delivered from seven demons (Luke 8:2; cf. Mark 16:9) and who, along with several other female followers of Jesus, provided for his ministry out of her means (Luke 8:3; Mark 15:40–41). She was also the first to witness and announce Jesus's resurrection, though the male disciples did not initially believe her (Luke 24:1–11; John 20:11–18). It is curious that this Mary was known by a toponym (a place name) rather than as the wife or mother of some male figure, as is far more common in the Gospels (see Mark 15:40; John 19:25; Acts 1:14; 12:12).[2]

The original texts of the Gospels never explicitly place Jesus in Magdala.[3] They do, however, speak of his wide-ranging mission throughout the entire region of Galilee:

1. De Luca and Lena, "Magdala/Taricheae," 2:287.

2. Bauckham, "Magdala as We Now Know It," 59.

3. In the Greek manuscripts that constitute the Majority Text, Matt. 15:39 names the "region of Magdala" as Jesus's destination in one crossing of the Sea of Galilee. In the oldest codices, however, this verse names the otherwise unknown "region of Magadan." "Magdala" makes sense as a scribal correction—but for that very reason is thought unlikely to have been Matthew's original reading.

> Jesus went throughout Galilee, teaching in their synagogues and proclaiming the good news of the kingdom and curing every disease and every sickness among the people. (Matt. 4:23; cf. Mark 1:39; Luke 4:14–15)

> Jesus went about all the cities and villages, teaching in their synagogues, and proclaiming the good news of the kingdom, and curing every disease and every sickness. (Matt. 9:35)

It would be surprising if Jesus had *not* visited so prominent a town as Magdala on the western shore of the Sea of Galilee at some point during this far-ranging ministry.

For students of the Gospels, Magdala is the jewel of archaeological sites around the Sea of Galilee. Its excavations show far more of the first-century Roman city than most in the region, where late Roman or early Byzantine remains predominate. Magdala was resettled as part of the Judean colonization of Galilee during the early first century BC under the Hasmoneans; though, as at many other sites in Galilee, there are signs of earlier settlement in the Hellenistic period.[4] It may have covered an area of at least 25 acres.[5] According to Josephus (*J.W.* 2.598–99; *Life* 132, 138), there was even a hippodrome, a facility built primarily with a view to chariot races, on the outskirts of the town, though this has not yet been located.[6]

A major feature of the public areas from the Hellenistic period onward is the Quadriporticus, a large, open courtyard originally surrounded on all four sides by columned porches (see fig. 8.1). A public fountain once stood in its center. It is not clear whether this space functioned as a commercial forum (or agora) or as an exercise space (a palaestra) in conjunction with the baths immediately to the north of it.[7] Whatever its functions, the Quadriporticus presented a magnificent entrance to the city for traffic entering from the lake.[8]

Magdala appears to have been an important center for the local fishing industry, especially for the preparation of fish for transport from the region. Magdala was also known as Taricheae in Greek and Latin sources (including Josephus), a name that appears to have been derived from a noun related to

4. De Luca and Lena, "Magdala/Taricheae," 2:303; Bauckham, "Magdala as We Now Know It," 13, 16.

5. De Luca and Lena, "Magdala/Taricheae," 2:299.

6. Bauckham, "Magdala as We Now Know It," 36.

7. De Luca and Lena, "Magdala/Taricheae," 2:325. Magdala certainly had an agora—not only because this would be expected of every town or city, but because excavations uncovered a number of market weights with the names of one or two individuals holding the office of *agoranomos*. Bauckham, "Magdala as We Now Know It," 25.

8. De Luca and Lena, "Magdala/Taricheae," 2:325.

Figure 8.1. The southern half of the large public square, once surrounded by four columned porticoes, known as the Quadriporticus.

drying, salting, and preparing fish.[9] Its domination of the fishing industry on the Sea of Galilee is the source of its notable wealth in comparison with other Jewish settlements in the region (other than those in which Antipas took a personal interest—namely, Sepphoris and Tiberias). Over the centuries, the shore of the Sea of Galilee has receded about 200 feet. The Quadriporticus was originally a waterfront construction. Mooring stones are still visible, anchored into the wall of the quay lining the east side of the Quadriporticus (see figs. 8.2, 8.3). The south end of the Quadriporticus also fronted the Sea of Galilee. Additional lakeside docks have been found along the shore to the north as well.

An important find directly related to the fishing industry based around the Sea of Galilee is the lower part of the hull of a small boat (see fig. 8.4). This was discovered close to the shoreline north of Magdala during a time of drought and plausibly dated to the late first century BC or early first century AD. It was 27 feet long and 7.5 feet wide, constructed from planks of a variety of species of wood, and repaired frequently before being allowed

9. On the identification of Magdala with Josephus's Taricheae, see De Luca and Lena, "Magdala/Taricheae," 2:283, 287–88, 291–98; Bauckham, "Magdala as We Now Know It," 8.

Figure 8.2. The quay along the eastern side of the Quadriporticus.

Figure 8.3. A number of mooring stones were built into the wall of the quay, used to secure the boats of fishermen bringing their catch (beyond the needs of their families) for processing or merchants bringing their wares from elsewhere in the region of the Sea of Galilee. Most of these were added during the mid-first century BC as an improvement to the older Hellenistic dock, though an original Hellenistic mooring stone is still visible to the rear of the quay.

to sink into oblivion.[10] Though nothing connects *this* boat with Jesus or his fishermen followers, this find represents a type of boat in use on this vast lake during Jesus's lifetime. It is smaller than would be required to transport thirteen adult males from one shore to the other but about right for a family of two or three fishermen with their gear, along with some business partners or hired hands, to use to ply their trade (cf. Matt. 4:21–22; Luke 5:2–3).[11]

Figure 8.4. The hull of a first-century AD boat discovered near the western shore of the Sea of Galilee.

10. Magness, *Archaeology of the Holy Land*, 203. See also Wachsmann, "Galilee Boat," 18–33.

11. Bauckham, "Magdala as We Now Know It," 27; Josephus refers to a boat of this size in *J.W.* 2.635; *Life* 163.

Figure 8.5. The principal north-south road of Magdala, running west of the bath complex. The road as currently seen has been narrowed by the construction of a high-level aqueduct (that is, raised above the ground) in the late Roman or early Byzantine period.

Magdala had at least one major north-south thoroughfare and multiple east-west streets intersecting it (see figs. 8.5, 8.6). Given the irregularity of some side streets, this didn't constitute a true Hippodamian grid network, such as characterized Roman Corinth, for example, but it is enough of one to suggest some level of conscious urban planning. The north-south road, a substantial thoroughfare with a width of 10 yards in some stretches, passed alongside the Quadriporticus and continued south to Tiberias and north through the remaining public and residential areas of Magdala and beyond. Immediately north of the Quadriporticus, this road passed an extensive public bath complex. In the Hellenistic period, it consisted of several cold-water pools. During the early Roman period it was adapted to include the typical features of the Roman bathhouse, including a sauna and public latrines. One of the rooms on the periphery of this complex was formerly identified as a synagogue, but it is now clear that it was a fountain house for the drawing of

Figure 8.6. The main north-south road as it approaches the better-preserved synagogue. The blockage at its end likely dates from the First Jewish Revolt.

Author photo, courtesy of the Terra Sancta Museum, Jerusalem

Figure 8.7. A small fishing boat from a mosaic that once adorned the floor of a room in the bath complex. The mosaic also included items associated with the baths and exercise yards: an oil flask and strigils (the tools used to scrape oil, dirt, and sweat from one's body after a rubdown), a discus, and a pair of weights used in conjunction with the long jump.

water.[12] The bathhouse, the fountain in the Quadriporticus, and the residential areas were supplied with fresh water from an underground spring channeled to and distributed from a water tower first erected in the late Hellenistic period.[13]

Magdala was home to a diverse population. Among the artifacts found are the usual signals in the material culture of a Torah-observant Jewish community—chalk or limestone vessels, cooking ware from Kefar Hananya, storage vessels from Shikhin, and mikvaoth (as at Gamala and Jotapata, for example).[14] Additionally, any animal bones uncovered tended to be from species deemed kosher.[15] A number of finds, however, also suggest a Gentile population among the Jewish majority, specifically certain household objects (like lamps) and signet rings decorated with animals, erotic scenes, or representations of deities or their symbols (like an eagle carrying a thunderbolt, symbols connected with Jupiter/Zeus).[16]

Some of the residents clearly enjoyed a high standard of living as, for example, those families that occupied three Roman-period houses discovered west of the road and water tower in the vicinity of the Quadriporticus. Excavations of one of these houses revealed a typically Greek peristyle arrangement, featuring a central, open-air courtyard surrounded by columned porches. The private rooms, kitchen, and front reception areas of the house were all accessed from this central courtyard. As would be expected, more modest residential areas have also been discovered, of which little more than the footprint of the buildings remain.

Two villas about 250 yards northwest of the Quadriporticus have also been excavated, one with fifteen rooms and a courtyard and its neighboring villa with at least ten rooms and a courtyard. The floors in a number of the rooms, particularly those associated with the stepped pools, are paved with flagstone. A number of the walls were plastered; one floor sports a simple but elegant mosaic (see fig. 8.8).[17] Each of these villas was equipped with a pair of stepped pools. While it remains disputed, it seems probable these pools are to be identified as mikvaoth, or purificatory baths, for use by the residents of the houses. This suggests, in turn, that the villas belonged to priestly families, for whom a higher degree of purity was often required (see chap. 5 under the heading "Sepphoris"). These mikvaoth are not plastered below the water line and were filled through the seepage of groundwater—the first known examples of this kind in the land of Israel (see fig. 8.9).[18] They were

12. Bonnie and Richard, "Building D1 at Magdala Revisited"; De Luca and Lena, "Magdala/Taricheae," 2:319–20.
13. De Luca and Lena, "Magdala/Taricheae," 2:305.
14. Zapata-Meza et al., "Magdala Archaeological Project," 109.
15. Bauckham, "Magdala as We Now Know It," 57.
16. De Luca and Lena, "Magdala/Taricheae," 2:329–30.
17. Bauckham, "Magdala as We Now Know It," 51.
18. Reich and Zapata-Meza, "Preliminary Report on the *Miqwa'ot* of Migdal," 68–69.

Figure 8.8. A red, black, and white mosaic from a room in the priestly villa, sporting typical image-free motifs—a meander design serving as the border, geometric shapes, and a central rosette.

Figure 8.9. One of the four groundwater-fed mikvaoth in the two priestly villas. These were interconnected with one another and with runoff channels that helped to keep the water levels consistent.

once covered under barrel-vaulted roofs, much like the mikvaoth found in the lower levels of elite priestly homes in Jerusalem.[19] Flagstone-paved rooms adjoining the pools may have served as spaces for undressing.

Mikvaoth are rarely found in the villages and cities located on the shores of the Sea of Galilee, since its waters would suffice for ritual purification. Having purpose-built mikvaoth indoors, however, would certainly serve the goal of convenience, especially if the requirement of total nudity for ritual purification to be effective, as recorded in the Mishnah, reflects pre-AD 70 practice.[20] The fact that these mikvaoth appear in pairs in each residential unit is somewhat puzzling. Was one reserved for use by women in the household and the other for men? Was one reserved for the *priestly* males to use, the other for remaining members of the household? Were they for the purification of different degrees of uncleanness?[21] At present, there is insufficient evidence to adjudicate between the possibilities. Given the fact that facilities for ritual purification are found in close proximity to many first-century synagogues in Galilee and Judea (as at Gamala, Modein, and the revolutionaries' makeshift synagogue at Herodium), one might naturally also wonder if these mikvaoth served the larger community in regard to synagogue attendance. The excavators think not, in part because the villas are still a few blocks removed from the synagogue, in part because of the practical difficulties involved in turning part of one's home into public space.[22]

Further north of the priestly villas sits a block of buildings used for both industrial and domestic functions (see fig. 8.10). The inhabitants of this block, like their more affluent neighbors to the southeast, were supplied with water through ground-level aqueducts from a public source. Several of the units in this and neighboring blocks have been found to contain shallow, square, plastered pools. These might have been used for the storage or sale of live fish (if filled with water), pickling and drying (if filled with vinegar or salt), or even reduction of the innards to garum, a fish-based sauce that was the ketchup of the Roman world. Fish thus processed could be exported to the Decapolis cities, Judea, Idumea, and beyond. While the vats could have been used in a variety of other industries, such as dying fabric,[23] the importance of the fish industry to Magdala tilts the probabilities in that direction.

19. Reich and Zapata-Meza, "Domestic Miqva'ot," 120.

20. Reich and Zapata-Meza, "Preliminary Report on the *Miqwa'ot* of Migdal," 70. It is difficult to discern with confidence, however, which regulations in the Mishnah, compiled around AD 200, actually reflect standard Jewish practice in the early Roman period.

21. Reich and Zapata-Meza, "Domestic Miqva'ot," 123.

22. Reich and Zapata-Meza, "Domestic Miqva'ot," 124. These archaeologists anticipate that a mikveh closer to the synagogue may yet be uncovered in future excavations.

23. De Luca and Lena, "Magdala/Taricheae," 2:309.

Figure 8.10. An industrial block immediately south of the better-preserved Magdala synagogue. Stone basins used for processing fish line the left side.

Perhaps the most exciting discovery at Magdala is its synagogue, a structure clearly dating, in its present form, to the first half of the first century AD.[24] The synagogue was built on Hellenistic-period foundations, though the use of the older structure remains uncertain. The large gathering room has a depressed central area surrounded by two rows of flagstones serving as seats, then another tier with stone benches lining the perimeter (see figs. 8.11, 8.12). Columns at the corners of the innermost row of seating supported the roof beams. The walls were plastered and painted in the style of the most basic frescoes from Pompeii (see fig. 8.13). Sometime after AD 43, the floor was decorated with two-color mosaics featuring geometric and meander patterns.[25] The care and expense that went into the construction and progressive beautification of this building testifies to its importance for the

24. A second synagogue was identified in the course of excavations in 2021, not far from this better-preserved and decidedly more ornate synagogue (Steinmeyer, "Archaeologists Discover New First-Century Synagogue"). That a town as large as Magdala should have had several synagogues is not at all surprising.

25. This date was established by the discovery of an ancient coin beneath the floor. De Luca and Lena, "Magdala/Taricheae," 2:312.

Figure 8.11. The synagogue in Magdala viewed from the east. Note the rows of seating around the perimeter and around the central depressed space, the placement of the columns, and the finely executed mosaic.

Figure 8.12. The Magdala synagogue viewed from the west. A main entrance led first into the study room and then into the synagogue's main hall beyond. Note the remaining benches in the study room (left) and the flagstones around the perimeter that served as an inner row of seats.

Figure 8.13. A small, surviving portion of the plastered wall of a small room on the south side of the same synagogue. The fresco's pattern is very similar to a style popular in Roman buildings (for example, the houses of Pompeii) in the first centuries BC and AD.

community—as well as to the presence of one or more local benefactors pouring considerable resources into it. The architectural focus was all on the center space, where there was likely a stand for reading, and expounding on, the scroll of the Torah.

A smaller room with two rows of seating around the perimeter sits to the west of the assembly hall, plausibly identified as a study room.[26] A small chamber on the southern side of the hall may have served for the storage of the Torah scrolls. These elements would be comparable to those identified within the first-century synagogue complex discovered at Gamala (see chap. 3, pp. 28–31).

We cannot be certain that Jesus visited and taught in this particular synagogue. Archaeologists have identified three building phases: (1) a late Hasmonean phase in which its function is uncertain; (2) an early Roman phase dated AD 29 or later (based on coin finds) in which the structure took on the unmistakable shape of a synagogue; (3) more renovations and upgrades in the period following AD 43 (again based on discoveries of coins beneath the

26. Aviam, "The Synagogue," 128–29.

Figure 8.14. A replica of the decorative stone table or base from the Magdala synagogue.

mosaic floor).[27] While it would be reasonable to suppose that the structure served as a community center and synagogue prior to the renovations of AD 29, this remains a supposition. However, we can be certain that this was not the only such structure in a town as populous as Magdala. And when we read that Jesus "traveled throughout Galilee, preaching in their synagogues and driving out demons" (Mark 1:39 NIV), it seems probable that he would not have omitted to do so here in Magdala as well—the town associated with Mary Magdalene.

A curious artifact discovered in the synagogue is a short table that may have served as a base for a lectern for the reading from a scroll of the Torah during a synagogue service or, alternatively, as an offering table (see fig. 8.14).[28] Of special interest are the signs of connection with the Jerusalem temple visible in its carvings.[29] On one short side is carved a menorah set within an arch supported by two pillars (perhaps the temple facade or the threshold of the holy of holies). The menorah is flanked by amphorae that may represent the

27. Bauckham, "Magdala as We Now Know It," 40, 43–44.

28. De Luca and Lena ("Magdala/Taricheae," 2:317) favor the latter option.

29. See, further, Aviam, "Decorated Synagogue Stone"; Aviam and Bauckham, "Further Thoughts on the Migdal Synagogue Stone."

libation vessels (Josephus, *Ant.* 14.72) or flagons of the oil that kept the lamp burning. Beneath the menorah is a square item that may represent the altar of incense. On the other short side, one sees, through columns, two wheels that may symbolize the chariot on which God's throne rested. On both long sides, one sees what appear to be arched colonnades, perhaps reminding the viewer of the colonnades that surround the perimeter of the temple's courts. On the top face is carved a number of symbols that have been taken to represent either the twelve loaves of the showbread as arranged on the table in the temple or pairs of the seven kinds of produce that were collected as first fruits to be delivered to the priests in the temple (dates, grapes or wine, wheat, barley, figs, pomegranates, and olives or their oil; cf. Deut. 8:8).[30] This artifact, like many similar temple-themed decorations and symbols represented in later synagogues throughout Galilee, likely served to reinforce a connection between the teaching and prayer that took place in the synagogue, on the one hand, and the temple, the architectural beating heart of Jewish religious practice, on the other.

The synagogue appears to have been largely dismantled, filled, and covered over by the late first century, likely in connection with Josephus's activities as a general fortifying the town in preparation for the Roman assault (see *J.W.* 2.572) or in connection with the Roman advance through Galilee. A number of its columns appear to have been incorporated into a barricade at the north end of a major north-south road.[31] Magdala's synagogue is thus an important addition to the repertoire of pre-70 synagogues discovered throughout Galilee and the Golan that supports the Synoptic Gospels' picture of Jesus's activity in such purpose-built structures.

30. On the decipherment of these symbols, see Aviam and Bauckham, "Further Thoughts on the Migdal Synagogue Stone"; Aviam and Bauckham, "The Synagogue Stone."

31. De Luca and Lena, "Magdala/Taricheae," 2:312. Josephus claimed the city to have had defensive walls (*J.W.* 3.462–65), but no archaeological evidence has been found for that to date. De Luca and Lena, "Magdala/Taricheae," 2:328.

9

CAESAREA PHILIPPI

Caesarea Philippi figures only once in the Gospel narrative as the general setting for Peter's climactic profession of Jesus's identity as the Messiah.

> Jesus went on with his disciples to the villages of Caesarea Philippi; and on the way he asked his disciples, "Who do people say that I am?" And they answered him, "John the Baptist; and others, Elijah; and still others, one of the prophets." He asked them, "But who do you say that I am?" Peter answered him, "You are the Messiah." And he sternly ordered them not to tell anyone about him. (Mark 8:27–30; cf. Matt. 16:13–20)

Jesus and his disciples thus temporarily moved north out of Galilee and Antipas's jurisdiction and entered the diminutive realm of Philip, another of Herod the Great's surviving sons. Herod had designated Archelaus, Antipas, and Philip co-heirs to his kingdom in his final will; Augustus ratified his deceased client's arrangements and divided the territory among the three in 4 BC. The following year, Philip significantly expanded the older Greek city of Panion and renamed it Caesarea as an expression of his gratitude and loyalty to Augustus Caesar, whom he acknowledged thereby as his patron.[1] To distinguish it from his father's seaside city of Caesarea, the new city was called Caesarea *Philippi*, "Philip's Caesarea."

Panion had been the site of the important battle in or shortly after 200 BC in which the armies of Antiochus III, the king of the Hellenistic kingdom of Syria and Babylonia, took control of Palestine away from the Ptolemies,

1. Wilson, *Caesarea Philippi*, 19.

Figure 9.1. The grotto of Pan together with a number of sacred areas that arose to the east of the grotto.

the Greek kings of Egypt (Polybius, *Hist*. 16.18.2; 28.1.3). The name Panion suggests that a shrine or sacred area dedicated to the Greek nature god, Pan, already existed here during the period of Ptolemaic control (which would be in keeping with the worship of Pan in Egypt under the Ptolemies). At the earliest stage, a large cavern located in the side of a rocky cliff was the focus of the worship of Pan (see fig. 9.1).[2] From the mouth of the cavern once flowed a powerful spring that remains one of the sources of the Jordan River, alongside springs from nearby Tel Dan. Seismic shifts in the nineteenth century altered the underground channels, with the result that the spring now emerges at some distance from the grotto. In the Hellenistic period, however, this was a perfect setting for the worship of one of the principal gods associated with nature. A number of shrines and sacred precincts would grow up around this cave during the first and the second centuries AD (see fig. 9.2).

After the Maccabean Revolt and the establishment of Judea as an independent kingdom again in 142 BC, the region of Panion remained in the hands of Antiochus's successors. After the decline of the Seleucid Empire, the region

2. Ma'oz, "Banias," 1:137, 140.

Figure 9.2. The courtyard immediately to the right (east) of the grotto, with several decorative niches that once most likely housed images of Pan and related figures such as Hermes (his father) and Echo (his woodland nymph lover). This particular sacred area might have been built as early as Philip's reign (Hartal and Tzaferis, "Banias," 5:1588).

became a disputed border between the Hasmonean kings of Israel and the local kings of Iturea, but it appears to have remained more securely in non-Jewish hands and to have retained, therefore, its pagan character. In 20 BC, the Roman emperor Augustus removed the region of Iturea, including Panion, from the jurisdiction of one Zenodorus and entrusted it to Herod the Great, his friend and client, in part out of regard for Herod's unflagging loyalty, in part out of faith that the brutal Herod could bring order to unruly Iturea. Herod, in turn, built and dedicated a temple to Augustus and Roma in the vicinity as a mark of his gratitude and ongoing commitment to his patron, just as he had done in both Caesarea Maritima and Samaria/Sebaste after Augustus added those territories to Herod's domain.[3] The facade of this temple is frequently featured on coins minted by Herod the Great's son Philip

3. Josephus, *J.W.* 1.404–6; *Ant.* 15.363–64. Augustus insisted that any temple that would be erected to honor him would also be dedicated to the goddess Roma (Suetonius, *Aug.* 52). This was a political move, as Augustus thus defused envy against himself by the Senate or any other party that could now see themselves honored alongside Augustus in the deified personification of their city.

Figure 9.3. Three representations of the Temple of Augustus and Roma in the area of Caesarea Philippi (top). Philip's name and his status ("tetrarch") are particularly clear in the legend on the coin on the right. The obverse of these coins featured Augustus and Julia Livia (left), Tiberius (center), and Philip himself (right).
Photo courtesy of Zak's Antiquities, Jerusalem. Used by permission.

(see fig. 9.3).[4] We know from these that it had four columns across the facade (the technical term is "tetrastyle"), an architectural commonplace for temples erected in Augustus's honor. Similar temples can be seen in Nimes (France), Pula (Croatia), and Pompeii (Italy). Connecting this temple to extant archaeological remains, however, is a subject for dispute. Josephus says only that Herod built this imperial temple "at a place called Paneion" (*J.W.* 1.404) or "in the territory of Zenodorus, near the place called Paneion" (*Ant.* 15.363–64).

The remains of two parallel walls can be seen in front of the grotto of Pan, likely part of what was once a monumental structure (see fig. 9.4). These walls stand 11.5 yards apart, the better-preserved western wall extending for almost 20 yards. The *opus reticulatum* brickwork substructure, once lined with marble-faced limestone ashlars, is a signature Roman architectural style that Herod frequently incorporated into his later building projects (the other examples in Israel-Palestine being found in Herod's third palace at Jericho and a monumental tomb north of Jerusalem's Old City). Some believe this to be Herod's temple to Augustus, possibly open to Pan's grotto in the rear.[5] Others suggest, however, that it was merely a grand entrance built by either Herod or Philip to enhance Pan's cult site.[6]

4. Luke 3:1; Josephus, *J.W.* 2.95, 168; *Ant.* 17.189, 319; 18.28.
5. Ma'oz, "Banias, Temple of Pan," 59; Ma'oz, "Banias," 1:140.
6. Wilson, *Caesarea Philippi*, 14–15; Netzer, *Architecture of Herod*, 222.

Figure 9.4. A portion of a wall that might have been part of a monumental entrance to the grotto of Pan or part of Herod's Temple of Augustus and Roma. Note the decorative niches that would, at one time, have housed statues, perhaps of nymphs and other figures associated with Pan, perhaps of members of the imperial household.

The same *opus reticulatum* brickwork has been discovered in connection with several artificially carved terraces located about 100 yards southwest of Pan's grotto. A large hall (about 11 by 16 yards) was part of this complex along with a parallel colonnade, the whole being accessed by a staircase. Some suggest that this was rather the site of Herod's temple to Augustus, pointing to its prominent location alongside and above the grotto of Pan, its obviously Herodian style, and the fact that Josephus speaks only of one building project of Herod in this area.[7] The layout is anomalous at best, however, for an imperial temple, and there is nothing to suggest that Josephus's account of Herod's building projects, though extensive, was exhaustive. As a result, others suggest that these are simply the remains of a palace that Herod built for himself at this bucolic location.[8]

A third candidate has been discovered 2.5 miles southwest of the grotto, at Horvat Omrit (see fig. 9.5). This temple would have been significantly more grandiose than either structure at the grotto, measuring 75 by 48 feet at the base and likely reaching 60 feet above the street level when it was intact. This temple was also located prominently at the gateway to Iturea, alongside a major north-south road leading from Beit Shean (Scythopolis) toward Damascus. Excavations revealed an older temple from the late first century BC

7. Netzer, *Architecture of Herod*, 220–21.
8. Ma'oz, "Banias," 1:141.

that had been expanded in the early second century AD (see fig. 9.6). The original temple had four columns across its front and was accessed only by a stairway at the front side—in the Roman style and specifically in the style of many other imperial temples throughout the empire. The exquisite workmanship of Herodian masonry, with stones finished with a smooth boss and fitted together perfectly and without mortar, is still visible in the interior spaces of

Figure 9.5. The temple at Horvat Omrit.

Figure 9.6. A view of the rear left corner of the original, Herodian-period temple at Horvat Omrit encased in the later expansion. Note the field stone and mortar fill that still closes the distance between the smaller temple and the perimeter of its expanded podium, save for this excavated corner.

the older structure.[9] This structure is a better architectural fit than anything discovered in the immediate vicinity of the grotto of Pan to date.[10] The principal objection to it is that Josephus leads the reader to expect a temple closer to the grotto. He does, however, give conflicting testimony, locating the temple "*at* a place called Paneion" in his *Jewish War* (1.404) but "*near* the place called Paneion" in his *Jewish Antiquities* (15.363–64).

Figure 9.7. A reconstructed section of the exterior wall of the temple at Horvat Omrit using original plaster decorative elements.

Some imagine the grotto of Pan in the side of the cliff—and the growing number of shrines around it—to have been the setting of Jesus's question and Peter's confession.[11] These readers suggest that the significance of Jesus's question is to be heard in terms of calling for a particular rejection of the worldview represented by those pagan shrines, or that the "rock" of Peter and his confession is to be understood in contrast to the rocky face of the cliff into which those shrines were built. These readers suggest that we hear resonances of Matthew's longer version of Jesus's reply to Peter bouncing off that particular cliff face: "I tell you, you are Peter, and on this rock I will build my church, and the gates of Hades will not prevail against it" (Matt. 16:18). Granted that the spring of water came up from a great depth in the back of Pan's grotto, there is no ancient evidence to support the suggestion that Pan's grotto was in fact known as "the gates of Hades." A number of caverns in Greece and Asia Minor were indeed believed to be portals to the underworld (for example, the cave next to the Temple of Apollo in Hierapolis), but they were always associated with the worship of Hades (Pluto, to the Romans), the brother of Zeus and god of the underworld, and not the nature god, Pan. It is tempting to look, alternatively, to the Temple of Augustus and Roma as the backdrop for Peter's bold confession, "*You* are the Messiah, the Son of the living God" (16:16), which would be heard at least as an *implicit* criticism of this imperial

9. At a later stage, it was expanded to become a hexastyle temple with columns all around the periphery.

10. See Overman et al., "Discovering Herod's Shrine to Augustus"; Overman, "Omrit, Horvat."

11. See, e.g., Phillips, "Peter's Declaration," 286, 293–94.

temple with its presumptuous claims about Augustus as the son of a deified emperor—the *deceased* god Julius Caesar rather than the one, true, *living* God worshiped in Israel.

The fact, however, is that neither Mark nor Matthew specifically invites the readers to imagine these structures, speaking instead very vaguely about Jesus's location. Mark merely sets the episode among "the villages of Caesarea Philippi" (Mark 8:27) and Matthew somewhere within "the district of Caesarea Philippi" (Matt. 16:13). Attractive as it is to say more, it is probably more an exercise in the interpreter's creativity than the clues the evangelists themselves have given their readers. Nevertheless, these are at least strong indications of the largely Gentile character of Philip's territory, where worship of pagan and imperial gods would be supported and promoted.[12]

CAESAREA PHILIPPI AFTER JESUS

Philip appears to have governed well and to have taken responsibilities to hear cases and dispense justice very seriously, traveling a regular circuit throughout his territory to do so (Josephus, *Ant.* 18.106–7). A few years after his death in AD 34, his nephew, Agrippa I, inherited Philip's territory and, in the ensuing years, would become king of the Jewish territories of Judea, Samaria, and Galilee as well. After Herod Agrippa I died suddenly in AD 44 (see Acts 12:20–23; Josephus, *Ant.* 19.343–50), Iturea was placed under the Roman governor of Syria until Agrippa I's son, Agrippa II, came of age. Caesarea Philippi became the capital of his small kingdom northeast and east of Galilee and the Decapolis (essentially the territory that had once been governed by Philip), which he ruled from 53 to the end of the first century AD. Agrippa II and his half sister Berenice appear in the pages of the New Testament in connection with Paul's detention in the other Caesarea, which the two visit in order to greet the new Roman governor Festus upon his arrival in the province (Acts 25:13), leading to Festus consulting with Agrippa concerning Paul's case. Agrippa II was no doubt better known during his lifetime for his involvement in supporting Vespasian and Titus in the suppression of the Jewish revolt of AD 66–70.

The centerpiece of the archaeological excavations in Caesarea Philippi is Agrippa II's palace, just a quarter-mile walk from the sacred area of Pan.

12. Josephus attests to some Jewish population of Caesarea Philippi before the First Jewish Revolt, narrating their unfortunate fate at that time. Josephus, *Life* 51–61, 74; Ma'oz, "Banias," 1:138.

Agrippa II appears to have inherited his great-grandfather's penchant for combining opulence with defensive functionality. His palace complex, covering a space of no less than 300 by 200 feet, was exceptionally well fortified, sporting defensive walls with semicircular towers guarding its narrow entrances. Access to the palace was thus easily controlled and defended. The water supply was assured by a subterranean delivery system, which could be accessed at various points through the covered pavement of the palace. After passing through passageways leading to smaller rooms or to stairways giving access to the upper level and the defensive perimeter, one comes to the larger, public areas of the palace's lower level—for example, a large basilica that was likely used for judicial actions and hearings. Large, vaulted chambers functioned as storerooms or perhaps served some other function for the administrative and military personnel attached to the palace. The royal living quarters would have been found on a second story. The complex, like so many ancient structures, was heavily pillaged for building materials in later periods. The palace may have been built only after the resolution of the First Jewish Revolt, possibly as a gift from the emperor Vespasian to his loyal vassal, paid for from some portion of the immense spoils Vespasian and Titus acquired from their military actions in Galilee and Judea.[a]

a. Wilson, *Caesarea Philippi*, 36–37.

10

MACHAERUS

When readers of the New Testament think of Herod Antipas, they will likely recall first and foremost his treatment of John the Baptist, whom he imprisoned and eventually executed (Matt. 14:1–12; Mark 6:14–29). Josephus corroborates the accounts in the Synoptic Gospels this far: Antipas had John arrested and executed because the latter's ability to draw and influence large crowds represented a potential threat to the stability of Antipas's realm (*Ant.* 18.116–19). The Gospels make the confrontation more personal, asserting that John had, in true prophetic fashion, challenged the propriety of Antipas's second marriage (Mark 6:17–18; Luke 3:19–20). Antipas had married Herodias, who had herself divorced her husband—a private citizen named Herod, who was also Antipas's half brother. At the same time, Herodias was the daughter of Antipas's half brother Aristobulus and, thus, Antipas's niece. According to the law of Moses, she was forbidden fruit on two counts. The two accounts need not be viewed as contradictory, all the more as the Gospels provide a rather clearer motivation for Antipas's decision to take action against John. It would not do to have a popular prophet pointing out his violation of the legal code that most of his subjects believed to have been divinely imposed on the Jewish people, ruler and subject alike.

The Gospels are silent on the question of *where* John was held and executed, but Josephus specifies the fortress and city of Machaerus as the place of John's incarceration and death (*Ant.* 18.119). Of the many fortress complexes that his father Herod had improved or constructed anew, Machaerus was the only one that fell within Antipas's own borders (see fig. 10.1). It was located in the southern end of Peraea, Antipas's territory east of the Jordan

Figure 10.1. The upper half of the imposing mountain of Machaerus. The aqueduct that supplied the fortress and lower city can be seen leading up to the mountain (bottom center). Two re-erected columns are visible atop the summit.

River and south of the Decapolis. As the only such fortified place in Antipas's domain, it makes good sense that he would choose to keep political prisoners under guard there. It is also quite plausible that Antipas had chosen to celebrate his birthday in the citadel on this site, which was the perfect blend of palace and fortress that marked so many of his father's constructions (see chaps. 21 and 22). If he had transported his retinue there for the celebration, Salome's request could indeed have been fulfilled with the immediacy narrated in the Gospels.

The fortress at Machaerus was first built by Alexander Jannaeus around 90 BC.[1] It was a link in a chain of fortresses built under the Hasmoneans to guard the eastern and southern borders of their realm. This chain included fortresses running north to south throughout Judea from Alexandrium (about 25 miles north-northeast of Jerusalem) to Dok outside of Jericho (about 13 miles east-northeast of Jerusalem) to Hyrcania (about 10 miles east-southeast of Jerusalem) to Masada (about 32 miles south-southeast of Jerusalem). When Jannaeus pushed the boundaries of his kingdom into the area east of the Jordan, he added Machaerus to protect his new territory. The fortress was destroyed during the civil wars between Jannaeus's two sons, Hyrcanus II

1. For a sketch of the excavated remains of the Hasmonean-period fortress, see Vörös, *Machaerus I*, 281.

and Aristobulus II, with the Roman triumvir Pompey the Great putting the weight of his military forces behind Hyrcanus. Since Machaerus was one of Aristobulus's supporters' strongholds, besieging and dismantling it became a high priority after Hyrcanus secured Jerusalem.

After his installation as king in 37 BC, Herod the Great gave significant attention to rebuilding, improving, and extending the chain of fortresses left to him by the Hasmoneans, particularly as a defense against the Nabatean Kingdom to the east and south. In every case, Herod gave as much attention to making the royal residences at these fortresses more luxurious as he gave to the fortifications themselves. In the case of Machaerus, he restored and improved the essential defenses of the Hasmonean fortress with its three bastions, raising each to a height of 90 feet above the steep approaches on every side, and built a veritable palace with all its amenities within the confines of the citadel.[2]

Only the slightest hints of the fortress's former strength and the palace's former luxury remain to greet the visitor. Like Masada and Herodium, Machaerus was seized by revolutionaries in AD 66 in preparation for the First Jewish Revolt and flooded with refugees as the revolution devolved (Josephus, *J.W.* 2.485–86). After Titus's legions secured Jerusalem, the newly installed military governor, Lucilius Bassus, undertook the necessary cleanup operations. His first target was Machaerus, which he surrounded with encampments of various cohorts of the Tenth Legion and a siege wall. One of the siege camps is clearly visible from the top of the citadel in the direction of the Dead Sea. Bassus was in the process of building a siege ramp opposite the northwest bastion, a strategy similar to the one that would be successfully used two years later at Masada. He abandoned this project, however, when he persuaded the revolutionaries in the citadel, with the promise of safe passage, to surrender. Those in the lower city, however, were not so fortunate but were massacred when they tried to escape (*J.W.* 7.190–209). The Romans tore the fortifications down to the foundations to ensure that it would never again provide a military advantage to the unruly province. The state of the site is silent testimony to the thoroughness with which they undertook their task.

The remains of a courtyard, the paving stones of which have been largely reconstructed, are now the most prominent feature of the site (see fig. 10.2). This courtyard was once surrounded by eight columns on each of its sides, supporting roofs that created four porches around the open space. At one end are the remains of a semicircular niche, which may have been the area of

2. Josephus, *J.W.* 7.172–77. For a detailed plan of the excavated remains of the Herodian improvements, see Vörös, *Machaerus I*, 288–89. Vörös (252–53) also provides a detailed plan of all the remains, color-coded by the time period to which each structure belongs.

Figure 10.2. A small section of the original Herodian flagstones of the large peristyle courtyard at the heart of Herod's renovations of the interior of the fortress. Note the semicircular exedra suggestive of a setting for a throne (Vörös, *Mount Machaerus*, 86).

Figure 10.3. A mikveh constructed in the Herodian period near the southwestern bastion of the fortress (Vörös, *Machaerus I*, 87; Vörös, *Mount Machaerus*, 69). The Hasmonean priest-kings would have provided the earlier iteration of the fortress with mikvaoth as well.

the royal throne, enabling Herod the Great and, later, his son Antipas to look out thence into the portico-surrounded courtyard. Was it perhaps here that Antipas sat as he entertained his guests on his birthday, with the center of the large, paved courtyard becoming Salome's dance floor? The space could indeed have been adapted for this purpose, though Herod the Great had also built two triclinia, or dining rooms, southwest of the courtyard, each room being able to accommodate between nine and twelve guests on three couches set around a central serving area. The walls of one of these rooms have been partially re-erected to give a clearer sense of its dimensions.

Adjacent to Herod's restored northwest bastion are the remains of a stairway that originally extended to an upper level, perhaps even to the walkway around the ramparts. The existence of a second story, probably the location of the royal bedchambers, is also suggested by the thick bases of columns in the triclinium—enough to support a roof that was itself bearing the load of another floor above. Herod would not have considered any palace habitable, it would seem, unless it had been equipped with the amenities of a complete Roman bath with its cold plunge, sauna, and hot tub (see fig. 10.4). The floor of the bathhouse was decorated with geometric mosaics (see fig. 10.5).

Figure 10.4. The frigidarium, or cold pool, from the small but complete bath complex that Herod the Great had built within the fortress of Machaerus (Vörös, *Machaerus I*, 113). Behind it stands a re-erected column in the Ionic style from the smaller courtyard.

Figure 10.5. A mosaic, reconstructed on the basis of the sections actually recovered, from the bathhouse atop Machaerus (Vörös, *Machaerus I*, 113).

A second, smaller paved courtyard, perhaps fitted with a garden, provided a place for rest and relaxation outside the bath complex, as was also common in the Roman baths of Italy. Along the east side of this second courtyard were a number of storerooms with ample capacity, of which only the footprints are now visible.

In the Herodian period, the citadel was accessed through the lower city. Now a barren hillside, this was once home to a fortified city with towers on the north and south sides, a high defensive wall, and a gate complex in the lower center. It is thought more likely that the place of John's incarceration was in this lower city, and not the citadel itself. Literary works and plays from the nineteenth century onward tended to imagine John languishing in one of the great cisterns beneath the summit, but in the arid conditions of the Peraean desert, these would all have been put to their proper use storing water.

PART 2

THE DECAPOLIS

11

THE "TEN CITIES"

When Jesus crossed over to the east shores of the Sea of Galilee, he landed in the largely Gentile territory of the Decapolis, the "ten cities." While these cities were not joined together in anything like a formal league or federation, they certainly shared a sense of fraternity as a group of neighboring Greek cities with a common cultural heritage. Ancient authors are not clear on *which* cities precisely constituted the "ten," suggesting rather that the number fluctuated over time and served as more of a definition of the region than a strictly formal designation.[1] The most stable list appears to have included Damascus and Canatha in the northeast; Hippos, Dium, Abila, Gadara, and Capitolias clustered east and southeast of the Sea of Galilee; Scythopolis and Pella flanking the Jordan south of the Sea of Galilee; and Gerasa and finally Philadelphia further south in the territory east of the Jordan.[2] Damascus and Philadelphia (modern Amman) were geographically the outliers among the group.

While some of these cities have a longer history, the majority were given a new start, or at least a new shape, by Alexander the Great and his successors, who continued his policy of planting colonies of military veterans and their families in strategic locations throughout the newly acquired territories as a means of establishing long-term, stable control.[3] Pella, Dium, and Gerasa appear to have been founded during the period of Ptolemaic control of the region (the third century BC) as military colonies for Macedonian veterans.

1. Browning, *Jerash and the Decapolis*, 11.

2. Browning, *Jerash and the Decapolis*, 14; cf. Pliny the Elder, *Nat.* 5.74; Ptolemy, *Geogr.* 5.14–22.

3. Browning, *Jerash and the Decapolis*, 12–13.

The defensive fortifications of Gadara and Philadelphia suggest that these were particularly important garrisons for active military.

These cities were indeed granted the status of *poleis* in the administrative sense (fully functioning, semi-autonomous Greek cities) and granted rights over substantial territories that included local villages whose residents would thenceforth owe a portion of their produce to the cities.[4] The veterans were also granted sufficient farmland of their own outside the cities to reward their service, sustain their families, and ensure their continued loyalty and assistance, should it be required. The cities were self-governing on the pattern of the Greek city, each with its council, judiciary, and gymnasium—the last being the means by which to continue to train new generations in the Greek language, the Greek literary and ethical heritage, and Greek athletics rooted in the skills required for success and stamina in combat (e.g., running, boxing, wrestling, javelin throwing).

During the era of Hasmonean expansion, particularly through the efforts of the Hasmonean king Alexander Jannaeus (103–77 BC), several of these cities, including Gadara, Hippos, Dium, Pella, and Gerasa, came temporarily under Judean control. Their resentment of the fact was revealed a few decades later, when Pompey the Great intervened in the family-feud-turned-civil-war between Jannaeus's two sons, Hyrcanus II and Aristobulus II, in favor of the former in 63 BC. As part of Pompey's redistribution of power in the region, he removed these Decapolis cities from Hyrcanus II's realm (Josephus, *Ant.* 14.74–75). The Decapolis cities hailed Pompey as their liberator when he restored their "independence" from Judean domination (in favor of Roman domination!). The cities were once again answerable to a Gentile imperial power, this time the Roman governor of Syria, who nevertheless respected their right to a good degree of self-governance over themselves and the villages in their hinterlands. So exuberant were these cities that they adopted a new dating system marking 63 BC, the year of their liberation, as year one of a new era.

Many of these cities and their associated villages remained home to a Jewish population, though these were in the minority. In AD 66, the hostilities between the Greek and Jewish residents of Caesarea Maritima spilled over into the territories of Judea and Galilee. Bands of Jewish marauders attacked many cities of the Decapolis and their neighboring cities. In response, perhaps both in retaliation and as a proactive attempt to ensure their internal security, the citizens turned against and, in many cases, slaughtered the Jewish inhabitants of their cities (Josephus, *J.W.* 2.457–80).[5]

4. *Poleis* is the plural form of *polis*, the Greek word for a city.

5. Browning, *Jerash and the Decapolis*, 30–31.

Jesus's ministry attracted the attention of residents of the Decapolis. Jesus performed at least one impressive exorcism in this region east of the Sea of Galilee—namely, his expulsion of the "Legion" of demons from the man who had been driven by the same to live out among the tombs. The demon-possessed man's transformation and testimony led to Jesus's fame being spread throughout the Decapolis (Mark 5:20). Matthew also tells us that "great crowds followed him from Galilee, the Decapolis, Jerusalem, Judea, and from beyond the Jordan" to hear Jesus's preaching and experience his healings (Matt. 4:25).

12

GADARA

The first three Gospels differ as to the location of the exorcism Jesus performed in the territory of the Decapolis (and variants among the manuscripts introduce further complications). Matthew's Gospel places the event, which in his account involved *two* possessed men, "in the region of the Gadarenes" (Matt. 8:28 NIV), hence near the city of Gadara. This was a city of the Decapolis that sat atop a hill overlooking the Sea of Galilee, perhaps 5 miles distant from the shore. Gadara's territory, however, extended down to the lakeshore.[1] Its inhabitants maintained a harbor on the lake for the city's interests in the fishing industry. Like most of the cities of the Decapolis, Gadara was founded during the Hellenistic period as a military colony while the region was under the control of the Ptolemies of Egypt.[2] Stretches of its original, third-century BC fortification walls are still visible, having been incorporated into the Roman-period city wall (see fig. 12.1). The base of a tower is still visible along the fortification wall, displaying the "header and stretcher" construction typical of the Hellenistic period (one layer of several rows of ashlars laid with their long sides facing out alternating with a second layer of ashlars laid with their short ends facing out). An underground mausoleum also dates from the Hellenistic-Roman period.[3] Most of the visible remains, however, date back to the second century AD.[4]

1. Bolen, "Where Did the Possessed Pigs Drown?," 209. McRay (*Archaeology and the New Testament*, 167–68) too quickly dismisses Gadara on the basis of distance, particularly in light of the notion of a city's territory.
2. Weber, *Umm Qais*, 6.
3. Weber, *Umm Qais*, 29.
4. Weber, *Umm Qais*, 8.

Figure 12.1. Remains of the city wall (right) and a tower (left) dating back to Gadara's Hellenistic foundation.

The city had two theaters by the second century AD, and a theater would doubtless have been part of the cityscape from Gadara's founding.[5] The South Theater is still largely unexcavated. It follows the Greek pattern of having been built into an existing hill for support of its cavea, the semicircular seating for the audience. With the development of concrete, the Romans could build new theaters wherever it pleased them without being limited by the natural topography. A second, later theater sits along the cardo, built of the local black basalt (see fig. 12.2). A stadium was built just outside the city's walls.[6]

Gadara appears to have been particularly devoted to the goddess Tyche, who represented Fortune or Destiny. A larger-than-life statue of the goddess was discovered on the site, perhaps once serving as a cultic idol in a Hellenistic- or Roman-period temple (see fig. 12.3). Tyche was also featured on several of the coins minted in the city during the early imperial period. Coins from second-century AD Gadara depict a temple to Zeus with four columns on the front side, attesting to its presence even though its remains have not been definitively identified.[7]

After Pompey reorganized Syria and Palestine, he dedicated significant resources to rebuilding Gadara, which had sustained extensive damage in

5. Weber, *Umm Qais*, 20.
6. Weber, *Umm Qais*, 32–33.
7. Weber, *Umm Qais*, 35.

Figure 12.2. The western theater.

Alexander Jannaeus's conquest. He may have further settled some of the many veterans of his eastern campaigns here.[8] Gadara would continue to see development and improvement during the Roman period and in the manner typical of Roman cities, beginning with the expansion of two perpendicular streets—a north-south cardo and an east-west decumanus. The latter has been excavated to a considerable extent, revealing glimpses of the grandeur of this Hellenized Roman city standing just a few miles from Jewish Galilee (see fig. 12.4). Near their intersection stand the remains of a second-century AD nymphaeum, an ornamental fountain that also served as a public water supply. It would have originally stood several stories tall, its black basalt substructure largely covered in delicately carved marble. Niches would have sported statues of nymphs and

Figure 12.3. A statue of the goddess Tyche from Gadara.

8. Weber, *Umm Qais*, 9.

Figure 12.4. Several reassembled columns provide a hint of the grandeur of the colonnade that once lined the decumanus.

other divine beings. Gadara was the birthplace of several noted Greek authors, including Philodemus, an Epicurean philosopher who left a large literary output and who personally trained Virgil after moving to Italy, as well as Theodorus, who became a tutor of the future emperor Tiberius.[9]

Figure 12.5. Restored late Roman shops lining the cardo.

The hinterlands of the city include several steep inclines. It is easy to imagine a freshly possessed herd of swine running down one of these into the Sea of Galilee to their doom. Excavations outside Gadara's city

9. Weber, *Umm Qais*, 4. Many of Philodemus's works are being painstakingly recovered from a charred library discovered in a villa in Herculaneum, a city devastated by Vesuvius alongside Pompeii in AD 79.

walls have also resulted in the discovery of several mausolea, two of which—the tomb of Lucius Sentius Modestus and the tomb of the Germani—date to the first century.[10] Such mausolea, if they could be opened, would indeed provide the kind of shelter for undomiciled outcasts such as we read about in Matthew 8:28 and Luke 8:27 (see fig. 12.6).

Figure 12.6. A pair of basalt doors that once gave entrance to a mausoleum outside the city walls.

10. Weber, *Umm Qais*, 14.

13

GERASA

Mark and Luke locate Jesus's exorcism of Legion in "the region of the Gerasenes" (Mark 5:1 NASB; cf. Luke 8:26)—that is, in the territory or hinterlands of Gerasa (modern Jerash). This is far *less* likely than Gadara. The herd of swine would have to gallop 30-plus miles from Gerasa in order to perish in the Sea of Galilee—or at least 15 miles if we think of the hinterlands of Gerasa extending to the approximate midpoint between the Decapolis cities of Gerasa, Gadara, and Scythopolis (better known as Beit Shean). Nevertheless, it is not surprising that these evangelists should think first of Gerasa when thinking about the Decapolis, for it was certainly the jewel in the chain of these ten cities.

The face of Gerasa visible today is largely the face of the second-century AD city, a period during which many of the cities of the Decapolis experienced significant growth. Approaching from the south, visitors pass through a massive, freestanding, triple-arched gate erected in AD 129/130 in honor of the emperor Hadrian's visit during his tour of the eastern provinces.[1] A hippodrome sits on the west side of the road stretching between this arch and the city (see fig. 13.1). While this likely predates Hadrian's visit, it still postdates the period of Jesus's active ministry.[2] It is, nevertheless, an excellent extant example of the kind of structure that was a staple of many Greek cities, with

1. Browning, *Jerash and the Decapolis*, 104.
2. Browning, *Jerash and the Decapolis*, 109.

Figure 13.1. The starting gates and a small portion of the stadium seating of Gerasa's hippodrome.

external dimensions of 250 by 860 feet and sixteen rows of seats yielding an estimated seating capacity of fifteen thousand.[3]

The city walls of the Roman period enclosed an area of 210 acres, a notable expansion of the Hellenistic footprint of the city. These walls were probably completed by the reign of Vespasian, around AD 75.[4] Another triple-arched gate provides entrance through the south wall, opening onto the Cardo Maximus, the principal north-south road through the city.

Dominating this entrance are the sacred precincts of the Temple of Zeus (see fig. 13.2). The present remains of the temple proper, with a footprint of 44 by 30 yards, represent a magnificent rebuild from about AD 161–65.[5] At the foot of a monumental stairway leading down from the temple is an expansive courtyard constituting the temple's sacred precinct. A massive altar once stood in the northern half, while smaller votive altars surrounded the courtyard (see fig. 13.3). Some such sacred site dedicated to Zeus was probably already standing here during the Hellenistic period. The earlier temple might have been situated within the rectangular precinct rather than set more dramatically on the hill above it; it might also have begun as a large open-air altar in the middle of the sacred precinct.[6] The precinct was significantly renovated beginning in the first half of the first century AD, judging by inscriptions on the premises recording two donors' significant gifts to the building project in AD 22 and again in AD 42.[7] This might have involved the building of the first actual *temple*, whether beside the altar or on the hill directly overlooking the sacred courtyard.

3. Browning, *Jerash and the Decapolis*, 109; Aubin, "Jerash," 3:217.
4. Browning, *Jerash and the Decapolis*, 112.
5. Browning, *Jerash and the Decapolis*, 119; Aubin, "Jerash," 3:216.
6. Browning, *Jerash and the Decapolis*, 115.
7. Browning, *Jerash and the Decapolis*, 35.

Figure 13.2. The Temple of Zeus in Gerasa.

Figure 13.3. The sacred precinct of the altar of Zeus with the oval forum in the background.

Figure 13.4. The south theater, next to the Temple of Zeus.

Standing next to the Temple of Zeus is a well-preserved theater dating in its present form from the late first century AD, though there is evidence of an earlier structure beneath the current one (see fig. 13.4).[8] Indeed, a Greek city would hardly have been without a theater from its earliest founding. The present theater has an estimated seating capacity of three thousand.[9] Of particular interest is an inscription now housed outside the theater bearing a dedicatory inscription to Domitian, dated to AD 90–91. Domitian's personal name has been effaced, bearing witness to the Senate's formal condemnation of his memory (see fig. 13.5).

Figure 13.5. Dedicatory inscription showing the *damnatio memoriae* of Domitian.

Beyond the sacred precinct sprawls the distinctive oval forum of second-century

8. Browning, *Jerash and the Decapolis*, 36, 126.
9. Aubin, "Jerash," 3:217.

Figure 13.6. The oval forum.

Figure 13.7. Gerasa's principal cardo.

AD Gerasa, with the cardo still visible as it leads north toward the heart of the city (see fig. 13.6). The forum itself is not quite oval, as the portion that abuts the sacred precincts of Zeus constitutes a straight line. The concentric paving, however, tends to fool the eye in this regard. It is almost 90 yards across at its widest point.[10]

The grandeur of an ancient cardo is better preserved in Gerasa than in most Roman sites (see fig. 13.7). It features the typical provisions for runoff rain and wastewater in the form of sewer channels laid beneath its surface. As it runs northward it intersects with the city's principal decumanus in a circular plaza once dominated by four freestanding groups of four pillars, each group

10. Browning, *Jerash and the Decapolis*, 131.

Figure 13.8. The north tetrapylon, situated over the intersection of the Cardo Maximus and a secondary decumanus.

supporting a rectangular roof. These appear to have served only an aesthetic function. Similarly, sheltering the intersection further north with another of the city's decumani, stood a tall, arched tetrapylon—also a nonfunctional monument merely adorning the ancient city, dating from the second half of the second century AD (see fig. 13.8).

Along the cardo, one passes an exceptionally well-preserved example of a nymphaeum, a richly decorated public fountain once graced with statues of nymphs and other water-related deities standing in the many niches across its 24-yard-wide facade (see fig. 13.9).[11] It is likely that the nymphaeum was once capped by a great half dome. This particular structure, one of the finest examples of its type, dates from the late second century AD.[12] Nevertheless, fountains and more ornate nymphaea were standard features of Greek cities in the Roman period.

Just before the nymphaeum is the once grand entrance to a temple to Dionysus that had been converted into a cathedral during the Byzantine era. Inscriptions to "the Arabian god," likely indicating Dusares, the principal god of the Nabateans, were found in the temple area, suggesting that

11. Browning, *Jerash and the Decapolis*, 144.
12. Browning, *Jerash and the Decapolis*, 143.

Figure 13.9. The nymphaeum, or fountain house.

Dionysius and Dusares were assimilated to one another and worshiped together here.[13]

Further north along the cardo lay a monumental entrance, called a propylon, to the sacred precincts of Artemis, the patron goddess of the city. While a temple to Artemis existed from the city's earliest period, probably on this very site, the structure presently visible reflects the grandiose expansion of the temple and its precinct begun under one of the Roman governors of Syria during the reign of Antoninus Pius.[14] On a landing near the top of this monumental stairway stand the remains of one of the massive altars to the goddess. The temple itself towers above a vast, colonnaded courtyard of 176 by 132 yards at the top of the stairs (see fig. 13.10). Another great altar stood immediately in front of the stairs leading up to the temple, which stood on an elevated base of 24 by 45 yards.[15] Sacrifices in the Greco-Roman world—including the temple in Jerusalem—took place in front of, and not within, the gods' houses.

13. Browning, *Jerash and the Decapolis*, 36.
14. Browning, *Jerash and the Decapolis*, 50, 164; Aubin, "Jerash," 3:217.
15. Browning, *Jerash and the Decapolis*, 160–61.

Figure 13.10. The Temple of Artemis.

While Gerasa and its hinterlands are almost assuredly not the site of the dramatic exorcism of the legion of demons from the possessed man of the Decapolis, its excavated remains nevertheless provide perhaps the most complete sense of the architecture, layout, and institutions of these Greek cities in the territory between the Jewish homeland to the west and the Nabatean Kingdom to the east and south.

14

HIPPOS

While Gadara remains the strongest candidate for the site of Jesus's dramatic exorcism on the combined basis of a Gospel's witness (Matt. 8:28) and geographic plausibility, another Decapolis city might recommend itself as an alternative—namely, Hippos. Situated atop a mountain perch 1,000 feet above the Sea of Galilee, Hippos would have readily illustrated—and might even have inspired—Jesus's maxim "A city on a hill cannot be hidden" (5:14 AT).[1] One can also readily imagine a herd of swine rushing down from this Gentile city, not a mile from the lakeshore, into the waters below.

Hippos was first a Ptolemaic outpost, then a Seleucid settlement, built over top of earlier, Iron Age remains. It, too, had been conquered by Alexander Jannaeus in or around 83 BC and "liberated" from Judean rule by Pompey in the aftermath of 63 BC (Josephus, *Ant.* 14.75). Briefly made part of Herod's kingdom by Augustus, it was restored to the province of Syria (and a good deal of autonomy) after Herod's death (Josephus, *J.W.* 1.396; 2.97).

In its current state, Hippos showcases the churches built here during the Byzantine period and otherwise preserves several late Roman structures. Almost nothing remains visible of the Hellenistic or early Roman city. Approaching from the east, the visitor passes through the area of an ancient gate between two fortified towers from the Hellenistic period, one round and one square.[2] The gate would have opened onto the main decumanus of the city, which extended to another gate on the west side. The remains of the street

1. Rousseau and Arav, *Jesus and His World*, 127.
2. A. Segal dates this to the late first century AD, however. "Hippos (Sussita)," 5:1787.

Figure 14.1. The well-paved courtyard in front of the Northwest Basilica, a church that incorporates many elements from the older Hellenistic temple.

probably represent a second-century AD renovation. The foundations of a Hellenistic-period sanctuary have been excavated, but the structure was overbuilt first by a Roman-period temple and, later, a Byzantine church. Corinthian capitals, column drums, and other limestone elements from the original sanctuary continued to be used in the later structures (see figs. 14.1, 14.2).[3] The original, Hellenistic sanctuary was probably destroyed by Alexander Jannaeus as part of his conquest (and purging) of this territory for his priestly kingdom.

Figure 14.2. The excavated foundations of the Hellenistic-period temple.

The water supply of Hippos was improved during the early Roman period through the construction of low-level aqueducts that brought water from the east into the city. Water channels can still be seen beneath and alongside the decumanus, as well as several portions of the aqueduct. At the heart of Roman Hippos was

3. Segal and Eisenberg, "Spade Hits Sussita"; A. Segal, "Hippos (Sussita)," 5:1785.

Figure 14.3. One of two adjacent winepresses at Hippos, dating from the Byzantine period. Grapes were trodden underfoot in the large basin to the left, and the juice ran through a channel into the lower collection basin on the right, where fermentation began. Wine was, incidentally, almost always drunk watered down, even at dinner parties. The host would determine the ratio of wine to water.

its forum, perhaps built over the Hellenistic agora or marketplace. Colonnades on at least two of the sides of the forum created shaded areas for merchants. A large cistern dug into the rock off the southwest side of the forum, catching runoff water from the decumanus and the forum, probably predates the Roman period. Channels around the forum testify to the intentionality with which such rainwater was harvested for use during the long dry season.

A freestanding monument in the forum, once thought to be a nymphaeum or fountain house, is now believed to have been an open shrine dedicated to the emperor, once sporting a cult statue of an emperor, built in the late second or early third century AD.[4] This brought the imperial cult into the very heart of the civic center—not a separate temple recessed from the bustle, but an open shrine in the midst of it. West of the forum stand the remains of an odeon, a small theater-like structure typically reserved for musical performances and poetic recitations.

4. A. Segal, "Hippos (Sussita)," 5:1785.

We may finally never know at which of these Decapolis cities the former demoniac or demoniacs resided.[5] What we do know, however, is that, as the man "went away and began to proclaim in the Decapolis how much Jesus had done for him," as Mark recounts the result of the exorcism (Mark 5:19–20), he would have been bearing witness to a largely non-Jewish population and possibly laying the foundations for a later mission to the Gentiles throughout that region.

5. McRay (*Archaeology and the New Testament*, 166–68) favors identifying the site of Kursi, a site 5 miles north of Hippos, with "Gergesa," a variant reading for the location for the exorcism in some manuscripts of Matt. 8:28, Mark 5:1, and Luke 8:26. Excavations there, however, have turned up only the remains of a Byzantine monastery, which is not in itself evidence of the commemoration of some Gospel event (Bolen, "Where Did the Possessed Pigs Drown?," 204–5, contrary to McRay, *Archaeology and the New Testament*, 167). A steep hill is located 1 mile south of the settlement. While surveys of the area have recorded the presence of caves, they have not noted the presence of tombs, which is another problem for locating the exorcism of "Legion" here (Bolen, "Where Did the Possessed Pigs Drown?," 206–7, contrary to McRay, *Archaeology and the New Testament*, 167, who erroneously speaks of tombs on-site).

15

BEIT SHEAN

The Gospels give no indication that Jesus ever visited the Decapolis city of Scythopolis, the only Decapolis city west of the Jordan River. Jesus might, however, have passed through on more than one occasion as he traveled from Galilee to Judea during his lifetime, most notably on his final journey to Jerusalem that, according to Luke, took him through Jericho. Jericho does not lie on the path from Galilee to Jerusalem that passes through Samaria (a path Jesus was remembered to have taken in John 4:1–4), but a route existed from Galilee past Beit Shean to Jericho. His ministry directly impacted residents of the Decapolis, and residents of Scythopolis, just 17 miles from the Sea of Galilee, might well have been among the growing audience that included people from the cities of the Decapolis (Matt. 4:25). We are also reminded that the Gospels do not pretend to be exhaustive accounts of Jesus's teachings, deeds, and movements (cf. John 21:25).

Scythopolis—or Beth Shean in the Israelite period (Beit Shean today)—is one of the most impressive archaeological sites in northern Israel. Located by a perennial freshwater stream along a major east-west trade route, Beit Shean was occupied for millennia prior to the Roman period. From the Neolithic period into the Greek age, the settlement appears to have been mostly confined to a large mound in the northern part of the site. The city that sprang up at the base of the tell dates primarily to the Hellenistic, Roman, and Byzantine periods. Beit Shean is distinctive in Israel for being one of a very few settlements that remained predominantly Gentile during the biblical period—and that not on the outskirts of the territory, but in the very heart of what would become the Northern Kingdom.

Beth Shean was the site of an Egyptian military outpost from the fifteenth through the twelfth centuries BC, one of several such outposts by means of which the Pharaohs maintained their hold on Canaan and Syria (see fig. 15.1). According to Joshua 17:11–16, the invading Hebrews did not displace the Gentile inhabitants of Beth Shean, though the Philistines do appear to have gained the upper hand over its residents by the tenth century BC. The bodies of King Saul, his son Jonathan, and two other sons of Saul were said to have been hung in disgrace from the walls of Beth Shean after the Philistines defeated his army on Mount Gilboa (see 1 Sam. 31), occasioning David's lament, "How the mighty have fallen!" (2 Sam. 1:19, 27). Material evidence of a Philistine occupation has not been forthcoming; it must, in any event, have been quite brief. The city was soon taken by David and appears as an administrative center under Solomon's rule (1 Kings 4:12). The foundations of an Israelite fortress from this period have been uncovered on the tell. Israelite control of the city came to an end two centuries later, when Beth Shean was destroyed along with so much else of the Northern Kingdom of Israel during the Assyrian invasions of the eighth century BC under Tiglath-Pileser III and his son Shalmaneser V.

Author photo, courtesy of the Rockefeller Museum, Jerusalem

Figure 15.1. A basalt stele recording the successful suppression of a local rebellion against the Egyptian presence in Beth Shean. The portrait shows the early thirteenth-century BC pharaoh Seti I, second ruler of the Nineteenth Dynasty, presenting offerings to Ra in thanksgiving.

Beth Shean would remain largely vacant until the third century BC, when it was resettled as a military colony by Ptolemy II (along with Philadelphia-Amman and Pella) and renamed Scythopolis.[1] The presence of hundreds of stamped Rhodian amphora handles once again helps confirm the date of reoccupation.[2] It was later granted the rights of an incorporated Greek city by Antiochus IV in the second century BC. The worship of Zeus and Dionysus is attested during this period, the latter being particularly reinforced in the renaming of the city as Nysa-Scythopolis, after

1. A. Mazar, "Beth-Shean," 5:1621.
2. Berlin, "Between Large Forces," 13.

Nysa, the mythical nurse of the infant Dionysus.[3] John Hyrcanus I attacked and annexed Scythopolis for the growing Hasmonean Kingdom around 108 BC, but the city's semi-independence was restored by Pompey the Great in 63 BC, though it would continue under the aegis of the Roman province of Syria.

The conquest by Hyrcanus I probably introduced a Jewish minority among the city's population. This minority continued to exist through the eve of the First Jewish Revolt. Indeed, the Jewish residents were so well integrated into the city's population that they fought *alongside* their fellow citizens against some bands of Judeans who attacked the city in AD 66 as part of a string of reprisals for the massacre of Jews in Caesarea Maritima by their Gentile neighbors. The tragic aftermath, however, was that the Gentile population of Scythopolis turned against their own Jewish fellow citizens because of the general fear of Jewish violence as the First Jewish Revolt gained momentum (Josephus, *J.W.* 2.466–80).

Little in the way of first-century AD remains are visible on the site. As with other Decapolis cities, Scythopolis underwent a major urban renewal program in the first half of the second century (under Hadrian and Antoninus Pius) and then again at the turn of the third (under Septimius Severus). Many of the excavated spaces and structures reflect the building activity of this period as well as the later Byzantine reconfigurations of the city.

Beginning in the first century, the tell was entirely dedicated to a temple to Zeus Akraios (Zeus "of the Summit") and to its sacred precincts.[4] Almost nothing remains save for its foundations and a number of fallen columns with their Corinthian capitals, but in its day it would have been a truly impressive structure, like the Temple of Zeus in the sister Decapolis city of Gerasa, looming over the city below. The extensive remains at the foot of the tell essentially represent the city of the second through the fourth centuries AD (see fig. 15.2). The landscape would have been somewhat more modest during Jesus's lifetime.

The oldest Roman-period remains are to be found in a small area about 200 yards south of the tell. This area was dominated by two small temples built at the top of two flights of stairs (see fig. 15.3). These originated in the first part of the first century, though they were renovated in the second century as part of the citywide facelift.[5] It is not clear to which gods or goddesses these temples were consecrated. A number of small altars and inscriptions found in this area suggest that one was dedicated to Kore, another name

3. Mazor, "Beth-Shean," 5:1625.

4. Mazor, "Beth-Shean," 5:1623, though he notes that some date this to the early second century AD.

5. Mazor, "Beth-Shean," 5:1630–31.

Figure 15.2. A view of the lower city from the top of the tell. The large open agora to the right (a consistent feature of the city during the Greek and Roman periods), the main north-south street that stretches alongside it, and the theater visible in the center top all had first-century iterations (Mazor, "Beth-Shean," 5:1628, 1630).

Figure 15.3. Two early Roman-period sanctuaries once stood at the top of each of the stairways pictured here. Note also the fountain in the bottom left.

for Persephone, the reluctant wife of Hades, god of the underworld (see fig. 15.4).[6] Kore and her mother, Demeter, were important deities in connection with the agricultural cycle. Kore's marriage to Hades necessitated her living in the underworld for four months of the year, causing her mother to pine away for her annually during that period. This manifested itself in the four months of winter, when Demeter's joy and consequent blessing of crops were absent. An inscription dated to the first century names one Cassiodoros in connection with the construction of the temple, calling him a "priest of a deity and the emperor, gymnasiarch and agoranomos," which indicates that the emperor cult was already established in Scythopolis by that time.[7] It also points to the existence of an as-yet undiscovered gymnasium complex from the first century, a principal institution for the transmission of Greek cultural knowledge and a venue for athletic training.

Figure 15.4. A votive altar dedicated to Lady Kore, daughter of Demeter and wife of Hades.

Between the two sets of steps ascending to the temples are the remains of a public fountain, with running water being delivered from the decorative lions' mouths. Adjacent to these sacred spaces was a latrine. While this particular installation dates to the second-century renovation of the Eastern Baths (which existed in some form in the first century),[8] it provides a good example of a standard feature of cities in the Roman period (see fig. 15.5). Water flowed continuously in a trough before

Figure 15.5. A section of the Roman-period latrine. Marble slabs with the necessary holes were once laid across the supports jutting from the wall. Such slabs were often appropriated for later building projects.

6. Mazor, "Beth-Shean," 5:1630.

7. Mazor, "Beth-Shean," 5:1630.

8. Mazor, "Beth-Shean," 5:1631. The well-preserved Western Baths, though not built until the Byzantine period, nevertheless give a good sense of the elements of a first-century Roman bath with its cold pools, warm pools, spacious caldarium (sauna), and courtyard for exercise.

Figure 15.6. The head from a larger-than-life statue of Athena and a small altar with the heads of Pan and Dionysus in relief (Silenus and another representation of Dionysus appear on the other sides), both found at Beit Shean and dated to the second century AD.

the seats, which would have been equipped with sponges on sticks for personal hygiene. The channels beneath the seats would have been flushed out regularly as well with the draining and changing of the water in the public baths north of the latrine.

The city was significantly expanded in the early decades of the second century AD, when the Sixth Roman Legion was stationed in the nearby camp at Legio (Carpacotna). While it is highly likely that a cultic site dedicated to Dionysus existed from the Hellenistic period, given the addition of "Nysa" (the baby Dionysus's nanny) to the name of the city, it is the remains of a magnificent second-century AD temple, located at the intersection of two major streets, that bear witness to the city's long-standing devotion. Four columns stood atop the temple's podium, each 4 feet in diameter and 30 feet high. The temple stood overall at least 45 feet above street level, and the width of the platform was 65 feet. The cella, or enclosed sanctuary where the cult statue would have been housed, had a distinctive, semicircular rear. Archaeological finds confirm that the residents of the city worshiped many of the gods of the Greco-Roman pantheon, including Aphrodite, the goddess of love, and Athena, the goddess of war and military strategy (see fig. 15.6).

Figure 15.7. The theater at Beit Shean.

Perhaps the most impressive structure from Roman Scythopolis is its great theater, located at the far southern end of the downtown area (see fig. 15.7). Originally built in the early first century AD during the reign of Tiberius,[9] it was renovated and expanded to three tiers in the second century and could accommodate around seven thousand viewers. When all three tiers were still intact, the structure was a sprawling 360 feet in diameter, the largest in the territory of Israel. The theater was decorated with exquisite carvings of floral and animal motifs. Especially noteworthy is the backdrop of its stage area, which was crafted from imported decorative marble and granite and still boasts exquisite detail, above all in its ornate Corinthian capitals.

At the fringes of the second-century city, a new attraction arose about 800 feet south of the theater—an amphitheater with internal dimensions of about 270 by 150 feet. The 10-foot wall around the inside of the arena, with seating beginning only above this level, shows that it was built with gladiatorial contests and fights against wild animals in mind—exactly the sorts of entertainment that would cater to the tastes of the soldiers of the Sixth Legion. Originally built with between eleven and thirteen rows of seats, it is estimated that the amphitheater could have accommodated five to six thousand people.

9. Mazor, "Beth-Shean," 5:1628.

Taken as a whole, the remains of Beth Shean / Scythopolis from the Egyptian through the late Roman periods remind us of the ongoing presence of Gentile culture, Gentile institutions, and Gentile populations deep in the land of Israel for the whole of the biblical period.

PART 3

THE REALMS OF THE ROMAN PREFECTS

16

THE REGION OF SAMARIA

The region known as Samaria in the time of Jesus was composed of the old territories of the tribes of Ephraim and Manasseh. Hilly and well watered, it was highly fertile agricultural land with expansive native forests that supplied abundant timber. After the death of Solomon, it became part of the Northern Kingdom, or kingdom of Israel, formed under Jeroboam I, leaving only the territories of Judah, Simeon, and Benjamin to Solomon's heirs. The Northern Kingdom was invaded by Shalmaneser V of Assyria and its conquest completed by Sargon II in 722 BC. Some portion of the Israelite population was deported, and the city of Samaria and other cities in the region were resettled by colonists loyal to Assyria. Unlike much of Galilee, the region of Samaria remained consistently inhabited—and farmed—between the Assyrian invasion and the Hasmonean period. The situation changed little as the Assyrian Empire yielded to the Babylonian Empire, and the Babylonian Empire, in turn, to the Persian Empire.

After Alexander's conquest of the lands between Syria and Egypt, he refounded the city of Samaria as a colony for military veterans, introducing a new population into the region. Along with Judea and Galilee, the territory passed first to Alexander's successors in Egypt (the Ptolemaic Empire) and then, in 200 BC, to the successors in Syria and Babylon (the Seleucid Empire). Its lands continued to be exploited for these empires, though they appear not to have had a more lasting impact on the region. This was no doubt due to their attention and resources being drained in their wars with one another and, increasingly, in civil wars within the empires. One archaeological indication of the fecundity of the region is the discovery and documentation of over twelve hundred stone field towers (structures for processing and storing agricultural products) with typical dimensions of about 18 by 18 feet. Many of these were found in the northwest, possibly in territory designated as "royal lands," owned by and farmed for the benefit of whoever was the ruler at the time, but they are plentiful also in the southern part of the region.[1]

It was, indeed, due to the dynamics of internal strife within the Seleucid Empire that members of the Hasmonean family in Judah first gained a foothold in the region of Samaria. One Seleucid rival, Demetrius II, awarded three districts of southern Samaria to Jonathan shortly after 145 BC in return for his continued support as a loyal vassal (1 Macc. 11:34–36; Josephus, *Ant.* 13.127). Jonathan's nephew John Hyrcanus I would acquire the rest of Samaria through military action by 107 BC. When Pompey established Roman oversight over the region in 63 BC, he detached all of Samaria from Hasmonean rule and set the region—and its rich resources—under the Roman governor of Syria. Augustus would turn around and award Samaria to his loyal vassal, Herod the Great, forty years later, only to restore it to the Roman province of Syria after the removal of Herod's primary heir, Archelaus, in AD 6. It would remain under Roman rule thereafter, save for a brief span (AD 41 to 44) during which the emperor Claudius added Samaria, along with Judea and Idumea, to the realm of Agrippa I—likely as a reward for the part Agrippa played in the negotiations between the Senate and Praetorian guard that brought Claudius to the imperial throne.

As a consequence of this history of colonization, not everyone in the region of Samaria was "Samaritan" in the sense of a person who worshiped the God of Israel and looked to Mount Gerizim as God's sacred mountain. There were also many "Samarians" who claimed no historic or ethnic connection with Israel. Just the opposite: these were Gentiles who were proud of their own Greek or Syrian or Phoenician heritage and culture. Many of these were descendants of the veterans of the armies of Alexander or Pompey. They would have made up the majority of the population of the *city* of Samaria that gave its name to the region and would have been the owners of a great deal of the fertile lands around it. Their population would increase and flourish under the patronage of Herod the Great.

The question of the Samaritans' origins and ethnicity is a highly contested one. Indeed, it is difficult to pierce through the partisan fog and hostility in our literary sources to arrive at a clear picture.[2] As worshipers of the God of Israel, the Samaritans regarded themselves as the native descendants of the

1. Dar, "Samaria," 5:929. It is not clear whether they date from the Hellenistic period or represent rather a consequence of the Hasmonean-period resettlement and exploitation of the area.
2. Purvis, "The Samaritans," 2:591–92.

tribes of Ephraim and Manasseh, even if they had also incorporated numerous proselytes along the way. They were faithful adherents to the law of Moses, which they possessed in a distinctive form (one that, notably, did not focus on Jerusalem as the sole location for a legitimate, central shrine), worshiping God at a site that had been divinely sanctioned long before Jerusalem was settled by Jews. A collection of Samaritan documents from the late fourth century BC found in a cave in Wadi Daliyeh reveals that the most typical names among Samaritans contained components of the name of the God of Israel (that is, names including the element *yhw-*, *yh-*, or *-yhw*, as in Yehoshua or Eliyahu), suggesting continued occupation by descendants of the Israelites.[3]

Judeans denied them this genealogical continuity, claiming the Samaritans to be the descendants of Gentiles resettled in the region after the Assyrian invasion of the Northern Kingdom and deportation of the *whole* of its population, who incorporated the worship of the God of Israel alongside their own so as to enjoy his protection in his land. This is the account provided in 2 Kings 17:22–34—the canonical, but perhaps still partisan and biased, account of their origins. It was likely composed after the return from exile and, thus, after Samaritans had been established as "other" in the minds of Judeans—and especially in the minds of the "congregation of the returning exiles" (Ezra 10:8 Tanakh), those Judeans who had been allowed to return from Babylon and who appear to have been particularly concerned with the purity of Israelite bloodlines.

When the people of Samaria offered to help rebuild the Jerusalem temple in the Persian period (Ezra 4:1–5), this "congregation of the exiles" soundly rejected their help, which also entailed a decisive rejection of any kinship. The Samaritans responded in kind, seeking to derail the building project. The first temple on Mount Gerizim appears to have been constructed around this time (late fifth century BC), quite possibly in response to exclusion from the rebuilding efforts and spiritual life of the temple in Jerusalem.[4] This hostility continued through the Hellenistic period, reflected, for example, in Ben Sira's contempt for "the foolish people that live in Shechem" (Sir. 50:26) and in a Qumran text (4Q372) that speaks of the thorough exile of the tribes of Joseph and their replacement with "fools" who "made for themselves a high place on an elevated mountain to excite the jealousy of Israel, . . . blaspheming against the tent of Zion."[5]

3. Dušek, "Importance of the Wadi Daliyeh Manuscripts," 7.

4. Josephus mistook the time of the building of the Gerizim sanctuary, placing it in the time of Darius III rather than Darius II (424–405 BC; see *Ant.* 11.302–12; Dušek, "Importance of the Wadi Daliyeh Manuscripts," 7–8).

5. Vermès, *Complete Dead Sea Scrolls*, 565–66.

When Antiochus IV violated the sanctity of the temple in Jerusalem, establishing a polytheistic cult there for the multicultural inhabitants of the Hellenized city of "Antioch-at-Jerusalem," the Samaritans sought a more amicable solution by dedicating their temple to "Zeus the Friend of Strangers" at their own initiative. Josephus claims that, on this occasion, it was the Samaritans who denied any kinship with Judeans, seeking to distance themselves from the population of Jerusalem that had dangerously provoked the king (Josephus, *Ant.* 12.257–64). It is possible, however, that this initiative came from the *Samarians* rather than the *Samaritans* themselves. Josephus uses the same term for both ethnic populations without distinction. Both Judean-Samaritan and Judean-*Samarian* relations would reach a low point in the Hasmonean period, when John Hyrcanus I laid siege to and destroyed the cities of Samaria and Shechem along with the Samaritan temple (111–107 BC; see Josephus, *Ant.* 13.254–56, 275–83).[6] It was probably at this time that Sychar was settled by Samaritan refugees (cf. John 4:5–6).[7]

This legacy of hostility continues into the first century AD and appears in the pages of the New Testament. Jesus himself is remembered at one point to have excluded the villages of the Samaritans from his disciples' mission, distinguishing them from "the house of Israel" (Matt. 10:5–6). The conflict over the true center for the worship of the God of Israel—as well as the tendency of Samaritans and Jews to avoid having dealings with one another—is reflected in John 4:20–21. In Luke 9:51–56, a Samaritan village refuses hospitality to Jesus and his disciples, since they were heading to Jerusalem. This same resentment over Galileans using Samaria as a shortcut to their temple in Jerusalem would result in the murder of some Galileans by some Samaritans two decades later (around AD 50), which would prompt, in turn, serious and widespread violence between Judeans and Galileans, on the one hand, and Samaritans (and/or Samarians?) on the other (see Josephus, *J.W.* 2.232–46; *Ant.* 20.118–36).[8] A more hopeful note is struck in the Acts of the Apostles, however, where Luke recalls the success of the apostles' work in Samaria (Acts 8:4–25) and implicitly includes the Samaritans once more as part of "the House of David," which is only fully restored after Judea, Galilee, and Samaria have responded to the proclamation about Jesus (9:31), in fulfillment of the prophecy of Amos 9:11 (Acts 15:15–17 NLT).

6. Magen, "Dating of the First Phase," 193; Magen, *Mount Gerizim Excavations*, 98.

7. Isser, "Samaritans and Their Sects," 3:571.

8. The Roman historian Tacitus mentions these events in passing along with the note that Judeans and Samaritans had been carrying on a long-standing feud (*Ann.* 12.54).

17

SEBASTE (SAMARIA)

The city of Samaria, located outside the modern village of Sebastiya and about 5 miles northwest of Nablus, became the capital of the Northern Kingdom of Israel during the reigns of Omri and Ahab (1 Kings 16:23–24), the remains of whose palaces and casemate fortification walls can still be seen at the site. The entirety of the Northern Kingdom came under Assyrian rule with Sargon II's conquest of the territory in 722 BC, followed by the deportation of some number of its inhabitants and the importing of colonists from elsewhere in the Assyrian Empire to continue to ensure that the fertile lands be exploited for the benefit of its new masters.

When Alexander the Great made his southward advance toward Egypt in 334 BC, the Persian governor of Samaria, Sanballat III, capitulated to him immediately. The inhabitants, however, revolted against Macedonian rule after Alexander had moved on, with the result that Alexander's forces destroyed the city of Samaria and refounded it as a Greek city. Alexander settled many Macedonian veterans in his newly minted city and rewarded them with ample parcels in the rich agricultural hinterlands of the city. The first nineteen courses of a large, round tower from the Hellenistic period still stand as a witness to the fortification of the city during this period (see fig. 17.1).[1] Inscriptions bear witness to the presence of a temple to Isis and Serapis in the Greek city from the third century BC (see fig. 17.2).[2] Scholars tend to believe this to have been a precursor to the early Roman-period Temple of Kore (better known as Persephone, the reluctant bride of Hades).

1. Parrot, *Samaria*, 99–100.
2. Avigad, "Samaria (City)," 4:1308; Berlin, "Between Large Forces," 10.

Figure 17.1. The remains of a round tower from the defenses of the Hellenistic-period city.

After the Hasmonean family reestablished Judean independence in 141 BC, its leaders began to execute their program of conquest and expansion. This brought the armies of John Hyrcanus I to the city of Samaria and its environs from about 113 to 107 BC, resulting in the destruction of Hellenistic Samaria, Shechem, and the temple and settlement on Mount Gerizim.[3] After Pompey's settlement of matters in Judea in 63 BC, Gabinius, Pompey's appointee for looking after Roman interests in the more immediate region from 57 to 55 BC, dedicated

Figure 17.2. A votive relief from the Hellenistic-period city of Samaria showing a couple making an offering before a goddess, perhaps Isis, who was known to have had a temple in the city.

3. Berlin, "Between Large Forces," 31. See also Josephus, *J.W.* 1.166.

Author photo, courtesy of the Rockefeller Museum, Jerusalem

Figure 17.3. A relief of the star-topped cap associated with the Dioscuri, the brothers Castor and Pollux, found on the site of the Temple of Kore. The reliefs may date from the Hellenistic period, when this temple was dedicated to Isis (Avigad, "Samaria [City]," 4:1308).

considerable resources to rebuilding and resettling the city of Samaria.[4]

It is to Herod the Great, however, that the city would owe the greatest single debt. Octavian, who typically showed great confidence in Herod's competence and loyalty, added the region of Samaria to Herod's domain in 30 BC. In gratitude, Herod refounded its principal city as Sebaste to honor his patron. This was the feminine form of the word *Sebastos*, the Greek translation of the Latin honorific title *Augustus* that Octavian had received from the Roman Senate at this time. Herod incorporated the city's Hellenistic-period fortifications into a new city wall that encompassed 185 acres, leaving the city with plenty of room for growth.[5] The lower courses of the round towers guarding Herod's western entrance to the city are still visible.[6]

Herod provided the city with a basilica that covered an area of about 74 by 35 yards. Adjacent to its east side, he built an expansive forum of 140 by 80 yards.[7] The outlet of an aqueduct discovered on the south side of the forum bears witness to Herod's provision of a water supply for his new city, bringing water from a spring 3 miles away. He also supplied the city with a theater and, in a valley in the northeastern part of the city, a stadium (see fig. 17.4).[8] Sebaste thus became a respectable city in which Herod could settle thousands of the non-Jewish veterans of his army, providing them also with adequate farmland to sustain them and their families (Josephus, *J.W.* 1.403; *Ant.* 15.298). Along with Caesarea Maritima, Sebaste would become a prime recruiting ground for new soldiers.

4. Netzer, *Architecture of Herod*, 81.

5. Netzer, *Architecture of Herod*, 84.

6. Avigad, "Samaria (City)," 4:1307; Netzer, *Architecture of Herod*, 85. The walls between those towers, however, date from a Severan period rebuild.

7. Parrot, *Samaria*, 111–12. Once again, however, it is the late second-century AD iteration that is now visible on the site. Avigad, "Samaria (City)," 4:1308.

8. Herod's stadium was originally ornamented in the Doric style; it was renovated in the second century AD in the Corinthian style. Parrot, *Samaria*, 113.

Figure 17.4. The late second-century AD rebuild of Herod's theater in Sebaste.

Such was Herod's devotion to his patron that he crowned the city of Sebaste with a grand temple to Augustus and Roma, the deified personification of the city at the heart of the empire. Herod would make similarly lavish statements of his allegiance and gratitude in response to Augustus's gift (or, better, trust) of two other regions to his oversight. Simultaneously with Samaria, Augustus entrusted the cities of the coastal plains to Herod's domain. In response, Herod erected a massive temple to Augustus and Roma at Caesarea Maritima in conjunction with his extensive renovations and expansions of that harbor city, locating it prominently above the inner harbor. He would erect a third such temple near the city of Panion (see chap. 9) when Augustus assigned the northern territories of Gaulanitis, Trachonitis, Batanea, and Auranitis to his oversight at some point between 23 and 20 BC (Josephus, *Ant.* 15.359, 363–64).

The Temple of Augustus and Roma in Sebaste was built on the highest point of the city, partially over the remains of the palaces of Omri and Ahab.[9] The temple itself had a footprint of about 115 by 80 feet. It was elevated 15 feet above a large forecourt of about 275 by 240 feet. A grand staircase led up from the courtyard to the temple proper (see fig. 17.5). As at Caesarea Maritima, the temple would be visible from a great distance around, exalting

9. Parrot, *Samaria*, 103.

Figure 17.5. The Severan-era stairway to the Herodian Temple of Augustus and Roma, built over the Herodian steps (Avigad, "Samaria [City]," 4:1307).

not only Herod's imperial patron but also Herod's devotion and loyalty to the same (see fig. 17.6).

It seems unlikely that Jesus's path ever intersected with Sebaste. While he and his disciples were known to traverse the region of Samaria on their trips between Galilee and Judea, Sebaste was 7 or 8 miles off that route, which passed through Shechem and alongside Gerizim.[10] Sebaste remains, however, a witness to the degree to which Herod the Great changed the landscape of his territory beyond the bounds of Judea, the degree to which he could do so with a view to making non-Jews feel perfectly at home, and the boundaries he was willing to cross, as far as his Jewish subjects were concerned, to show his commitment to his emperor using Rome's own language of devotion. By the time of Jesus, of course, Sebaste along with all Samaria was under the direct oversight of the Roman prefect. The residents of Sebaste, however, would have regarded this as a natural development rather than a foreign imposition. Indeed, as a city founded as a veteran colony by Herod and continuing to

10. Shechem has not been extensively excavated, though work at Tel Balatah has uncovered significant remains from the Bronze and Iron Ages as well as some evidence of Hellenistic-period habitation. See Campbell, "Shechem."

Figure 17.6. The podium that once supported Herod's Temple of Augustus and Roma. Note the four bases for the pillars that once adorned the front of the temple, a typical architectural feature for temples dedicated to Augustus.

supply first Herod, then Archelaus, and then the Roman prefects with new recruits, they would have looked to Caesarea Maritima and the prefect's headquarters as a symbol of opportunity and of ongoing partnership. Indeed, these Sebastene recruits would be among the most enthusiastic enforcers of Roman rule over Judea and its surrounding regions.

18

MOUNT GERIZIM

Jesus and his disciples were remembered to have visited the Samaritan village of Sychar as they returned to Galilee from a Passover festival in Jerusalem. It was here that Jesus engaged a woman of the village who had come to "Jacob's well" to draw water (see fig. 18.1). In the course of their conversation, the woman brought up a point of perpetual disagreement between the Samaritans

Jordan Duerrstein

Figure 18.1. An ancient well in Balata, immediately east of modern Nablus, traditionally revered as Jacob's well. The modern cap obscures the dimensions of the actual well, which is over 7 feet wide and 100 feet deep (Rousseau and Arav, *Jesus and His World*, 131).

Carl Rasmussen

Figure 18.2. The gate and grand staircase giving access to the sanctuary platform from the east.

and the people of Judea and Galilee—namely, the place that God had chosen as the center for his worship, particularly for the sacrificial cult.

> The woman says to him, "Sir, I see that you are a prophet. Our forebears worshiped on *this* mountain, but *you* say that Jerusalem is the place where one must worship." Jesus says to her, "Believe me, woman, that the hour is coming when you will all worship the Father neither on this mountain nor in Jerusalem." (John 4:19–21 AT)

The unnamed Samaritan woman, of course, was indicating the sacred spaces atop Mount Gerizim as the historic center of her ancestors' worship.

A sanctuary was built atop Mount Gerizim in the Persian period (the mid-fifth century BC).[1] The sacred precincts—measuring about 100 yards square in their initial phase—were approached through gates on the north, east, and south sides.[2] During the Hellenistic period, a much grander approach was constructed from the east, which appears to have become the primary point of access. Pilgrims passed through a two-chambered gate, ascended a broad, high staircase, and entered the sacred area through another gate at the top (see fig. 18.2). Access from the south remained in place; the northern

1. Magen, "Gerizim, Mount," 5:1746; Magen, *Mount Gerizim Excavations*, 167–69.
2. Magen, *Mount Gerizim Excavations*, 143.

Bukvoed / CC BY 3.0 / Wikimedia Commons

Figure 18.3. Lintels decorated with triglyphs that once adorned the entrances to the reception hall of the Hellenistic citadel.

Figure 18.4. Broad paved courtyards southeast of the temple platform provided as (outdoor) accommodations for pilgrims.

Carl Rasmussen

gate was reduced in size and may have been used only by temple personnel.[3] The sanctuary itself was also replaced by a more splendid temple in the early second century BC.

A good deal of the peripheral structures from the Persian and especially the Hellenistic period remain, including two expansive courtyards to the southeast and slightly below the sacred precincts believed to have been provided as temporary accommodations for pilgrims to the site and the remains of a Hellenistic-period fortified citadel southeast of those courts and south of the temple precincts proper (see figs. 18.3, 18.4). During the

3. Magen, *Mount Gerizim Excavations*, 98–102.

Andrew Witt

Figure 18.5. The area of the Twelve Stones, the remnants of the holy place of the Persian-period sanctuary.

Byzantine period, however, a grand octagonal church was constructed in honor of Mary that wholly obscures any remains of the Samaritan temple apart from one area to the west—the area called the Twelve Stones, which appears to have marked the holy place of the earlier Persian-period sanctuary (see fig. 18.5).

In both its Persian- and its Hellenistic-period iterations, the temple itself was likely similar to the one in Jerusalem in terms of overall structure, being based on the same specifications for the tabernacle in the (Samaritan version of the) Pentateuch.[4] It would likely have been oriented toward the east, such that its front came into full view as soon as one passed through the eastern gate into the courtyard. Over four hundred thousand burnt animal bones found on the site attest to the robust cultic activity of the sanctuary during the centuries it was in active use.[5]

Once Simon, the last surviving brother of Judas Maccabaeus, had established Judea's independence from Seleucid rule, he and his descendants invested themselves heavily in military campaigns seeking to recover territory formerly belonging to historic Israel for the Hasmonean Kingdom. Simon's son John Hyrcanus I devoted considerable efforts to completing his father's

4. Magen, *Mount Gerizim Excavations*, 143.
5. Magen, "Gerizim, Mount," 5:1747.

Figure 18.6. Remains of courtyard houses from the western quarter (Area A).

reconquest of Samaria (Josephus, *Ant.* 13.254–56, 275–83), territory that was highly desirable for its abundance of fertile land and its strategic location adjacent to the coastal plains. After besieging the Greek city of Samaria, he and his elder sons conquered Shechem and besieged Mount Gerizim itself, destroying the temple and the priestly residences and facilities that had grown up around it. These efforts appear to have taken place between 113 and 107 BC.[6] While his motives for doing so are a matter for conjecture, it seems likely that, as a ruler whose power and authority were invested entirely in his position as high priest in Jerusalem, he would have deemed allowing the Gerizim temple to remain standing and operational to present a significant obstacle to uniting Samaria and Judea under his rule. This act may represent the nadir in Judean-Samaritan relations.

There is no indication that the Samaritan temple was rebuilt after Hyrcanus's conquest. When the woman at the well of Jacob in Sychar pointed to "this mountain" as the place to worship God, she was indicating a place where the Samaritans could already have designated their own "wailing wall" to lament the loss of their temple—and that at Judean, not Roman, hands.

There are significant remains of late Hellenistic residences surrounding the temple complex, particularly spreading down the gentle slope to the south and, to a lesser extent, the west and north. These are, for the most part, blocks of courtyard houses with a few more elite mansions, one sporting decorative stucco and frescoes (see fig. 18.6). More wood went into the construction of these houses than would have been the case in Judea and Galilee, in large part

6. Josephus (*Ant.* 13.254–56; *J.W.* 1.62) places these events early in Hyrcanus's reign, but archaeological evidence requires that he be corrected on this point. See Berlin, "Between Large Forces," 31; Barag, "New Evidence"; deSilva, *Judea Under Greek and Roman Rule*, 58–59.

Figure 18.7. A central courtyard in the mansion, giving access to three small, upper-story bedrooms, possibly for seasonal workers of the olive presses. Note the two partial staircases on the extreme right (Magen, *Mount Gerizim Excavations*, 55–56).

because Samaria had large forests. Special stones called "corbels," cut so as to protrude beyond the interior wall face by perhaps a foot, were incorporated into the walls to provide support for the upper-story's floors and ceilings, which were usually made of planks of wood laid across the corbels and sealed with plaster. The walls of the upper-story rooms may also have been lined with wood for better insulation against the cold and winds of the Samarian winters.[7] Numerous bathtubs, built-in or freestanding, were discovered throughout the residential and industrial areas, attesting to the inhabitants' and workers' concern for ritual purity. One complex, called "the mansion," merits special mention. This was a sprawling complex that incorporated an olive oil processing installation and, in all likelihood, clusters of small bedrooms for seasonal workers (see figs. 18.7, 18.8, 18.9).

There is little indication of urban planning. Residential areas sprang up as the needs of the population (the priestly staff, their families, and those involved as "support staff" for the temple) dictated.[8] The temple city was not fortified with a defensive wall, which would have been regarded with suspicion by the successions of Hellenistic overlords (Macedonian, Ptolemaic, Seleucid). The exterior walls of adjoining residences created a kind of fortification line, with gates being built to give some measure of control over access to

7. Magen, *Mount Gerizim Excavations*, 91.
8. Magen, *Mount Gerizim Excavations*, 89–90.

Figure 18.8. Stone remains of olive presses used in the two stages of oil extraction—the round crushing press in the upper left, the stone weights and other apparatus from the beam presses in the lower right and the center.

Figure 18.9. A large courtyard with surrounding rooms northwest of the oil processing room in the mansion.

the compounds. These informal defenses could not withstand the assault of Hyrcanus I and his forces, as a layer of destruction found throughout the remains of the residential and industrial areas attests. These buildings also apparently remained deserted after 107 BC until the late Roman / early Byzantine period (reflected particularly in the record of coins found—or, rather, *not* found).[9] The ruins stood as a testimony, decade after decade, to Judean hostilities against Samaritans, and no doubt continued to feed the animosity harbored in return.

9. Magen, "Gerizim, Mount," 5:1747.

19

JUDEA

The region of Judea was the Jewish heartland, the territory most consistently under the control of, and inhabited by, the historic people of Israel. It was the land parceled out to the tribes of Judah, Simeon, and Benjamin during the conquest of Canaan, the seat of the governments of Saul, David, and Solomon, and the realm of the Southern Kingdom (the kingdom of Judah) after the secession of the northern tribes upon Solomon's death. Judah was conquered by King Nebuchadnezzar II of the Babylonian Empire in 596 BC. In the course of suppressing an ill-advised rebellion a decade later, Nebuchadnezzar destroyed Solomon's temple and left Jerusalem—at the time the only Judean settlement worthy of being designated a "city"—in ruins. Both events were accompanied by deportations of members of the elite and skilled laborers from Judea to Babylon as resources to be exploited for the interests of the empire's capital.

Not fifty years later, in or around 539 BC, Cyrus, king of the Persian Empire—which had by then swallowed up the Babylonian Empire—gave permission for many people who had been deported and relocated under Babylonian rule to return to their native lands, including the Judeans. While many Judeans opted to remain in Babylon, which would thereafter remain a major center for diaspora Judaism, tens of thousands returned in a number of waves. The rebuilding of the temple—and thus the inauguration of the Second Temple period—was accomplished by 515 BC, and the restoration of the walls surrounding the City of David by the middle of the fifth century BC.

Yehud, as Judea was then called, remained a province of the Persian Empire until Alexander the Great's eastward advance in 334 BC, became a province of the Ptolemaic Empire by 301 BC, and was seized by the Seleucid Empire in 200 BC. The primary interest of all these empires was the extraction of wealth and agricultural supplies from the territory to fund their kings' domestic and foreign agendas. Judea itself remained quite underdeveloped, with Jerusalem as its most significant city—and even it was small and unimpressive by Hellenistic standards.[1] Hebron, Ziph, and Adoraim were also (relatively) major population centers at this time.[2] During this period, Jerusalem and its environs showed little evidence of participating in the Mediterranean economy with its luxury items, remaining essentially an agrarian-based economy supporting the temple state and its foreign overlords.[3] Locally made goods were the norm.

Judea regained its autonomy under the high priestly kings of the Hasmonean dynasty, an independence it enjoyed essentially from 141 to 63 BC. Jerusalem grew appreciably during this time, and new settlements were founded throughout Judea and the lands into which the Hasmonean dynasty expanded. With the intrusion of Rome into the eastern territories, Judea remained both independent *and* answerable to Rome's representatives, first under Hyrcanus II (63–40 BC) and then under Herod the Great (37–4 BC) and his eldest surviving son, Archelaus (4 BC–AD 6). At this point its fate parallels that of Samaria. Judea came under direct Roman administration with the removal of Archelaus in AD 6, with a brief period of Herodian rule again under Agrippa I from AD 41 to 44.

While the Hasmonean rulers had extended their borders to the coast and, thus, opened up the way for trade across the Mediterranean, it was really only under Herod that the Judean elites would acquire a taste for foreign wines and wares. Even then, there was a surprising consistency of distinctively "Jewish" material culture among Judeans and Galileans—the kinds of clay storage vessels and tableware, the stone vessels of various sizes and styles, the styles of lamps (largely made from clay from the area of Jerusalem itself), the ritual immersion pools, and the manner of constructing tombs and practice of secondary burial in ossuaries.

As was the case for both Galilee and Samaria, Judea's economy was also primarily agricultural and pastoral, with land well suited to olives, grapes, and pasturing flocks. This was enhanced by the ancient equivalent of the tourist industry, where Jerusalem and its temple were concerned. The Fourth Gospel foregrounds this more fully than the others by narrating Jesus's and his disciples' frequent trips to Jerusalem for one festival or another (John 2:13,

1. Berlin, "Between Large Forces," 8.
2. Richardson, *Herod*, 137.
3. Berlin, "Between Large Forces," 3–4.

23; 5:1; 7:2, 10; 12:12). We should also recall that the Torah's regulations concerning tithes included a second tithe *specifically* for spending in Jerusalem at such festivals (Deut. 14:22–27). Between the various tithes (to whatever extent they were observed in practice) and the taxes imposed by the Hasmoneans, by Herod, and by his son Archelaus during their reigns, the priestly and ruling elites based in Jerusalem siphoned off significant wealth from a largely peasant or agrarian population to maintain their institutions and lifestyles.

20

BETHLEHEM

The town associated with the birth of Jesus in both Matthew and Luke (Matt. 2:1, 6; Luke 2:4, 15) is characterized by a long history of Christian veneration at traditional locations assigned to the various events known from the infancy narratives of the Gospels, rather than disciplined archaeological recovery of Herodian and early Roman-period structures. Bethlehem also remains a densely populated city in the Palestinian Territories, and the needs of the living necessarily take precedence over archaeological endeavors.

The Church of the Nativity is often the first and *only* site visited in the city. The structure that greets pilgrims is largely from the time of Justinian (emperor from AD 527 to 565) and richly rewards those interested in church history from the Byzantine through Crusader periods. What it offers to those interested in the first century is largely limited to an altar and shrine over the traditional spot of Jesus's birth (see fig. 20.1), a second shrine at a site where a feeding trough (a "manger") once stood (see fig. 20.2), and a network of caves that were in use in the first and second centuries AD. The history of the veneration of this place is indeed ancient. Origen already bore witness to the displaying here of a cave and a manger traditionally associated with Jesus's birth by the early third century (*Cels.* 1.51). A church would be built over the spot by Constantine. In the early fifth century, Jerome, resident in Bethlehem, would lament the removal of the more ancient and unimpressive manger (which he speaks of as having been made of pottery rather than stone) with an ornate, silver substitute (*Hom.* 88)—a symbolically significant swap, capturing so vividly the manner in which centuries of Christian devotion can

Figure 20.1. The shrine in the Church of the Nativity commemorating the traditional location of Jesus's birth in the cave below. The aperture at the center of the fourteen-pointed silver star allows pilgrims to touch the rock of the cave floor.

Figure 20.2. Two stone feeding troughs from the Iron Age found in Megiddo. The "manger" in which the newborn Jesus was laid (Luke 2:7, 12) may have resembled these, the design of which changed little between the Iron Age and the Crusader period.

Figure 20.3. The southern half of the lowest of the three reservoirs of Solomon's Pools, dating from the second century BC. The stairway cut into the rock gives some indication of its massive size.

create more than merely temporal distance from the realities of Jesus's own lived experience.[1]

The practice observed in Nazareth may help us imagine the birth of Jesus in Bethlehem in a somewhat more authentic manner. Many artistic depictions and traditional carols portray something like a barn or a cave isolated from any residential area—an artistic trend that reflects the much later practice of keeping barns with their livestock in an outbuilding on one's farm. In first-century Nazareth, one finds purpose-built residences in close proximity to (usually above, sometimes adjoining) cave-like structures, whether natural or purposefully dug out, which were used for keeping livestock as well as the processing and storage of agricultural produce. The "little Lord Jesus, asleep on the hay," might indeed have been in such a cave, but it would have been only a few meters from a Bethlehemite's residence across an enclosed courtyard.[2]

A significant but often overlooked archaeological site in the Bethlehem area is the system of reservoirs known as Solomon's Pools, a 3-mile trek from

1. Jerome's reproach can be found in Ewald, *Homilies of Saint Jerome*, 222.
2. See also Murphy-O'Connor, *Holy Land*, 230.

Figure 20.4. The northern half of the middle reservoir of Solomon's Pools.

the Church of the Nativity. Jerusalem's growth depended on the increase and regularization of its water supply. During the late Hellenistic and early Hasmonean periods, great efforts were made to increase the supply of water to Jerusalem. Solomon's Pools were an important node in that supply. The combined capacity of the three reservoirs is approximately 40 *million* gallons. The pools were fed by four nearby springs and by aqueducts leading from wadis as far as 8 miles further south. Other aqueducts conducted the water from these reservoirs to Jerusalem. We do not know who initiated this project and built the first pool. Ben Sira credits Simon the Just, high priest from 219 to 196 BC (cf. Josephus, *Ant.* 12.224–25), with improving the city's water supply, including building "a reservoir like the sea in circumference" (Sir. 50:3). It is possible that Ben Sira was referring to the oldest (the lowest) of these three reservoirs, though other possibilities in the near vicinity of Jerusalem also exist (see fig. 20.3). The middle and upper pools were in service by the time of Herod the Great, who is likely to have been responsible for the construction of at least one of these pools (see fig. 20.4). Both Herod and Pilate also built new aqueducts to tap additional sources of fresh water for Jerusalem from the southern hill country and increase the volume conveyed from Solomon's Pools. Pilate appropriated funds from the temple to pay for his project and was no doubt caught off guard when what he intended as a benefit to the city aroused opposition and gave rise to public demonstrations that he dispersed with extreme prejudice (Josephus, *Ant.* 18.60–62).

21

HERODIUM

As the shadow of Herod the Great looms over the narrative of Jesus's birth in Bethlehem (Matt. 2:1–12), so the shadow of Herodium, one of Herod's palace-fortress complexes, loomed over Bethlehem—or, at least, on its near horizon, sitting just 3 miles southeast of the Church of the Nativity. Unlike Herod's other palace-fortress complexes (like Jericho, Masada, or Machaerus), Herodium was an undeveloped site prior to Herod's building activity. This had been the location of a minor victory fought by Herod in 40 BC against the last claimant to the Hasmonean throne, Mattathias Antigonus. His victory in this skirmish allowed his party to push on to Masada (where Herod left his family members and eight hundred armed supporters) and Herod to escape to Rome, with whose power and backing he would eventually assert himself as king over the region. The site evidently impressed itself on his mind and heart. At some point close to 20 BC, Herod began construction here on a massive palace complex and fortress (see fig. 21.1). It became the administrative center for the district, attracting thereby a resident population of officials in the local government, their support staff and families, and the families of those who would work in the support industries required to sustain what became, essentially, a small town, not to mention a regular military presence of Herod's auxiliaries.

Herod selected a prominent hill for his palace-fortress. The whole structure was surrounded by two high, concentric circular walls that provided corridors and galleries to allow access to the multiple levels of the various components of the complex. Four towers were constructed at the four points of the compass, the east tower having the greatest diameter (60 feet, as opposed to 50 for the remaining towers). Based on patterns observable elsewhere in Herod's palatial architecture, the east tower, at least, would likely have originally stood several stories above the level of the walls and have been furnished with well-appointed rooms and halls and an open, roofed top level enjoying splendid views and catching evening breezes (see fig. 21.2). The remaining towers, which may or may not have extended above the wall, also had plentiful interior rooms, though many of these would have been needed for storage, barracks for at least part of the resident cohort, lookout stations, and other such functions.

Figure 21.1. The artificially enhanced cone of Upper Herodium seen from amid the remains of Lower Herodium.

Figure 21.2. The base of the eastern tower and the garden-courtyard of Upper Herodium.

Author photo, courtesy of the Terra Sancta Museum, Jerusalem

Figure 21.3. A Corinthian column capital from the colonnades lining the courtyard within Upper Herodium.

The diameter of the space within the round fortification walls is about 200 feet, providing ample room for the palace. Upper Herodium was accessed by means of a monumental stairway consisting of about two hundred steps, covered by a roof laid atop arched supports and climbing to a grand entryway that opened into the large, inner, rectangular courtyard—a garden with colonnades on three sides and exedras on the two short sides (see fig. 21.3).[1] This space, which filled the eastern half of Upper Herodium, would remain open to the sky above. The western half housed several elements. First, Herod's triclinium or dining hall—a large, ornately frescoed and tiled room of about 30 by 50 feet—sat in the southwest (see fig. 21.4).[2] Second, in the northwest area of

Figure 21.4. The formal dining room. The benches around the periphery were added by the revolutionaries who seized the fortress in AD 66 and converted this space into a synagogue.

1. On the monumental stairway and its various phases of construction, see Netzer, *Palaces of the Hasmoneans*, 147–51. Josephus provides a description of the complex in *J.W.* 1.419–21; *Ant.* 15.323–25.

2. Foerster and Netzer, "Herodium," 2:619.

the circle, a small but complete Roman bath facility was installed, consisting of a dressing room (apodyterium) with a mosaic floor, a furnace-heated sauna (caldarium), a domed warm room (tepidarium; see fig. 21.5), and a cold pool (frigidarium). The walls were plastered and frescoed in the Pompeian Second Style.[3] Between and behind the dining room and bathhouse were a number of well-appointed rooms that may have served as royal bedchambers. The palace originally had at least a second, if not also a third, floor constructed over the remains currently visible within to provide a level for private living quarters for Herod, his family, and his guests.[4] It is likely that the whole was equipped with the means to catch rainwater and lead it to several of the cisterns dug into the mountain.[5]

Figure 21.5. The domed tepidarium from the bath complex inside Upper Herodium.

Figure 21.6. Herod had a small theater built into the exterior of the hill somewhat lower than the main level of the palace. Here we see it with partial reconstruction to recover something of its former stature (see, further, Netzer, *Palaces of the Hasmoneans*, 144–46).

3. Foerster and Netzer, "Herodium," 2:620.
4. Netzer, *Palaces of the Hasmoneans*, 104.
5. Netzer, *Palaces of the Hasmoneans*, 106.

Figure 21.7. Herod entertained visiting dignitaries in an ornately frescoed room behind the gallery at the top of the theater's seating area.

Figure 21.8. Lower Herodium, looking northwest across the pool and garden complex.

The conical fortress-palace was just one part of the grander complex of Herodium, the most lavish parts of which sprawled out at the foot of the hill (Lower Herodium; see fig. 21.8). There Herod built a large pool, 210 by 135 feet and 10 feet deep—deep enough to accommodate small, recreational boats.[6] A columned circular pavilion rose from the center of the pool while columned porticoes surrounded the pool on its northern, western, and southern sides. Lush gardens planted in imported soil surrounded the pool as well,

6. Foerster and Netzer, "Herodium," 2:622.

Figure 21.9. The pool and garden complex of Lower Herodium.

with a large garden area of 360 by 190 feet on its eastern side (see fig. 21.9).[7] Another bath complex, richly decorated with frescoes and molded stucco work, was built at the southwest corner of the pool complex. Herodium was supplied with water chiefly by an aqueduct that brought water from a spring near Solomon's Pools, 3 miles south of Bethlehem. The spring was sufficient not only for human needs but also for filling the great pool and irrigating the lavish gardens that surrounded it. A great deal of water was also carried by pack animals some distance up Herodium to be stored in one of several cisterns hewn into the limestone mountain.[8]

A number of service areas, including stables and storage facilities, have been identified north of the pool complex. As Herodium served as the administrative center for the district, several of the structures originally built in the vicinity of the pool complex probably served as venues for government offices and as residences for the administration's staff. A long, thin stretch of leveled surface, beginning at the southeastern corner of the pool and garden complex, sits at the base of the mound, variously identified as a stadium or

7. Netzer, *Palaces of the Hasmoneans*, 109.
8. Netzer, *Palaces of the Hasmoneans*, 106.

Figure 21.10. An ornately carved building standing at the western end of the "stadium" in Lower Herodium. This may have served as a triclinium for a memorial feast that formed part of Herod's funerary rites, a tradition honoring his Nabatean roots. The hall's sides are 10 feet thick, likely to provide support for a heavy, ornamental, vaulted ceiling (Foerster and Netzer, "Herodium," 2:623–24).

as a staging ground for Herod's funeral procession, which set out from Jericho with Herod's body and may have stopped here before some portion of the entourage made the final journey to Herod's tomb itself (Josephus, *J.W.* 1.670–73; *Ant.* 17.196–99; see fig. 21.10). There is no reason to suppose it did not serve both purposes at different times. A second palace was built at the foot of the mound, overlooking this "stadium."[9] Taken as a whole, the royal facilities at Herodium constituted the largest such complex in the Mediterranean, to be outdone over the next century only by Nero's "Golden House" (*Domus Aurea*) in Rome and Hadrian's villa at Tivoli.[10]

Herod's mausoleum was discovered not far to the east of the ancient stairway that connected the lower palace to the upper fortress (see fig. 21.11). Its base measures 30 feet squared. Fragments of a beautifully decorated

9. Murphy-O'Connor, *Holy Land*, 322–23. Several of the structures of Lower Herodium were significantly modified in the early Byzantine period, when it served as a monastery and also housed three small churches.

10. Broshi, "Archaeology of Palestine," 3:29.

Figure 21.11. The finely worked, but scant, remains of the base of Herod's mausoleum on the slopes of Herodium below the palace-fortress.

Author photo, courtesy of the Israel Museum, Jerusalem

Figure 21.12. The reconstructed rose-colored sarcophagus believed to have contained the remains of Herod the Great, together with a number of architectural fragments bearing witness to the artistry of the mausoleum itself.

sarcophagus were found within the ruins of the monument, along with some larger pieces suggestive of the monument's original stature and appearance (see fig. 21.12). The monument and sarcophagus appear to have been smashed with a vengeance in antiquity by people who bore a personal hatred for Herod and what he represented—possibly the revolutionaries who had taken over Herodium along with sister palace-fortresses Masada and Machaerus during the First Jewish Revolt, or perhaps the guerrilla fighters who seized this location during the Second Jewish Revolt. Prior to this desecration, the monument probably resembled the so-called Pillar of Absalom, a first-century BC tomb in Jerusalem's Kidron Valley, though Herod's monument had a more ornate upper level involving a decorative circle of columns around the central core and soared to a projected height of 70 feet.[11] After his burial, the slopes of Upper Herodium were covered further with fill, burying the theater and sealing off access to the upper palace, making the whole a monument to Herod's memory.[12]

11. Netzer, *Palaces of the Hasmoneans*, 141–44.
12. Netzer, *Palaces of the Hasmoneans*, 139.

22

MASADA

One of the most famous sites outside of Jerusalem shaped by Herod's imagination was Masada. This was a fortified site at the far southeast corner of Herod's realm, from which a watchful eye could be kept on the kingdom of the Nabateans to the south and southeast. While this was already a military outpost during the Hasmonean period, likely built under Alexander Jannaeus (103 to 73 BC),[1] Herod dramatically improved Masada's fortifications and built several palaces on its grounds over the course of his reign.

The most impressive of these, and the most obviously *designed* to impress, was the Northern Palace complex. The remains suggest a concerted effort on the part of Herod's architects to conquer nature by accomplishing the seemingly impossible—the construction of a fully equipped palace on three tiers descending down the cliff face, giving the impression of a palace suspended in the air. The upper level consisted of a large reception hall flanked by private rooms for Herod's use and that of his family (see fig. 22.1). The floors were decorated with mosaics featuring black and white geometric patterns without figures of animals or humans (apparently in deference to Jewish sensibilities concerning images; cf. Exod. 20:4; Deut. 5:8), while the walls were plastered and decorated with frescoes and molded stucco work. At the front of this level was a large, semicircular, columned porch, possibly including a garden area, offering views of the lower levels of the palace and, of course, the chasms below to either side of those levels.[2]

1. Yadin and Netzer, "Masada," 3:973; Netzer, *Architecture of Herod*, 80. Josephus (*J.W.* 7.285) claims it had already been fortified by Jonathan, Alexander Jannaeus's great-uncle.

2. Netzer, *Architecture of Herod*, 90–91.

The landing of the second level was 20 yards below the upper level. Most of its structures are lost, apart from the foundations of what was likely a large, circular hall that might have been used for banquets and receptions, given the breathtaking views. A number of rooms were built between this circular hall and the cliff face behind, one of which housed part of the stairwell connecting the upper and middle levels.[3] The third and lowest level, another 15 yards below the middle level, was clearly designed for entertaining, likely serving as a triclinium or dining room (see fig. 22.2). Signs of its former grandeur—its

Figure 22.1. The reception hall on the upper level of the Northern Palace. Two smaller bedrooms are clearly visible on the right; the larger bedroom is on the left.

Figure 22.2. The triclinium on the third, lowest level of the Northern Palace.

3. Netzer, *Architecture of Herod*, 91–92.

columns and plastered, frescoed walls—remain visible and have been somewhat restored. This room, hanging over a cliff in the Judean desert, could have been transported to Pompeii, where it would have fit right in with the architecture and interior decoration of its neighbors there. A pathway off to the east leads down to a small bath complex built into the cliff face, once complete with cold, tepid, and hot rooms, though much of this has since collapsed into the ravine below.

Figure 22.3. A portion of the caldarium, showing the hypocaust system supporting a (reconstructed) secondary floor. Note also the reconstruction of a portion of the ceramic tubes within the walls, just behind the plaster surfacing, that conducted the hot air throughout the walls as well.

Immediately south of the Northern Palace, on the main level of the mesa, was a bath complex, complete with all the typical elements of a Roman bath. It was equipped with a large courtyard that likely served as a palaestra, or exercise yard, as well as the usual dressing room, tepidarium, frigidarium, and caldarium. The last is the largest room in the bath, its secondary floor supported 2 feet off the ground by two hundred miniature columns, creating the space through which furnace-heated air passed to bring the room to its desired temperature (see fig. 22.3). All the rooms were adorned with frescoed walls, mosaic-covered floors, or both.[4]

The largest royal residence in the fortress was located on its western side, though the Western Palace complex incorporated many more pedestrian functions as well. The royal apartments occupied the southeastern quarter. These included public areas where Herod could receive and entertain guests and dignitaries, private chambers, and another complete Roman bath facility (see figs. 22.5, 22.6, 22.7). The northeastern quarter of the complex was given to workshops (including a pottery installation), kitchens, food storage rooms, and other service areas. Storerooms occupied the southwestern and

4. Yadin and Netzer, "Masada," 3:978; Netzer, *Architecture of Herod*, 95.

Figure 22.4. A complex of more than sixteen storerooms, several of which have been reconstructed, kept the fortress well supplied with all the required staples—flour, oil, wine, dried dates and figs, dried legumes, and weapons and raw materials in abundance—to withstand a long siege.

Figure 22.5. A formal reception area, perhaps more specifically a triclinium, from the Western Palace.

Figure 22.6. An exquisite mosaic from a waiting area adjacent to the throne room in the Western Palace.

Figure 22.7. Another geometric mosaic gracing the floor of a room in the bathhouse of the Western Palace. The damage is from alterations made to the room by insurrectionists and their families who occupied Masada in AD 66–74, here turning the space into a functional kitchen.

an administrative wing the northwestern quarters.[5] Three smaller, freestanding palace structures were built in the area to the immediate southeast of the Western Palace, each to some extent an imitation of the nucleus of the latter. These were likely intended to serve as residences for members of the extended royal family or visiting dignitaries.[6] A stepped pool with plastered basin and sides had been dug amid these complexes (see fig. 22.8). It is not clear whether this was the work of Herod, providing additional recreation for his guests (or perhaps a public mikveh for guests and permanent staff), or of the insurrectionists who occupied the site from AD 66 to 74, for whom it would indeed have served as a public mikveh.[7]

Even though Masada was surrounded by desert on three sides and a toxic sea on the fourth, there was no shortage of fresh water for its occupants. Herod's engineers had diverted a great deal of local runoff water from the winter rains toward a dozen cisterns dug into the base of the mesa that had a combined

Figure 22.8. The plastered, stepped pool in the vicinity of the Western Palace.

5. Yadin and Netzer, "Masada," 3:977; Netzer, *Architecture of Herod*, 83–85.
6. Netzer, *Architecture of Herod*, 85–86.
7. Yadin and Netzer ("Masada," 3:985) favor the latter option. The fall of Masada is more traditionally dated to AD 73, but see Cotton, "Date of the Fall of Masada."

capacity of over 52,000 cubic yards (see fig. 22.9).[8] A steady stream of servants and pack animals brought water from the lower cisterns to other cisterns on top of the fortress to keep them, the bathhouses, and other luxuries well supplied throughout the year. At the south end of Masada, Herod constructed a massive swimming pool capable of holding almost 150,000 gallons of water. This was not a reservoir, a function served by a deep, plastered cistern sunk into the rock not far from the pool, but rather a

Figure 22.9. A massive cistern dug out from the southern end of the plateau.

Figure 22.10. A columbarium, or dovecote, from Masada. Doves were an important source of fertilizer, eggs, and meat in the Greco-Roman period. The top level of this structure likely served as a guard post and watchtower.

8. Yadin and Netzer, "Masada," 3:975.

Figure 22.11. The remains of a second, round columbarium.

bold statement of the luxury Herod could afford himself and his guests here in the midst of the desert.

Almost the entire perimeter of the plateau (all but the Northern Palace) is surrounded by a stone casemate wall, stretching over 1,500 yards. Casemate walls are made of two parallel walls, the outer one generally being thicker, with open space left in between. This allowed the perimeter wall to be far more functional—it created seventy usable, if narrow, rooms on the plateau.[9] In the event of a siege, the wall could be quickly strengthened at the projected point of assault by filling in one or more rooms with rocks and soil. Thirty guard towers were built at intervals along the wall, which also included four gates. Two of these gates were for strictly internal use, opening onto paths that led down to two sets of cisterns; the remaining two gave entrance to the fortifications from the Snake Path and from a broader path on the west side of the mountain.[10]

Together with Herodium and Machaerus, Masada bears witness to how far Herod the Great went to assure the security of his realm as well as his own personal safety while, at the same time, assuring himself of a particular—and

9. The insurrectionists and, later, refugees who occupied Masada during the First Jewish Revolt made good use of these as residences for families. On their part in the revolt and their fate, see Cohen, "Masada"; Mason, *History of the Jewish War*, 514–75; Magness, *Masada*, 163–200; deSilva, *Judea Under Greek and Roman Rule*, 151–53.

10. Yadin and Netzer, "Masada," 3:975.

exceedingly high—standard of living *wherever* he might find himself within his realm. This is not to say that Herod was *unusually* exploitative of the people he ruled—some measure of exploitation was quite usual for Hellenistic kings. When his people, however, faced significant hardship—as, for example, during a famine that struck the region in 28 BC—Herod could display remarkable, even sacrificial, generosity. The scale and lavishness of his building projects, whether for the public, for the defense of the realm, or for his own enjoyment and projection of status, may also be regarded as an indication of the prosperity that his realm enjoyed under the Roman peace and his own stable rule—alongside, of course, the standard degree of exploitation of one's subjects.

Figure 22.12. During the period of the First Jewish Revolt, a Herodian structure (possibly a stable) was converted into this small synagogue.

23

QUMRAN

When Jesus was criticized for healing a man on the Sabbath day, he defended his actions with the question: "Suppose one of you has only one sheep and it falls into a pit on the sabbath; will you not lay hold of it and lift it out?" (Matt. 12:11). The implication would be that, if one was willing to rescue a sheep on the Sabbath, one should even more readily rescue a human being from distress, as Jesus had just done. Jesus was fortunate that no Essenes were present on this occasion, for they would have answered, "We wouldn't." According to their rule of life, "No man shall assist a beast to give birth on the Sabbath day. And if it should fall into a cistern or pit, he shall not lift it out on the Sabbath" (CD XI, 13). Indeed, so strict and absolute was their manner of hallowing the Sabbath by abstinence from "work" that Essenes did not defecate on the Sabbath, for this involved digging and filling in a hole for the excrement. It seems unlikely that they would have agreed with Jesus's claim that "the Sabbath was made for human beings, not human beings for the Sabbath" (Mark 2:27 AT).

Interest in the Essenes was greatly reinvigorated by the discovery and publication of the Dead Sea Scrolls beginning in 1947.[1] These scrolls had been hidden in the caves surrounding, or in close proximity to, the derelict building

1. The Essenes were, however, already well known through other literary descriptions, including Josephus, *J.W.* 2.119–61; *Ant.* 18.11, 18–22; Philo, *Hypoth.* 11.1–18; *Prob.* 12–13; Pliny, *Nat.* 5.70–73. The similarities between the communities described in these texts and the community life envisioned in several of the Dead Sea Scrolls have convinced most scholars that all of them are together describing Essene groups, some from an outsider's and others from an insider's perspective.

compound at Qumran, a site overlooking the shores of the northwest corner of the Dead Sea (see fig. 23.1). Most scholars believe the Qumran settlement to represent a monastic, celibate elite among the larger Essene movement, whose members were to be found marrying and raising families throughout the cities and towns of Judea.[2] A few regard the settlement as a more rigorous splinter group that found even the Essenes too lax in their pursuit of covenant faithfulness and holiness. Either way, the residents of Qumran represented the strictest wing of the strictest sect of Judaism.

Author photo, courtesy of the Jordan Museum, Amman

Figure 23.1. Some of the pottery jars that held a number of the scrolls being stored in the caves around the settlement of Qumran.

Author photo, courtesy of the Jordan Museum, Amman

Figure 23.2. Fragments of the Rule of the Congregation (1QSa).

2. Two documents found among the Dead Sea Scrolls appear to prescribe the "rule" or "way of life" for these different communities—the Rule of the Community for the celibate men of Qumran, the Damascus Document (or Damascus Covenant) for the Essenes living in enclaves among the general population and raising families.

The Essenes in general regarded themselves as the community of the "new covenant" prophesied in Jeremiah 31:31–34 (CD III, 12–16; VI, 19–20; VIII, 21; XV, 5–11). For them, the "new covenant" did not imply the setting aside of an "old" covenant. Rather, the Essenes believed that the "new covenant" meant the perfect and consistent fulfillment of the law of Moses. The Qumran elite studied the law and its interpretation in shifts night and day, and it no doubt formed the principal subject at their communal meals. While they made a distinction between priestly and lay members within their group, they also extended priestly degrees of purity to all members of the sect so that they might become together "a kingdom of priests" before God in fulfillment of Israel's special calling (Exod. 19:6 NASB). They would offer together the spiritual sacrifices of worship, prayer, and perfect obedience, and thus make atonement for "Israel" (1QS VIII, 4–9; IX, 4–6).[3] They were highly critical of the way the temple cult in Jerusalem was being administered, believing the priests there to be calculating the time for the annual festivals incorrectly (because the temple priests followed the lunar rather than the solar calendar) and to be careless in their safeguarding of ritual purity and their dispelling of pollution.[4] Their rigorist interpretation and living out of the law, however, coexisted alongside a strong affirmation of God's gracious initiative—that it was only by God's favor that the member of the sect had joined the elect company and was empowered to walk in uprightness before God (1QS XI, 5–16).

The origins of the Essenes in general and the Qumran community in particular, together with the early history of the sect, remain topics of significant dispute. Some number of the sect appear to have settled at the site of Qumran around 100 BC, where the core chapter would take root and flourish with only brief interruptions until AD 68, when the armies of Vespasian captured the settlement and killed most of its inhabitants in the course of suppressing the First Jewish Revolt.[5]

Perhaps the most striking feature of the archaeological site is the evidence it provides of the sect's obsession with water. Aqueducts run throughout the site, channeling water from the sporadic streams running down from the hills to the west of the settlement into large cisterns (see fig. 23.3). Such provisions were, of course, essential for a community trying to live in an arid environment, but they were not undertaken only for survival. Rather, these water channels also served to fill a system of plaster-lined ritual baths throughout the site. There are at least ten such shallow pools to be seen among the ruins,

3. Betz, "Essenes," 3:450.

4. A number of complaints lodged by a leader of the sect against the temple leadership are preserved in a singularly important sectarian text, Some Works of the Law (4QMMT).

5. Magness, *Archaeology of the Holy Land*, 112.

Figure 23.3. A portion of the water channel that runs throughout the site with a mikveh in the center background. Note the raised areas on the steps that create a low divider, probably to separate those entering the mikveh polluted from those exiting purified.

Figure 23.4. One of the many mikvaoth within the Qumran compound.

enough to service the hundred or so members who would have occupied the site at any given time (see fig. 23.4). These reflect the sect's intense interest in ritual purification, likely in connection with their sense of their community as a place where they joined with the angels in the worship of God and served as a kind of substitute priesthood on behalf of Israel.[6]

Purificatory immersions were undertaken by each member of the sect prior to participating in the common meal in the refectory, a large assembly hall (see fig. 23.5). The meal was also a spiritual event, surrounded with blessing and anticipating the meals that would one day be eaten in purity in the messianic kingdom. It was prepared by members of the sect who came from priestly families and was served individually (rather than from a common tray) on

Figure 23.5. The long assembly hall identified as the refectory from the presence of an adjoining room with over a thousand pieces of tableware.

6. Magness, *Archaeology of the Holy Land*, 130.

Figure 23.6. A reconstructed pottery kiln from the workshop at Qumran.

Figure 23.7. This chamber, in which several jars containing hundreds of silver coins were found, is believed to have been used by the bursar (or treasurer) of the sect's communal funds.

clay plates and in clay vessels kept neatly stacked in a pantry. The fellowship meal was also a time for congregational study, preaching, and prayer. It was a gathering that replaced participation in the Jerusalem temple cult that had, in their view, strayed from following God's law correctly.

This communal lifestyle was supported by communal labor, whether tending livestock, cultivating crops, or crafting pottery. A pottery workshop with a large kiln, for example, made the table vessels used by the community, the distinctive jars that first held the food stores of the community and were later used to store their most treasured scrolls, and perhaps also wares to be sold to outsiders (see fig. 23.6). The community was also supported as new members liquidated all their property and possessions and handed over the money to the financial administrator of the community at the conclusion of their three-year initiation process (see fig. 23.7). The members of the sect also tended large farms on the plains beyond the hills to the west and to the south of the settlement while others tended livestock, thus making the sect largely self-sufficient in terms of food.

Some of the community's members were involved in the production and curating of the scrolls that contained the shared Scriptures of Israel, other edifying but noncanonical texts also read by Jews outside the group, and the literature peculiar to the sect itself (such as its rule of life, its liturgies, and its distinctive form of biblical commentary). These were produced and stored in a two-story scriptorium and library, only the ground floor of which remains in part (see fig. 23.8). The scriptorium was connected also to several rooms for study, to judge from the number of oil lamps found there. The members of the community would meet in small groups through the different watches of the night, so that the entire night was sanctified by prayer and study (see fig. 23.9).

A three-story tower that might conceivably have served as a kind of barracks for at least some of the sectarians once stood on the compound's northern edge. It is likely, however, that very few of the sect's members slept within the compound. Rather, most members appear to have lived in caves and tents in the area surrounding the settlement. Based on the size of the refectory, the sect is believed not to have exceeded between 100 to 150 members at any one time.[7]

From one perspective, life in this community was strictly regulated and leadership was authoritarian and absolute, very much resembling the kind of religious group modern sociologists would label a cult. From another perspective, joining oneself to this group opened one up to a lifetime of work, study,

7. Magness, *Archaeology of the Holy Land*, 112.

Figure 23.8. The room identified as the scriptorium, given the discovery of several inkwells and plaster benches amid its ruins.

Figure 23.9. A small room believed to have been dedicated to the study of the Scriptures and the rule books of the sect.

and prayer spent in the assurance that one was indeed walking in the light of God's law moment by moment. It meant becoming part of a community that understood itself to fulfill Isaiah's call to prepare the way of the Lord in the desert (1QS VIII, 15–16; cf. Isa. 40:3).

It seems highly unlikely that Jesus encountered the sectarians living at Qumran (though he might well have rubbed shoulders with Essenes living in the towns and cities of Judea). Nevertheless, there is a great deal that this sect, and more particularly its *library*, can tell us about the world of Jesus. First, we learn that the text of some of the books that would emerge as part of the Hebrew Bible circulated in slightly varied forms in the first centuries BC and AD. Our English Bibles typically follow the Masoretic Text, which was edited by Jewish scribes in the late Byzantine and early medieval periods. If we were to compare the Masoretic Text of Jeremiah 10:1–10 with the same passage in a scroll of Jeremiah from the caves around the Qumran settlement, we would find that the latter version lacked our verses 6–8 and verse 10—namely, the material that interrupts the prophet's praise of the one and only God with sideways glances at the gods of the nations. Interestingly, the Greek translation of Jeremiah known from the same period (the Septuagint) *also* lacks these verses. We are thereby reminded that there was a bit more fluidity to the wording of some of these books among the manuscripts available in the first century than we might assume—or be comfortable with!

The Qumran library also tells us something about the "reach" enjoyed by literature outside of what would become the fixed canon of post-AD 70 Judaism. Partial manuscripts of the Wisdom of Ben Sira, Tobit, and 1 Enoch, all of which were also known to and passed along by other Jewish groups, were

Figure 23.10. A vast field of over a thousand simple trench graves lies on the eastern part of the plateau of the sectarian complex, most of which have been found to contain the bones of males, in keeping with literary descriptions of the sect as a community of celibate men (Magness, *Archaeology of the Holy Land*, 121).

found among the Dead Sea Scrolls. Perhaps it should occasion less surprise, then, when we find echoes of these books also in the teachings of Jesus, in the letters of his brothers (James and Jude), and in the other writings of the New Testament, since we find them among the treasured possessions of even so marginal and isolated a group as the Qumran community.[8]

Finally, a number of the writings among the Dead Sea Scrolls appear to have been composed by members of the sect, including a number of commentaries on the prophetic books of the Hebrew Bible. The starting point for the interpretation one finds in these commentaries (called *pesharim* in Hebrew) is the conviction that the events in the sect's own history, and particularly the events and trials in the life of the "Teacher of Righteousness" (an individual who was regarded as *the* authoritative interpreter of the law of Moses), were foretold in the prophetic books of Scripture (see fig. 23.11). Thus, these commentaries move back and forth between quoting passages from the biblical text and making connections with the life of their teacher and the ongoing story of his followers, legitimating the sect as the outworking of God's plan from long ago—an approach that will be very familiar to readers of the Gospels and Acts. Interestingly, the Qumran sectarians also read the Psalms of David as prophetic texts, as did the writers of the New Testament (quite prominently in the sermons of Acts and the Letter to the Hebrews).

Author photo, courtesy of the Jordan Museum, Amman

Figure 23.11. A portion of a commentary on Isaiah.

8. To learn more about these texts and the imprint of their teachings on Jesus, James, and Jude, see deSilva, *Jewish Teachers of Jesus, James, and Jude.*

24

JERICHO

According to all three Synoptic Gospels, Jesus, along with his by then considerable entourage, passed through Jericho on his final journey to Jerusalem (Matt. 20:29; Mark 10:46; Luke 18:35). Here he healed a blind man named Bartimaeus ("son of Timaeus," his father bearing a Greek name) and, according to Luke, encountered Zacchaeus, a man who had risen high in the ranks of those who collected a variety of taxes on people, property, and goods, and who typically exploited their position to line their own pockets (Luke 19:1–10). During the Hellenistic and Roman periods, the center of Jericho had shifted from the mound known today as Tell es-Sultan (the site of the Bronze Age remains of old Jericho) to the royal palaces and estates a little over a mile to the south, known today as Tulul Abu el-Alayiq. The oasis of Jericho was one of the most fertile areas of Judea and had been set apart, together with the Jezreel Valley in the north and the oasis of Ein Gedi, as royal lands, owned directly by whatever foreign power dominated the region, starting with the crown's appropriation of desirable lands in the Persian period.[1] The estates in Jericho were particularly well suited to growing date palms and the opobalsamum plant, the latter producing particularly lucrative perfume and medicinal products. After the Persian, Ptolemaic, and Seleucid Empires enjoyed the fruit of this land, each in its turn, it came under the jurisdiction of the high priests and kings of the Hasmonean dynasty and, eventually, Herod the Great.

1. Rousseau and Arav, *Jesus and His World*, 132.

The Hasmonean Palaces and Related Structures

Jericho was sufficiently close to Jerusalem to serve as a convenient retreat for its rulers (about 14 miles), but sufficiently far that it offered a significantly different (and more pleasant) climate during the winter season. John Hyrcanus I (134–104 BC) was the first in the Hasmonean line to build a palace near the site of the Jericho estates. This complex included a massive courtyard house, a garden area with two small swimming pools, and multiple stepped pools (mikvaoth). His son Alexander Jannaeus buried his father's palace beneath a high mound, on which he built his own, more heavily fortified palace. He also built a far more extensive recreational area composed of two much larger swimming pools, an open-air pavilion, and an expansive garden space (see fig. 24.1). At some point, a bath complex was built, perhaps for the enjoyment also of the resident administrative staff that oversaw the business of the estates as well as the traveling staff that would move with the royal family between Jerusalem, Jericho, and their other palaces and fortresses. Alexander's queen and successor, Salome Alexandra, built a further two palaces, essentially mirror images of one another, for their two sons, Hyrcanus II and Aristobulus II, though this would not resolve the rivalry between them. All these facilities

Figure 24.1. The twin pools that formed the centerpiece of Alexander Jannaeus's recreational facilities beside his palace. Herod reduced the dividing wall to make one large pool out of the two.

Figure 24.2. A mikveh and reservoir from one of the twin palaces of Hyrcanus II and Aristobulus II. The reservoir is fed by the water channel at the top left. A small opening at the level of the lip of the reservoir allows water to flow into the mikveh, thus maintaining its state of ritual purity.

included ritual immersion pools (see fig. 24.2). The juxtaposition of palace and immersion pool captures the twin impulses that characterized the Hasmonean dynasty—a desire to portray themselves, through architecture as well as symbols (like coinage), as successful Hellenistic monarchs alongside a commitment to preserve the distinctive values, practices, and culture of their Judean heritage, which gave them their greatest claim to legitimacy in the eyes of their subjects.[2]

The estates were worked by large numbers of resident farmers and others involved in the processing of the opobalsamum, dates, and other crops as well as by members of an administrative class. A residential area was discovered between the industrial area and the palaces consisting of nine separate buildings, built side-by-side in what appears to be a planned development. These are courtyard-style houses with plastered rooms and floors, a luxury in first-century houses. This suggests that they were prepared for a managerial class rather than the agricultural and industrial workers themselves.[3]

2. See, further, Regev, "Hellenization of the Hasmoneans Revisited."
3. Netzer, *Hasmonean and Herodian Palaces*, 2:145.

Figure 24.3. The footprint of the Hasmonean-era synagogue with the somewhat restored bases of the twelve pillars that once supported the roof.

At the westernmost end of the row of residences, closest to the palace grounds, a Hasmonean-period synagogue was uncovered, likely intended to be used by members of the administration-in-residence, for palace and support staff, and perhaps also for the agricultural and industrial workers (see fig. 24.3).[4] A mikveh with a reservoir (an *otzar*) adjacent to the structure and what appears to be a handwashing basin inside the structure, tied into a flowing water channel, attest to the attention given to ritual purity in connection with gathering at this location (see fig. 24.4).[5] The synagogue was also provided with a two-level niche in its northwest corner, possibly for storing the Torah scrolls. A triclinium and kitchen were added at a later stage, providing the synagogue with a private dining facility. The whole appears to have been destroyed in the earthquake of 31 BC, after which Herod built his second palace and its gardens over top of some portion of the complex.[6]

4. Netzer, *Hasmonean and Herodian Palaces*, 2:159, 186–88.
5. Netzer, *Hasmonean and Herodian Palaces*, 2:184–87; Netzer, "Jericho," 5:1799.
6. Netzer, *Hasmonean and Herodian Palaces*, 2:184–87.

Figure 24.4. The mikveh (right) and otzar (left) beside the synagogue. Fresh, ritually pure water flows into the reservoir from a water channel running beneath the synagogue (top center).

Figure 24.5. A four-room courtyard house adjacent to the east side of the synagogue, predating the latter. A small room in the back center appears to have been accessible only from above, likely a security provision for a storage room.

The Royal Estates and Their Produce

The royal estates at Jericho comprised at least 125 acres of land dedicated primarily to the raising of the balsam plant (which could grow only in very limited areas of the world) and date palms. This was an important source of wealth first for the Hasmonean rulers and then for Herod and his heirs. Rome, of course, benefited from the fruit of royal estates during periods of direct rule. Since these crops require an unusual amount of water both for growing and for processing, significant efforts were made to ensure the supply of water—as a web of plastered water canals throughout the estates bears witness.

Two large winepress installations have been found on the estate. The smaller of the two had a treading area of about 5 yards squared, marked by a primitively executed mosaic tile floor. Its contents drained into a settling tank of approximately 1 cubic yard and then to a collecting basin of 2 yards squared. The larger of the two consisted of *three* treading areas of about 6 yards squared each, also draining into settling tanks and finally to a collecting basin. A mikveh sits 15 yards to the northeast in obvious relationship to the winepress (since there are no other buildings in the vicinity).[7] Throughout Judea and Galilee, indeed, mikvaoth can often be found in close proximity to agricultural installations involved in the production of liquids (chiefly wine and olive oil). This suggests a widespread interest in guaranteeing the ritual purity of the liquids produced by ensuring the ritual purity of the workers involved in the production process (see fig. 24.6).[8] Such a guarantee would have been important both for goods heading for the temple, whose personnel and rites constituted a large market for oil and wine (beyond the tithed produce), and for Jews concerned to eat ritually pure food in a state of ritual purity themselves, such as the Pharisees, who organized informal societies called *ḥaberim* (Hebrew for "associates") for this purpose.[9]

The number of such facilities presupposes a broad acceptance of the principle of the sufficient purity of the *tevul yom* (the person who has "immersed that day"). Many of the prescriptions for purification found in the law of Moses call not only for immersion in water but also for the passage of time—the arrival of evening—for any pollution to be dispersed and purity to be restored. Such a requirement would render the placement of ritual immersion pools beside olive- and wine-pressing facilities moot since an immersion at the beginning of the workday would not suffice for purification.

7. Netzer, *Hasmonean and Herodian Palaces*, 2:25–29.
8. Adler, "Second Temple Period Ritual Baths," 63–65.
9. Adler, "Second Temple Period Ritual Baths," 66–67.

Figure 24.6. A mikveh and its reservoir (otzar) located in the industrial area of the royal estates of Jericho. The water channels bringing fresh water to the reservoir and allowing for overflow from both the reservoir and the mikveh are clearly seen here.

The Pharisees appear to have taught, however, that immersion alone sufficed to restore purity from a great many pollutions immediately.[10] Sadducees and Essenes opposed this principle as unscriptural, but the presence of mikvaoth beside so many agricultural sites suggests that the Pharisaic teaching carried significant weight in many quarters. It was a highly practical principle, and the dispute may throw light on how the Essenes, crafting a clever pun, would come to call Pharisees "seekers of smooth things" (Heb., *halaqoth*) in their "legal rulings" (Heb., *halakhoth*) because these rulings often sought to make purifications more practical for the demands of daily life.[11] The presence of mikvaoth among agricultural installations here in Jericho, moreover, suggests that the Pharisaic ruling came to be accepted by the Hasmonean rulers at some point—likely in the period after 76 BC when Salome Alexandra and her older son, Hyrcanus II, allied themselves with the Pharisees to the detriment

10. Adler, "Second Temple Period Ritual Baths," 69–71; Schiffmann, *Qumran and Jerusalem*, 128–29.

11. See Schiffmann, "Pharisaic and Sadducean Halakhah." The Essene position on this is reflected in 4QMMT (Some Works of the Law).

Figure 24.7. A small winepress from the industrial area of the royal estates (see Matt. 21:33; Mark 12:1).

of the Sadducees, who had enjoyed prominence under her husband, Alexander Jannaeus.

These particular winepresses were used to process date wine rather than the more typical wine made from grapes (see fig. 24.7). Dates would be soaked in water, pitted, then pressed on these slightly sloped floors. Stone rollers were used to express the syrup and juice. Significant quantities of water would be added to dilute the thick syrup, which would flow on into the settling tanks and into the collection vat for fermentation.[12]

The more important cash crop in Jericho was the balsam plant. Balsam was processed at many stages to squeeze every last drop of profitable substance from the plants.[13] First, the most valuable sap (opobalsamum) was extracted directly from cuttings in the trunks and branches of the plants. Olive oil was added, and the mixture was boiled, so that the scent of the opobalsamum disseminated throughout the oil, resulting in a coveted, expensive perfume. Second, carpobalsamum was extracted from the seeds, which

12. Netzer, *Hasmonean and Herodian Palaces*, 2:133–35. See also Pliny, *Nat.* 14.19.102.

13. Netzer, *Hasmonean and Herodian Palaces*, 2:135–38. On balsam, see also Pliny, *Nat.* 12.111–23.

Figure 24.8. A plastered pool believed to have been used in connection with the extraction of opobalsamum from the branches of the balsam plant.

would be laid out in the sun in plastered workspaces and covered with olive oil. Again, the sap would leach into and diffuse its scent into the oil. Third, after the final harvesting each year, the balsam plants were pruned, and the twigs and branches, after being beaten and bruised to facilitate extraction, were set in stepped pools with water (see fig. 24.8). The sun would sufficiently heat the water to extract the oils. The water was then collected and distilled over the ovens in the work area, allowing the oil to be retrieved for use. Finally, the bark of the plants could be used in the production of medicinal products.

Herod's Palaces

Herod, who had formally joined himself to the Hasmonean house by marriage to Mariamne, a granddaughter of Hyrcanus II, and who had already been made king of the Judeans by Rome, built his first palace in Jericho on the south side of the Wadi Qilt at some remove from the Hasmonean palaces in 35 BC. The dimensions of the whole were far from modest—almost 300 by 150 feet, a little more than a third of which was taken up by a magnificent peristyle courtyard and a dining hall. The palace would remain functional

Figure 24.9. A corridor in Herod's third palace, showing the Roman building techniques of *opus reticulatum* (the square-ended bricks laid at a forty-five-degree angle) and *opus quadratum* (the more common pattern of rectangular bricks laid on top of one another).

throughout Herod's reign, though Herod built two more palaces in Jericho during his lifetime. The second, constructed after the earthquake of 31 BC, was built over a portion of the ruins of the Twin Palaces and some peripheral buildings from the Hasmonean period. This was perhaps appropriate, since Herod himself had supplanted the Hasmonean line with his own. This palace was more geared toward recreation. The southern wing was dominated by two swimming pools surrounded by porticoes and was equipped with a complete Roman bathhouse. The northern wing was built around a large peristyle courtyard with an unusually elevated central space, which was made into a garden with the plants at eye-level to those strolling through the porticoes about its perimeter. Herod incorporated the Hasmoneans' twin pools (now joined into one) and a newly laid out garden into the plan of the second palace.

Sometime after 15 BC, the year in which Augustus's right-hand man, Marcus Agrippa, made a visit to Herod's realm, Herod began construction on a third palace. The building techniques employed suggest that Agrippa had sent skilled craftsmen from Italy to assist Herod with whatever building projects he wished to undertake (see fig. 24.9).[14] The third palace is a genuine architectural marvel, spanning the Wadi Qilt. On the north side of the wadi stood

14. Netzer, *Palaces of the Hasmoneans*, 48.

a complex containing two large dining halls (triclinia), a complete Roman bath (see fig. 24.10), a kitchen and other ancillary facilities, and a peristyle courtyard (see fig. 24.11). This northern complex had other features as well, but the erosion of the wadi's cliff face at a certain point caused them to

Figure 24.10. The remains of the laconicum, or sauna, from the bath complex in Herod's third palace. Note again the Romanesque brickwork of both kinds.

Figure 24.11. The larger of two courtyards in Herod's third palace, once surrounded by columned porticoes. A broad semicircular niche probably marks the conspicuous placement of Herod's seat when holding court or otherwise receiving guests in this space.

collapse completely into the shallow canyon centuries ago. On the south side of the wadi was a formal garden backed by a retaining wall with twenty-four decorative niches and a small theater in the center. To the east of this was a large swimming pool (the largest among the palace complexes). Between them, built on a high mound, was a great domed room that likely served as a venue for banquets and other functions. A bridge connected the north and south halves of the palace complex and led to a grand stairway ascending to the domed hall. It was here in his third Jericho palace that Herod would die in 4 BC.

The palaces of Jericho are uncommonly exposed. Herod tended to favor walls, towers, and garrisons surrounding his palaces, but Jericho was an exception. He did, however, refortify and upgrade the Hasmonean fortress situated on a mountain directly overlooking the palaces of Jericho, renaming the complex Cypros in honor of his Nabatean mother, Cypris. Cypros does not give evidence of being nearly so well fortified as Masada, Herodium, or Machaerus, but it was at least built with a view to easy defense by a small detachment of soldiers in times of trouble.[15]

Herod brought Greek and Roman entertainment to Judea like no ruler before him, planting theaters and hippodromes in Caesarea Maritima, Sebaste, and Jerusalem itself. He provided a stunningly innovative structure for Jericho in this regard, 1 mile north-northeast of his third palace—a hippodrome with seating in the form of a theater at one of the short ends of the racetrack.[16] Presumably, the building could be fitted with a wooden stage for dramatic performances (similar to the one used with the theater at Pergamum in the Roman province of Asia), which could be removed so as not to obstruct the view of athletic events. The theater was built into an artificial mound, atop which sat a building with a central, colonnaded courtyard and a number of rooms. Their purpose is entirely one of conjecture as only the foundations remain. It seems likely that the building would have been furnished at least with the means by which Herod could entertain friends and dignitaries in conjunction with the events held in the theater and hippodrome.

Jericho increasingly attracted more of Jerusalem's elite, who found it fashionable to winter in the vicinity of their rulers, along with their own retainers and the local support industries necessary to maintain their lifestyle. Over seventy tombs from the period have been surveyed, bearing the characteristic signs of Jewish burial (for example, the use of ossuaries for secondary burial

15. Netzer, *Hasmonean and Herodian Palaces*, 2:279–80.
16. Netzer, *Palaces of the Hasmoneans*, 64–67.

of the bones after the flesh had decayed). This suggests a sizable Jewish presence in the first century BC and AD.[17] It was, however, a seasonal destination for the elite class, who flocked here only for the winters and left before the oppressively hot summer season.

17. Hachlili, "Herodian Jericho," 3:17; see also Hachlili, "Second Temple Period Jewish Necropolis."

25

JERUSALEM: HEROD'S TEMPLE

Herod's most celebrated building program was his renovation and expansion of the Jerusalem temple. When Jesus's disciples came to Herod's temple, they responded to the sight much like tourists, exclaiming, "Teacher, look! What massive stones and huge buildings!" (Mark 13:1 AT). Herod had hoped for—and had designed the new and improved Temple Mount precisely to evoke—just such a response. Work commenced in 20 or 19 BC, sometime during the eighteenth year of Herod's reign.[1] Such an expensive building project required serious motivation. Herod no doubt wished to benefit the people under his rule in the regions of Judea and Galilee—those people groups most attached to the Jerusalem temple. Given the pride with which Herod showed off the temple to important Roman visitors like Marcus Agrippa, Augustus's right-hand man, it seems that Herod also wanted to create a landmark in the heart of his realm that would impress even those accustomed to the sights of the empire's capital, Rome. Herod may also have regarded this as a way to compensate for the legitimacy that his predecessors (and, for a period, ongoing rivals) enjoyed by means of a status that he would never enjoy. The Hasmonean dynasty was a series of rulers who also served, quite visibly, as high priests in the temple. They enjoyed privileges and a prestige that Herod could never attain as a layperson. But Herod *could* so completely reshape the temple complex that none who gathered therein, whether to officiate or to worship, could fail to feel the weight of his gravitas nonetheless.[2]

1. So Josephus, *Ant.* 15.380, though he places this three years earlier in *J.W.* 1.401.
2. Netzer, *Hasmonean and Herodian Palaces*, 1:129.

Figure 25.1. The layout of Herod's temple.

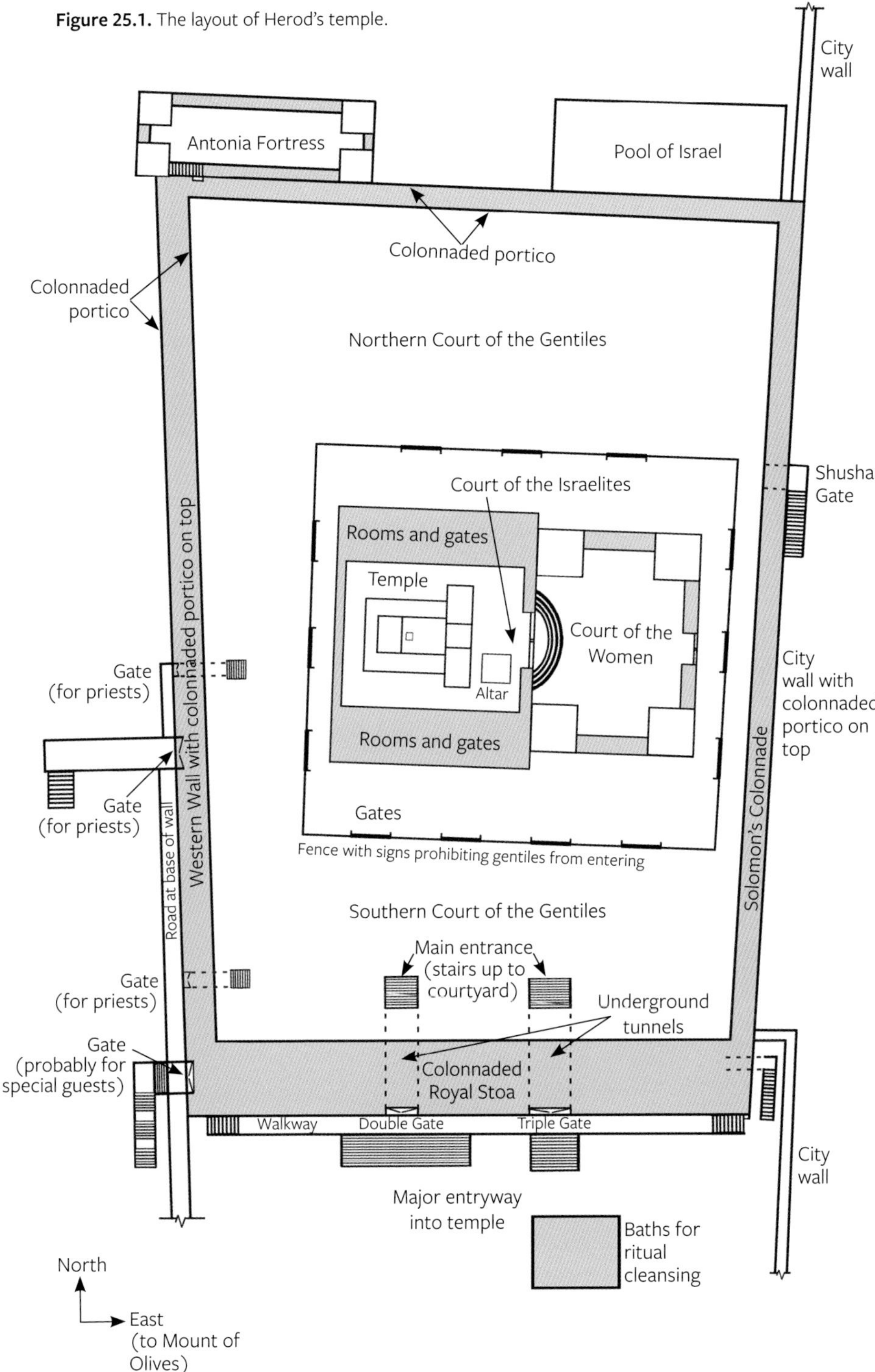

The sanctuary itself was completely rebuilt within two years by members of the priestly caste trained specially for this purpose so that no laypersons should enter into the sacred spaces set apart for priests alone. To avoid delays and to assure the priests and general populace that the work, once started, would be finished, reconstruction of the sanctuary began only once all the required building materials were brought to the site. The holy places retained the original internal dimensions of Solomon's temple, though Herod took the liberty of building the sanctuary higher and creating a significantly larger and more impressively ornamented facade. All this took place without any disruption of the temple service.

The essential features of the project—probably the temple courts and the surrounding porticoes—were completed by 12 or 11 BC (Josephus, *Ant.* 15.420–21). Work would continue in some fashion, however, for decades to come. According to John's Gospel, the Jewish authorities objected to Jesus's claim to be able to rebuild the temple in three days by declaring, "For forty-six years this temple has been under construction, and *you* are going to raise it in three days?" (John 2:20 AT), indicating that some work was still underway in AD 26 or 27. Because of occasional earthquakes and subsidences to the foundations at various points calling for significant repairs, the work could not be said to have stopped until the early years of the seventh decade AD, during the reign of Herod's great-grandson Herod Agrippa II, just a few years prior to the destruction of the entire complex in AD 70.

The destruction of the temple in AD 70 was so complete, and the repurposing of surviving building materials over the centuries so thorough, that nothing of the sanctuary or its surrounding buildings and porticoes remained for archaeologists to study and reconstruct, with the result that we depend entirely on literary sources for a picture of what Herod's temple complex looked like (see fig. 25.2). Josephus, himself an eyewitness as a frequenter of

Figure 25.2. The model of Herod's temple complex from the Israel Museum, based largely on the literary descriptions in Josephus and the Mishnah (tractate Middot).

the temple, provides extensive descriptions of the sanctuary and its courts (see *J.W.* 5.190–226; *Ant.* 15.391–95). Josephus also provides a description of the retaining walls and the gates that gave entrance to the temple precincts (*J.W.* 5.184–89; *Ant.* 15.396–402, 410–12), though here extensive archaeological work can supplement—and largely confirm the accuracy of—his account.[3]

Figure 25.3. A silver sela, or tetradrachm, minted by the revolutionary government during the Second Jewish Revolt.

A series of silver tetradrachms from the Second Jewish Revolt (AD 132–35) provide a rare, near-contemporary representation of Herod's temple as it was remembered two generations after its destruction (see fig. 25.3).[4] While the accuracy of such a representation is open for debate, it is interesting to find an image of the temple that resembles so closely the facades of Roman temples from the same period, including the tetrastyle (or four-pillared) temples of Augustus and Roma that Herod erected in Caesarea Maritima, in Samaria, and near Caesarea Philippi.

Roman influence on Herod's redesigned and expanded temple complex appears to have been significant, seen also in his investment in the grand, artificially expanded temple platform and the colonnades lining the perimeter of the courtyard.[5] The sacred precincts around the sanctuary were expanded to the north, west, and south till the space was almost doubled. The platform was an uneven rectangle measuring approximately 1,530 feet along the east side, 915 feet along the south side, 1,590 feet along the west side, and 1,040 feet along the north side, creating an area of 36 acres (or the equivalent of about 26 football fields).[6] This was not merely an act of vanity on Herod's part (though the fact that the expansion made this the largest temple complex in the Roman world during Herod's lifetime suggests that vanity was *one*

3. This is not to overlook the major discrepancies between literary accounts—between Josephus's own two accounts and the account in the Mishnah, tractate Middot. Scholars are increasingly convinced that the Middot describes an earlier iteration of the temple complex rather than the Herodian rebuild (Levine, *Jerusalem*, 223–26).

4. One or more ossuaries may also feature stylized representations of the temple's facade (see Grossberg, "Behold the Temple").

5. Levine, *Jerusalem*, 232.

6. The figures are from Ritmeyer, *The Quest*, 20; Galor and Bloedhorn, *Archaeology of Jerusalem*, 77; and Bahat, "Herodian Temple," 3:43–44, with some small discrepancies. Levine (*Jerusalem*, 228) gives slightly larger measurements of 1,620 feet (west), 1,050 feet (north), 1,550 feet (east), and 930 feet (south).

motive!). It was also highly practical. The population of Jerusalem swelled during the great pilgrimage festivals, which could draw tens of thousands of worshipers to the city above and beyond the city's sixty thousand or more residents. Herod's expansions made it possible for the temple's outer courts, at least, to accommodate far more worshipers during these peak seasons. This pilgrimage activity incidentally fed a robust tourist economy in Jerusalem along with its support industries, being significantly facilitated during the Roman period by its improved infrastructure for land travel as well as a reduction of piracy at sea.

Herod accepted the existing retaining wall on the eastern side as his own eastern boundary without attempting to push it further down into the Kidron Valley, extending it, rather, to the south and to the north. A clear seam on the eastern retaining wall shows where Herod's southern expansion began, continuing 105 feet further south (see fig. 25.4). The stones on the right side (the north side) are cut in a style common during the Hellenistic and Hasmonean periods—a clean margin of about 2 inches in width around a rough, flat center. The stones to the left (the south side) are cut in Herodian fashion, with

Figure 25.4. The seam on the eastern retaining wall showing the point at which Herod's southward extension of the temple platform began. Note the difference in the masonry on each side as well as the indications of the double gate on the Herodian (left) side of the seam.

a clean margin around a smooth, finished center. While Josephus attributed the retaining wall to the right of this seam to Solomon, most archaeologists look to the late Hellenistic or Hasmonean period for these earlier expansions to the Temple Mount.[7] Ben Sira, a teacher and scribe active around 200 BC, says that the high priest of that time, Simon son of Onias, "repaired the house, and in his time fortified the temple. He laid the foundations for the high double walls, the high retaining walls for the temple enclosure" (Sir. 50:1–2). Several such works were also undertaken under the leadership of Judas Maccabaeus and his brothers (see 1 Macc. 4:59–60; 12:35–37; 13:52), such that it is impossible to tell precisely when the first southward expansion of the platform had been undertaken.

On the Herodian side of the seam, one can see the remains of a double gate that most likely allowed access to the storerooms beneath the temple platform, though perhaps also to the platform itself.[8] The threshold stone is still visible above the springer of an arch that once supported the elevated entrance, likely accessed by a stairway that has long since disappeared as well. Smaller stones were used to block the original gateways at some point in the temple platform's transformation into a giant fortification in the Umayid, Crusader, or Mamluk periods. It seems likely that the southeastern corner of the retaining wall was once fitted with a number of windows, now also blocked, that opened onto the storage areas within so as to provide light and ventilation.[9] Another gate existed at about the midpoint of the eastern retaining wall (about 300 yards north of the southeastern corner), buried now beneath the Ottoman-period Golden Gate.[10] Beyond this are the remains of a Herodian tower that marked the northeast corner of the temple compound (see fig. 25.5).[11]

The southern wall of the new complex, some 100 feet further south than the original southern end of the platform and running 915 feet from east to west, was entirely Herodian. The architects did not merely fill the area of the expansion with rocks and soil but rather engineered enormous barrel-vaulted supports for the temple platform above, creating vast areas for storage and other uses under the temple platform in the process (the so-called Solomon's

7. See, e.g., E. Mazar, *Complete Guide*, 21–22.

8. Ritmeyer and Ritmeyer, *Secrets of Jerusalem's Temple Mount*, 36. On the various points of entry to the Temple Mount around the perimeter, see Bahat, "Herodian Temple," 3:47–51; Galor and Bloedhorn, *Archaeology of Jerusalem*, 81–85.

9. Ritmeyer and Ritmeyer, *Secrets of Jerusalem's Temple Mount*, 36.

10. Galor and Bloedhorn, *Archaeology of Jerusalem*, 84–85. It seems most likely that this gate predates Herod's building activity, but whether it represents the work of a Hasmonean king, Nehemiah, or Solomon himself remains unknown. Fleming, "Undiscovered Gate."

11. Ritmeyer and Ritmeyer, *Secrets of Jerusalem's Temple Mount*, 81–82.

Figure 25.5. Massive Herodian ashlars in the lower courses of this protrusion from the eastern retaining wall mark the location of a tower at the northeast corner of the temple platform.

Figure 25.6. Several Herodian ashlars at the southern end of the eastern wall still retain the "handles" by which the stones were lifted by cranes to be set on logs and then pulled along by teams of oxen. These would ideally have all been chiseled off and the surface smoothed when the work was completed (Ritmeyer and Ritmeyer, *Secrets of Jerusalem's Temple Mount*, 47–49).

Pierotti, *Jerusalem Explored*, plate 25a

Figure 25.7. A nineteenth-century view of the vast storerooms created within the southeast corner of Herod's expansions and supporting the platform for the courtyard and Royal Stoa above.

Stables; see fig. 25.7). Renovations by Islamic authorities on the top of the former Temple Mount, now known as the Haram es-Sharif, exposed the northern edge of these underground structures to view when these authorities created a broad descending stairway for the purpose of giving easier access to the Al-Marwani Mosque, into which the vaulted spaces had been transformed.

A street ran alongside the southern wall at the level of the gates, set above arched structures that also served as shops on the wall's far west and far east sides. These shops, in turn, opened onto a broad, 40-foot-wide plaza below the street.[12] Between the two wings of shops, a grand stairway led from the plaza to the level of this street. Its steps alternate between narrow and deep steps, a feature thought to have been put in place to regulate the pace of the many thousands of pilgrims that would pour up this stairway during festivals (see fig. 25.8). An eleventh-century building obscures three-quarters of the (now walled-up) Double Gate that served as the main point of access to the temple complex from the south side. The original lintel of the right gate as well as parts of the relieving arch set above the lintel are still visible (see fig. 25.10). This was an arch designed to distribute the weight of the many courses of stones above the gate toward the sides of the gate, relieving the pressure on the unsupported lintel so that it did not crack. The interior of these gates,

12. E. Mazar, *Complete Guide*, 47–48.

now largely inaccessible, is extremely well preserved. They opened into an arched foyer with high domes decorated with floral and geometric designs (see fig. 25.11). This led to a straight passageway and eventually a staircase that brought the worshipers dramatically into the middle of the Court of the

Figure 25.8. A segment of the Herodian southern steps to the Temple Mount, showing original steps amid modern replacements.

Figure 25.9. The massive Herodian ashlars in the bottom row of the retaining wall at the landing above the southern steps are original. The courses above the first one represent later rebuilding activity.

Figure 25.10. The Herodian lintel and relieving arch of the Double Gate are visible above the decorative arch that dates from the Umayyad Period (seventh century AD).

Pierotti, *Jerusalem Explored*, plate 25b

Figure 25.11. A lithograph showing the interior of the Double Gate as it appeared in 1864.

Gentiles (or "court open to all," 4 Macc. 4:11 AT) about 45 feet above the entry level.[13] The overall plan and grandeur of the south side of the platform and its entrances suggests that this was the principal path by which worshipers approached.

The great stairway south of the retaining wall was bisected into unequal halves by two buildings. The more eastern building may have been a gathering place for priests, perhaps also serving some administrative or judicial function.[14] The western building included many small mikvaoth, baths used for purification (see fig. 25.13). It is not clear whether these mikvaoth were for public use—a last opportunity for ritual purification before entering the temple precincts—or reserved for the use of the temple personnel, since large, public pools were available throughout the city and several others were to be found around the Temple Mount.[15] Behind the eastern, administrative building stood a triple gate. Almost nothing of the original gates remains. This gate might have been reserved for the use of priests, a sort of service entrance that provided access to the vaulted spaces underneath the temple platform ("Solomon's Stables") as well as to the platform itself, with pilgrims using

Figure 25.12. The excavated area of the two buildings that bisected the southern steps.

13. Galor and Bloedhorn, *Archaeology of Jerusalem*, 81.

14. The latter is suggested by m. Sanh. 11.2; see Levine, *Jerusalem*, 231; E. Mazar, *Complete Guide*, 57–58.

15. On the purposes for such purification, as well as those instances not also dependent on the passage of time (requiring the arrival of sunset on the day of immersion), see Adler, "Ritual Baths near the Temple Mount."

Figure 25.13. A large mikveh dating to the late Second Temple / Herodian period (Geva, "Stratigraphy and Architecture of Area Q," 7:5), located south-southeast of the temple platform. It is unclear whether it was for public use or for use by the temple personnel. Grossberg ("Miqweh with Surrounding Staircase") suggests on the basis of the size of the installation that it served recreational as well as ritual purposes, but this seems highly unlikely. At such close proximity to the temple, the pool was likely sufficiently in demand for ritual purposes (so also Geva, "Stratigraphy and Architecture of Area Q").

the Double Gate to access the temple platform.[16] It has also been suggested that the eastern end of the street in front of the southern wall sloped down on arches of decreasing height to the southeastern corner of the retaining wall, creating a possible path for bringing in the large numbers of lambs that would be required in festival seasons.

On top of the new platform, columned porticoes lined the perimeter on the western, northern, and eastern sides. According to Josephus, these were double porticoes, having two aisles formed by three rows of columns, the outermost row being joined to the walls. These were reputedly about 52 feet wide and 42 feet high. Along most (if not all) of its southern side, Herod had a much grander columned structure built—something akin to a basilica in the Roman world, though larger than most known from that period (see fig. 25.14). According to Josephus, this Royal Stoa consisted of four long parallel rows of forty columns each, all crowned with ornate Corinthian capitals, spanning a length of at least 600 feet. The middle aisle was 44 feet wide and 100 feet

16. Ritmeyer, *The Quest*, 86–87; Baruch and Reich, "Second Temple Period Finds," 88–93.

Author photo, courtesy of the Israel Museum, Jerusalem

Figure 25.14. Detail of the Royal Stoa and sanctuary from the model of Herodian Jerusalem.

Figure 25.15. Decorative fragments believed once to have adorned the Royal Stoa, found in significant numbers in the rubble around the south wall of the Temple Mount, giving some indication of the splendor of this structure.

Figure 25.16. The eight courses of massive stones laid in opposite directions at the southwest corner of the temple platform's retaining wall. For a sense of scale, note the three steps in the bottom right.

high, the side aisles 30 feet wide and 50 feet high, if Josephus's figures are to be trusted (*Ant.* 15.411–16).[17] The vast covered spaces created thereby served a variety of purposes for different groups congregating there, including conducting commerce related to the business of the temple.[18] It is possible that Herod had an apse created at the eastern end of this stoa, providing a place for the Sanhedrin (which was reputed to have met in this building in the early decades of the first century) to hold its gatherings. The architraves and friezes were richly decorated, though strictly with geometric and floral motifs in keeping with the prohibition of images in Exodus and Deuteronomy (see fig. 25.15).[19]

The southwest corner of the retaining wall shows careful reinforcement through the use of massive ashlars, the customary 3 feet in height, but 40 feet long and 8 feet thick.[20] These were set perpendicular to, and overlapping, one another, giving tremendous strength to this corner (see fig. 25.16). At this same corner, against the western wall, once stood a monumental stairway that rested on an arch that extended over the street running alongside the western wall of the temple platform and that descended on piers after taking a turn to the south (see fig. 25.17).[21] The landing of this stairway towered 60 feet above the level of the street below, likely giving direct access to the Royal Stoa and thence to the temple complex. The street

Figure 25.17. The remains of Robinson's Arch and the pier on which it landed (left); a model of Robinson's Arch (right) housed at the Israel Museum.

17. E. Mazar, *Complete Guide*, 33–34; Levine, *Jerusalem*, 234.

18. Galor and Bloedhorn, *Archaeology of Jerusalem*, 86; Levine, *Jerusalem*, 235–36.

19. E. Mazar, *Complete Guide*, 30–32.

20. The typical size of the ashlars used in the retaining wall and courtyard walls was a little more than 3 feet high by 4 to 6 feet long. Galor and Bloedhorn, *Archaeology of Jerusalem*, 78–79.

21. The arch is named Robinson's Arch in honor of Edward Robinson, the American archaeologist who identified it in the early nineteenth century.

Figure 25.18. The row of Herodian-period shops preserved under the pier of Robinson's Arch.

below was a major north-south pedestrian road in Herod's time, running up from the Pool of Siloam in the south at least as far as the northwest corner of the Temple Mount. It was a broad 30 feet wide, supported on arches that created a level surface and also allowed for the subterranean drainage channels along its length.[22] A number of small stone cells beneath the pier of Robinson's Arch remain remarkably well preserved. Artifacts related to commerce found in these areas identify them as shops, such as one

Figure 25.19. A large stone slab bearing the inscription "to the place of trumpeting" was discovered in the rubble below the southwest corner of the Temple Mount, marking this as the place from which a priest sounded the beginning and end of each Sabbath (Josephus, *J.W.* 4.582).

22. The street currently visible likely reflects Agrippa II's repaving program initiated in AD 62 to resolve the unemployment problem that resulted from the cessation of labors on the temple complex itself. E. Mazar, *Complete Guide*, 37; Josephus, *Ant.* 20.219–20.

Figure 25.20. A mikveh in the area immediately west of Robinson's Arch. Of special interest is the low dividing line that runs along the steps, marking a side for the person to enter prior to being cleansed and a side to exit purified. Several such mikvaoth have been found in the area south and southwest of the Temple Mount.

would expect to find lining a major street (see fig. 25.18).[23] Their presence reminds us of the lively business that would have been conducted at many points along this main thoroughfare.[24]

Herod extended the existing temple platform northward, southward, *and* westward. Thus the new southern retaining wall, its northern counterpart, and the full 1,590-foot length of the western retaining wall were all Herodian. The most celebrated stretch of the Herodian Temple Mount's retaining wall remains the "Western Wall" (in Hebrew, called the *kotel*), also popularly known as the "Wailing Wall" since it had long served the Jewish community as a site of mourning (see fig. 25.21). The bottom seven courses of stones—or ashlars—are original to Herod's project and still stand as they were before the time of the Roman destruction of the temple's fortifications. While the eighth through the eleventh courses use Herodian ashlars, they are thought to represent later repairs to bring the height of the walls back to the level of the platform. (The Romans had tried to destroy not just the temple precincts and its surrounding walls but also the retaining walls themselves, giving up when the work proved futile.)

Charles Warren, an avid explorer of the Temple Mount in the 1860s, discovered by tunneling down that an additional fourteen courses of these ashlars are to be found below the level of the present-day prayer plaza, grounding the retaining wall in the bedrock 50 feet below the modern surface.[25] The street

23. The discovery of several more such structures in the excavations beneath the Western Wall Plaza suggest that shops did indeed line significant stretches of this road.

24. E. Mazar et al., "Jerusalem," 5:1810.

25. Bahat, "Jerusalem Down Under," 32.

level in the time of Herod was considerably lower than it is now—at least another eight to ten courses of ashlars (about 25 feet) below the present surface (see fig. 25.22). In the southernmost portion of the *kotel* (in the far right

Figure 25.21. The portion of the retaining wall exposed in the Western Wall Plaza. The surface of the former temple platform is about level with the eleventh course of stones.

Figure 25.22. More perfectly preserved Herodian ashlars in the Western Wall, below the present surface of the Western Wall Plaza.

side of the women's section of the so-called Wailing Wall) half of the lintel of Barclay's Gate is visible just a few courses above the level of the plaza. This gate would have extended far below this level, giving access from the Herodian street below to the temple platform by means of an internal stairway. Since the Herodian wall also rose considerably higher than the temple platform, it towered almost 100 feet above street level in the southern part of the western side. At some points (notably the southeast), the top of the temple's precinct wall towered as high as 45 yards above the streets below.[26] As one moved further toward the north, however, the ground level would rise significantly, and, thus, the temple complex's walls would not seem to rise nearly so high.

Excavations along the exterior of the Western Wall have uncovered several further details about Herod's project. Not far to the north of this section of the Western Wall once stood an arch now known as Wilson's Arch that was the last of a number of arches supporting a bridge spanning the Tyropoeon Valley, creating a level passage from the Upper City west of the Temple Mount across the valley to the temple platform, chiefly to support an aqueduct that brought water from Solomon's Pools to the temple (so Josephus, *Ant.* 14.58; *J.W.* 1.143; 2.344; 6.323, 374).[27] Further north along the western wall, accessible via the Western Wall Tunnels, lies the so-called "master course" of stones (see fig. 25.23). The largest stone in this course is 42 feet long by 11 feet high by 14 feet deep, the depth being estimated based on ground-penetrating radar. It is estimated to weigh about 600 tons. Three other stones of decreasing lengths bring the overall length of this stretch of oversized ashlars to 100 feet. The size and weight of these stones compensated for a large open hall on the inner side of this retaining wall, perhaps intended to serve as a storeroom for the temple.[28] By using such massive stones, the engineers avoided the need for flying buttresses, such as are familiar from medieval cathedrals, to support the wall.

The dressed ashlars are especially well preserved in the area of the Western Wall excavations, as they have been protected from more than a millennium of erosion as later layers of occupation buried them under the rising ground. Each row of ashlars sits about one-half of an inch further back than the course below it, a measure that served both to reinforce the strength of the retaining

26. Bahat, "Herodian Temple," 3:43–44.

27. Bahat, "Western Wall Tunnels," 177–180; Bahat, "Jerusalem Down Under," 32–34; Bahat, "Herodian Temple," 3:47–48. Onn and Weksler-Bdolah ("Wilson's Arch," 120–21) suggest that Wilson's Arch supported the landing of an external staircase like Robinson's Arch. The two possibilities need not be mutually exclusive. The present structure of Wilson's Arch represents an Ummayid rebuild. Bahat, "Jerusalem Down Under," 34–38.

28. Bahat, "Western Wall Tunnels," 181.

Figure 25.23. The master course (second row from the bottom) in the Western Wall.

wall and to counteract the optical illusion created by a perfectly level surface (which would make the wall appear to bend outward as it rose).

Just north of the master course are indications of another gated entrance into the temple complex, now referred to as Warren's Gate.[29] This is the fourth of the four gates known to have existed on the west side.[30] Like Barclay's Gate, Warren's Gate gave access to the temple platform by means of a stairway built into the retaining wall.

Herod's retaining wall has largely survived, but very little remains of the walls that once stood atop the platform enclosing the temple and its courts above. What little of these walls had been observed (before access became impossible due to ongoing construction of private property in the Old City) suggests that the whole was ornamented with pilasters at regular intervals. Pilasters are decorative quasi-pillars built into and protruding slightly from the wall itself. Herod had used this decorative technique when building a

29. Bahat, "Western Wall Tunnels," 181–82.

30. Barclay's Gate sits almost 90 yards north of the southwest corner of the retaining wall and Robinson's Arch, Wilson's Arch about 110 yards north of that, and Warren's Gate 44 yards still further north of that. Galor and Bloedhorn, *Archaeology of Jerusalem*, 83–84.

monument for the tombs of the patriarchs in Hebron, about 20 miles to the south of Jerusalem—a monument that thus provides a good approximation of the overall appearance of the walls around Herod's temple platform (see fig. 25.25).

Figure 25.24. North of Warren's Gate another portion of the Herodian street running alongside the western retaining wall was uncovered. It is not clear what the pillars on the left signify, whether part of a colonnade running alongside the street or perhaps part of a plaza or market area, several of which were to be found around the Temple Mount according to Josephus (*J.W.* 5.331; see also Bahat, "Western Wall Tunnels," 188–89).

Figure 25.25. The exterior of Herod's monument to the tombs of the patriarchs in Hebron, suggestive of the finished appearance of the Temple Mount.

As for the layout and look of the sanctuary and its inner courts, we have only the literary descriptions in Josephus and the Mishnah to inform us. One of the very few archaeological remains of Herod's temple compound itself is a complete copy of an inscription in Greek (the appropriate language for the intended audience) that once stood in multiples fixed at intervals around the perimeter fence, or balustrade, that separated the "court open to people of all nations" (the so-called Court of the Gentiles) from the inner courts that were forbidden to non-Jews. The inscription reads: "No man of another nation is to enter within the fence and enclosure round the temple. And whoever is caught will have himself to blame for his death which will follow" (see Josephus, *Ant.* 15.417; *J.W.* 5.193–94; fig. 25.26).[31] The rumor that Paul had taken a Gentile from Ephesus named Trophimus across this line would incite a mob to attack Paul, resulting in his being arrested and taken into protective custody (Acts 21:28–29).[32] It was Jesus's perception of a violation of the sanctity of this "court open to all" that the evangelists remembered to have prompted Jesus's prophetic action in the temple (Matt. 21:12–13; Mark 11:15–16; Luke 19:45–47).

Author photo, courtesy of the Istanbul Archaeological Museum

Figure 25.26. The only surviving complete copy of the temple balustrade warning inscription. A fragment of a second is housed in the Israel Museum.

Beyond this balustrade (or *soreg*, in Hebrew), stairways of fourteen steps brought Jewish worshipers to the platform of the temple itself along with its inner courts.[33] The first of these courts, the Court of Women, could be entered from the eastern, northern, or southern sides. It was a relatively spacious court

31. Translation from Magness, *Archaeology of the Holy Land*, 154.

32. P. Segal ("Penalty of the Warning Inscription") presents a strong case that the death penalty would not be left to God to enact but would be carried out by God's agents, the priests.

33. It is not at all clear precisely where the temple sat within the space of its precinct. Ritmeyer (*The Quest*, 241–77) argues at length that it was so oriented that the holy of holies rested above the so-called Foundation Stone, which is also at the center of the Dome of the Rock (or Mosque of Omar) today. Levine (*Jerusalem*, 237–38) places the altar above the Foundation Stone in an attempt to honor the claim in m. Mid. 2.1 that the greatest amount of space in the outer courtyard was to the south, followed by the east, the west, and the north sides of the temple and its inner courts. Sporty ("Location of the Holy House" [1990]; "Location of the Holy House" [1991]) argues that it sat further north than the Dome of the Rock, aligned with the Golden Gate. Wherever it sat, it would seem more important to the parties concerned to

of 73 by 73 yards with chambers designated for special functions (the storing of wood and oil, the cleansing of lepers, the purification of Nazirites) in each of its four corners. This court was open to all Jews and appears to be the site for the performance of nonsacrificial rites. Fifteen more semicircular steps allowed those who were bringing sacrifices to ascend through a large gate of Corinthian bronze (Nicanor's Gate) into the innermost court, the Court of Israelites. This was a narrow space of 73 by 5 yards, enough to hand off animals to the priests, who would perform the slaughter of the animal and the distribution of its parts (whether for complete burning or for sharing between God, the priests, and the worshiper). The priests' court was surrounded by chambers serving various functions. Before the sanctuary, on the southern side of the priests' court, was the great altar of burnt offerings, measuring 50 feet squared and 25 feet high (see fig. 25.27). The area for slaughter and butchering was located to the north of the altar.

Behind both the altar and the area for butchering towered the 200-foot-high marble facade of the sanctuary itself. The grand doors that gave entrance into the holy places appear to have been fronted by four pillars (a change from the two pillars of the first temple) and the architrave over the entrance ornately decorated and further embellished with a great gold vine with grape clusters. Elements of the facade, including the parapet surrounding its top, were covered in gold plate, such that the pilgrim would see it gleaming in the sunlight from afar as soon as the temple came into view. This would be particularly dramatic for the pilgrims approaching from the north or the west, as they would catch sight of it only after rounding the tops of the mountains on those sides of the city. Behind the facade, the sanctuary itself was both narrower and shorter. It is believed that storerooms

Figure 25.27. The altar in the temple likely resembled, on a much grander scale, this four-horned altar from an Israelite shrine in Beersheba.

maintain a fixed location for the holy places from the period prior to Herod's renovations to the period subsequent to the same than for the sanctuary to be "centered" on the new platform.

and access paths were built into its sides at multiple levels for the wealth that belonged to the temple and that was deposited there on trust. What lay within the sanctuary, only the priests could see.[34]

Given Josephus's description, the temple's massive retaining walls and approaches, courts, and gleaming facade gave Jesus's disciples just cause to be impressed by the sight of this structure that stood at the heart of Jewish religious experience. As a later rabbi would testify in the Babylonian Talmud, "Anyone who has not seen Herod's Temple has never looked upon a beautiful building" (b. B. Bat. 4a, AT).

The Fate of the Temple

Jesus responded to his disciples' admiration for the temple structure in a manner that would surely have dampened their enthusiasm at seeing it: "You see these great structures? Surely a stone will not be left standing upon a stone that will not have been cast down!" (Mark 13:2 AT; cf. Matt. 24:1–2; Luke 21:5–6). In AD 66, insurgent elements across a wide spectrum of the population of Judea and Galilee initiated a full-scale revolt against Rome. This was motivated in part by decades of provocation by the local Roman authorities, in part by tensions between Jews and non-Jews that erupted into violent pogroms in cities like Caesarea Maritima, in part by socioeconomic tensions between rich and poor in the region, and in part by the irrepressible conviction that God's land belonged to God and to God's people and not to Gentile overlords. The revolt ended in disaster for the people of Galilee and Judea, climaxing in the siege and destruction of Jerusalem and its temple, which had become the fortified base of several revolutionary groups, in AD 70.[35]

What Jesus was remembered to have predicted about the destruction of the temple proved true as the Roman army methodically tore down the fortifications surrounding the temple complex so that it could never again be used as a stronghold for rebellion. The damage to the Herodian street running alongside the Western Wall of the temple complex that was caused as soldiers—or, perhaps more likely, Jewish prisoners of war—threw down each successive course of the massive ashlars from the wall around the temple platform above is still visible today (see fig. 25.28). At one end of the excavated

34. I depend throughout these paragraphs on Lee Levine's synthesis of the primary literary sources into a coherent description (*Jerusalem*, 238–42).

35. On the First Jewish Revolt, see Smallwood, *Jews Under Roman Rule*, 293–330; Berlin and Overman, *First Jewish Revolt*; Goodman, *Rome and Jerusalem*; Mason, *History of the Jewish War*; deSilva, *Judea Under Greek and Roman Rule*, 143–53; and, of course, Josephus, *Jewish War*.

Figure 25.28. Visible damage caused by the impact of the toppled ashlars and Robinson's Arch on the Herodian street running alongside the western retaining wall of the Temple Mount. In the background, heaps of these toppled ashlars have been left where they lay in AD 70.

portion of the street, archaeologists have left a hundred or so such stones piled up as they found them, a testimony to the Romans' thoroughness. Along the easternmost side of the southern retaining wall, one can see damage to the limestone ashlars caused by the burning of the shops adjacent to the wall (see fig. 25.29). Limestone and marble are susceptible to fire, which can reduce them to powder (producing the lime that is a necessary ingredient in ancient mortar and Roman cement). As the wooden beams that supported the roofs of the structures built against the southern wall burned, the heat caused parts of the temple platform wall to burn away, leaving the impressions of the arches that supported those roofs.

In Rome, the Arch of Titus, erected shortly after Titus's death in AD 81, still proclaims his victory and enshrines the memory of Judea's brutal recapture. The friezes on the interior of the arch present scenes from the triumphal procession awarded to Titus by the Roman Senate in honor of his victory. One

Figure 25.29. Damage done to the eastern side of the southern retaining wall, and charred outlines of arches left, by the conflagration of AD 70. The descending height of the arches suggests, incidentally, that a flight of shallow steps or, more likely, a ramp existed on this side of the southern wall.

Figure 25.30. The scene from the Arch of Titus showing the spoils of the temple being carried in procession to celebrate Titus's recapture of Jerusalem.

scene documents the fate of representative spoils from the temple, which are carried aloft by wreathed Romans. These include the great seven-branched golden candlestick, the table for the showbread, and the trumpets associated with the temple cult (see fig. 25.30).[36] The ultimate fate of these artifacts is unknown, but it is reasonable to believe that Vespasian put them on display among other prominent treasures in his so-called Temple of Peace, erected in Rome in AD 75 (cf. Josephus, *J.W.* 7.160–61).

36. Josephus (*J.W.* 7.148–50) also refers to these treasures being carried as spoils of war in this triumphal procession.

26

JERUSALEM: THE CITY

Jerusalem grew significantly throughout the Hasmonean, Herodian, and early Roman periods. When Jonathan first established himself as high priest and de facto leader of the Judean people in 152 BC, Jerusalem's fortifications surrounded only the City of David (the "Lower City") and the temple precincts. As Jerusalem's population increased over the next five or six decades, homes and shops spilled over onto Mount Zion west of the City of David, across

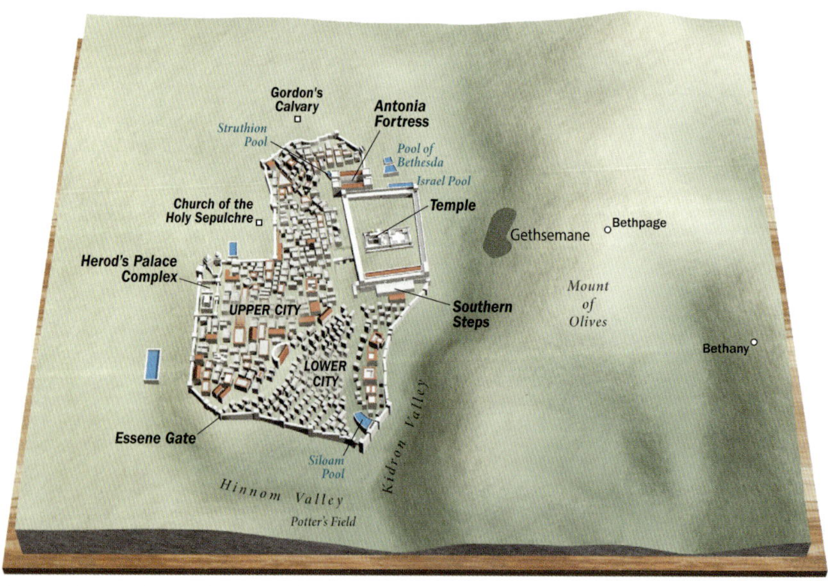

Map 26.1. Jerusalem in the time of Jesus.

Figure 26.1. The base of a Hasmonean tower, embedded in the First Wall, at the southern tip of Mount Zion. The foundations for the ancient, preexilic wall are visible immediately below it.

the Tyropoeon Valley, and onto the plateau west of the Temple Mount that would come to be called the Upper City.[1]

By the time of Alexander Jannaeus, Jerusalem's fortifications, known as the First Wall, enveloped between 150 and 160 acres. This wall essentially followed the line of Hezekiah's wall, which marked the city's peak expansion during the First Temple period.[2] The line followed the contours of the Lower City and the southern slopes of Mount Zion, stretching northward along the present line of the Old City wall, and then turning abruptly eastward at what is now the Jaffa Gate (see figs. 26.1, 26.2, 26.3). This gave Jerusalem excellent lines of defense around the eastern, southern, and western sides on account of the depth of the Kidron and Hinnom Valleys. The north side would always remain more vulnerable to attack. Herod would reinforce the First Wall and create new, stronger towers in the area of the wall's northwest corner (the Citadel), one of which survives in the base of the so-called Tower of David.

1. Halpern-Zylberstein, "Archaeology of Hellenistic Palestine," 2:10.
2. Levine, *Jerusalem*, 106–7; Galor and Bloedhorn, *Archaeology of Jerusalem*, 69.

Figure 26.2. A Hasmonean tower outside the east wall of the Old City, marking the line of the First Wall.

Figure 26.3. The line of the First Wall and a Hasmonean tower (center) visible in the Citadel.

By some point late in the Hasmonean period or early in Herod's reign, a sufficient mass of Jerusalem's residents, shopkeepers, and artisans had once again outgrown the city's walls to the north of the First Wall and west of the Temple Mount to require action. A second wall was constructed around an additional area of 60 to 70 acres, affording the new residential and commercial area protection.[3] According to Josephus (*J.W.* 5.146), this wall followed a northward path from the Gennath Gate, which sat about halfway between the northwest corner of the First Wall and the Temple Mount, and turned to join the Antonia fortress. The First and Second Walls would have demarcated the contours of the Jerusalem that Jesus knew throughout the whole of his earthly life. At this point, the city could be estimated to have a stable population of between sixty thousand and seventy thousand people, a number that could triple or quadruple during peak religious pilgrimage festival seasons.[4] Excavations have uncovered only sparse indications of growth into the area of the New City north and west of the Second Wall, which would eventually be enclosed by a Third Wall in the decades following Jesus's resurrection and ascension.[5] Perhaps a good deal of this space was used for agriculture as well as a tenting ground for some of the many pilgrims coming to Jerusalem for the three major festivals.[6]

Pools and Water Supply

Two of Jesus's most memorable miracles happened in or around the great pools of water in Jerusalem. He healed an invalid beside the Pools of Bethesda (John 5:1–20). He sent a man who had been born blind to wash his eyes in the Pool of Siloam, where he regained his sight (9:1–12). These were two of several pools and reservoirs in and around Jerusalem, a city that required a constant and substantial supply of water not only for the everyday needs of its residents but also for the special needs of the temple and its regulations for purity.

3. Levine, *Jerusalem*, 106. On the nature of this district, see Josephus, *J.W.* 5.331; Levine, *Jerusalem*, 335.

4. Levine, *Jerusalem*, 343.

5. Agrippa I (AD 41–44) would begin (Josephus, *J.W.* 5.151–53), and either his son Agrippa II or the insurrectionists of the First Jewish Revolt complete, a Third Wall that encompassed an even larger suburb that had grown up north of the First and Second Walls and the Temple Mount. How much area it enclosed is disputed. The minimalist view is that it followed the line of the current northern wall of the Old City (Magness, *Archaeology of the Holy Land*, 161); the maximalist view, based on discoveries of portions of what was certainly a wall of *some* kind during the Roman period, claims it followed a line about 1,300 feet north of the Old City wall. Galor and Bloedhorn, *Archaeology of Jerusalem*, 72–74; Levine, *Jerusalem*, 317.

6. Geva, "On the 'New City,'" 305–9.

Figure 26.4. A view of the interior of the Sultan's Pool (Serpent's Pool).

A massive reservoir stood just outside the first-century walls of the city to the southwest of the Citadel and west of Mount Zion. Now known as the Sultan's Pool, this may have been the reservoir known as the Serpent's Pool in the first century (see fig. 26.4). Like many of Jerusalem's pools, it was originally constructed as a means by which to collect and conserve runoff water during the rainy season, though it is unclear if it dates to the Hasmonean or Herodian period.[7] The fact that it is now used as a stadium for outdoor concerts testifies to its vast capacity. A similarly massive reservoir sits half a mile west of the modern Jaffa Gate, with a capacity of almost 8 million gallons, now known as the Mamilla Pool (see fig. 26.5). Its dating is widely disputed, though the ongoing use, repair, and replastering of such reservoirs can make determination of their time of origin difficult, if not impossible, to determine.[8]

7. Shimon Gibson (*Final Days of Jesus*, 95), following Magen Broshi ("Serpent's Pool"), believes this pool to have been constructed in the medieval period and the Serpent's Pool to have been located north of the city. More recently, David Gurevich ("Water Pools," 117) has offered evidence for its existence by the late Hellenistic period.

8. Gibson ("Excavations at the Bethesda Pool," 27–28) believes the Mamilla Pool to be medieval in origin, Gurevich ("Water Pools," 130) favors a Byzantine date, while Levine (*Jerusalem*, 215) believes it to be Herodian.

Figure 26.5. The Mamilla Pool. For scale, note the two visitors left of the center.

There were also several pools and smaller reservoirs within the city or close by its walls. The Struthion Pool (Josephus, *J.W.* 5.467) was originally a large, open-air pool to the north of the temple platform measuring about 16 by 60 yards and 8 yards deep (see fig. 26.6). Fed by an aqueduct, it was certainly in place by the early Herodian period as part of the moat structure around the newly built Antonia fortress (*J.W.* 5.149–51, 241),[9] though it might have had a Hasmonean predecessor. Later, under Hadrian, it would

Figure 26.6. The Struthion Pool. Less than a quarter of the pool is visible here in large measure due to Hadrian's construction of the vaulted roofs and bisecting of the pool.

9. Gurevich, "Water Pools," 117.

be covered over with two large, vaulted structures, which, in turn, supported part of Hadrian's expansive forum inside the Damascus Gate (see chap. 27).

A larger pool, known as Hezekiah's Pool or the Amygdalon Pool (Josephus, *J.W.* 5.468), sat immediately northeast of Herod's citadel and the Phasael Tower. Still clearly visible today from the Tower of David, it has dimensions of about 50 by 100 yards—about the size of a football field—and a depth of 6 or 7 yards.[10] This was also a basin constructed to catch and conserve runoff rainwater. Another, even larger collection basin called the Pool of Israel was constructed north of the eastern half of the northern wall of the temple complex. The pool has long since been filled in (and is now beneath a parking lot), but probes conducted in the nineteenth century suggest that it had dimensions of 41 by 120 yards and a depth of 25 to 30 yards.[11] Its date of construction is uncertain; it was either created in tandem with Herod's Temple Mount expansion project or predated the same and set the northern limit for it.[12]

Readers of the Gospel of John, of course, will be most interested in two particular pools—pools that, unlike all of the aforementioned, may have served ritual purposes and not merely as water collection basins. The first is the Pools of Bethesda, located north of the Temple Mount and the (now buried) Pool of Israel, currently found within the complex of the Church of Saint Anne. It can be difficult for visitors to imagine the ancient pool here, as it has been extensively overbuilt first by a Roman temple of Asclepius, then a Byzantine church, and finally a Crusader chapel. One must mentally remove all of this to begin to picture the large open space surrounded by steps that was the ancient pool (see fig. 26.7). This pool may have been referred to in the Copper Scroll, one of the documents from the Dead Sea Scrolls, as *Beth Eshdathayin*, which appears to mean "House of the Twin Pools."[13]

John tells us that the Pools of Bethesda had five porticoes, or roofed colonnades (John 5:2).[14] For a long while, the number five had been interpreted as symbolic, perhaps of the five books of Moses that belief in Jesus and Jesus's words had superseded. It was nearly impossible for scholars to imagine a pool with five porches until the pool itself was excavated, showing that it was, in fact, two separate pools. Four porches surrounded the two pools, and a fifth

10. Gurevich, "Water Pools," 106.

11. Levine, *Jerusalem*, 214.

12. Netzer, *Architecture of Herod*, 136, versus Gurevich, "Water Pools," 115–16.

13. McRay, *Archaeology and the New Testament*, 187.

14. These porticoes were dismantled and the dividing wall considerably thickened when the pools were renovated in the fifth century AD. Rousseau and Arav, *Jesus and His World*, 156.

Figure 26.7. The excavated portion of the southern basin of the Pools of Bethesda, showing the extensive construction over the site in the late Roman, Byzantine, and Crusader periods.

Figure 26.8. A reconstruction of the Pools of Bethesda (Israel Museum).

porch was constructed over the dam between the two pools (see fig. 26.8).[15] Much of the south pool and almost all of the north pool remain unexcavated due to private ownership of the many homes and other buildings built over the ancient layers of remains beneath. Both were slightly trapezoidal. The dimensions of the southern pool were 215 feet (on the south side) by 160 feet

15. Origen (*Comm. Jo.* 5.2) had spoken of the pool in these terms in the early third century, probably informed by his own visit to the site in Jerusalem. Murphy-O'Connor, "Argument for the Holy Sepulchre," 77.

Figure 26.9. The excavated portion of the western edge of the southern basin of the Pools of Bethesda, showing the pattern of alternating sets of steps and landings. It is not known how many of the pool's four sides would have had such a means of access.

(on the east side) by 190 feet (on the north side) by 160 feet (on the west side). The northern pool was smaller on every side (175 feet by 130 feet by 165 feet by 130 feet).[16] Some credit Simon the Just, high priest around 200 BC, with the construction of both pools or, at least, the larger, southern pool (cf. Sir. 50:3); others prefer to regard this as part of Herod the Great's building program.[17]

While it is possible that this pool was used for drawing water for everyday use, it has plausibly been suggested that the southern pool served as a public mikveh (see fig. 26.9).[18] There would have been a great need for large mikvaoth such as this pool, particularly during the great pilgrimage feasts of Passover, Pentecost, and Booths, when tens of thousands of worshipers thronged to Jerusalem to participate in the rituals within the temple precincts and, thus, would have required ritual purification of their bodies prior to entering the holy courts of the holy Lord. Indeed, the Pools of Bethesda and Pool of Siloam were well positioned to allow pilgrims to enter the *city* itself in a

16. McRay, *Archaeology and the New Testament*, 187.

17. B. Mazar, *Mountain of the Lord*, 202, versus Gibson, "Excavations at the Bethesda Pool," 22–23.

18. Gibson, "Pool of Bethesda in Jerusalem"; Gibson, "Excavations at the Bethesda Pool," 26.

Figure 26.10. The barrier between the northern and southern basins of the Pools of Bethesda.

state of ritual purity, if this was indeed a desideratum of the time.[19] While the temple itself was surrounded with dozens of ritual immersion pools, the majority of these were suitable for use only by an individual or small numbers of individuals. It might follow, then, that the northern basin of the Pools of Bethesda functioned as a reservoir for the southern pool and was not touched directly by people. Allowing ritually clean water to flow from the northern pool *into* the southern pool would ritually cleanse the water in the latter. This might explain the presence of the sluice gate discovered in the dam between the pools, perhaps installed both to adjust the level when it dropped too far and to refresh the ritual purity of the water (see fig. 26.10).[20]

In the second century AD, a shrine to Asclepius, the god of healing, was erected over the Pools of Bethesda. The choice of these pools for a healing sanctuary dedicated to Asclepius suggests that the legend of the healing powers of its waters persevered into the second and third centuries.[21] The relative altitude of the Asclepius shrine compared to the earlier pools again reminds us,

19. Gurevich, "Water Pools," 128.

20. Von Wahlde, "Puzzling Pool of Bethesda," 45–46.

21. See John 5:4, an explanatory verse that does not appear in the earliest manuscripts of John's Gospel. Gibson ("Excavations at the Bethesda Pool," 28–29, 42) argues that the so-called

along with the Struthion Pool, of the depth at which much of Herodian Jerusalem—the Jerusalem of Jesus—lies buried after centuries of continued occupation and building, beginning with the Hadrianic period.

The other pool prominently featured in the Fourth Gospel is the Pool of Siloam, where Jesus sent the man born blind to wash his eyes and receive his sight. This pool was located in the southernmost portion of the City of David, hence at the southernmost tip of Jerusalem itself. From Byzantine to recent times, a small pool in this vicinity was identified as the Pool of Siloam (see fig. 26.11). It is located at the outlet of Hezekiah's tunnel, dug to conduct water from the Gihon Spring into the City of David during the First Temple period (cf. 2 Kings 20:20). This pool's dimensions were reduced to about 50 by 15 feet as a consequence of the construction of a Byzantine church that was thought by its builders to mark the site of the great healing story recorded in John 9 (which was itself, in turn, supplanted by a mosque that still occupies the site). Originally its dimensions were perhaps 80 by 80 feet.[22]

Figure 26.11. The small pool traditionally identified as the Pool of Siloam.

A sewage pipe repair project in 2004, however, led to the discovery of a much larger stepped pool just 100 feet south of that site, and this is now generally identified as the Pool of Siloam known from the first century.[23] It had

healing sanctuary consists rather of ruins of early Roman-period dwellings from the neighborhood of Bezetha described by Josephus (*J.W.* 5.148–52).

22. Rousseau and Arav, *Jesus and His World*, 159.

23. This identification is not uncontested. Szanton argues that the pool formerly known as the Pool of Siloam was correctly identified and that the larger pool is actually the Pool of Solomon, which Josephus also locates in this area (*J.W.* 5.145). He believes that the increased water supply provided by the various aqueducts and other pools allowed the water in these pools to be used for different purposes—Siloam for ritual purification, Solomon for bathing and recreation. Szanton, "Ritual Purification," 37–39.

Figure 26.12. The more-recently discovered Pool of Siloam. Note the several landings between the groupings of five or six steps.

been hidden under 10 feet or more of soil, which accumulated in the pool after it went out of use in the period following the First Jewish Revolt. This pool stretched 50 yards across on its northeast side, which has been fully excavated. Angles in the corners suggest that it widened slightly as it reached southwest, taking on a trapezoidal shape.[24] Like the Pools of Bethesda, the Pool of Siloam has several sets of steps separated by landings along the northeast side (see fig. 26.12). It appears not to have had any steps on the two adjacent sides; nothing of the southwestern side has been recovered as of the time of writing.

The pool appears to have undergone two building phases. In the earlier phase, the pool along with its steps had a simple plastered floor. Stray coins of Alexander Jannaeus (Hasmonean king from 87 to 78 BC) were found in the plaster, suggesting that the pool was constructed in the later Hasmonean or the early Herodian period (the span of time during which Alexander's coins were in wide circulation).[25] At a later date, flagstones were laid on top of the

24. Reich and Shukron, "Pool of Siloam in Jerusalem," 244; Reich and Shukron, "Second Temple Period Siloam Pool," 75.

25. Reich and Shukron, "Pool of Siloam in Jerusalem," 245; Reich and Shukron, "Second Temple Period Siloam Pool," 79.

plaster for greater durability, likely in response to the amount of damage being done to the plaster by the number of people using the pool.[26] A paved and colonnaded esplanade north of, and adjacent to, the pool gave access—and aesthetic flair—to the facility.[27]

While it is possible that the pool was just one more source for drawing water, the configuration of its steps suggests that, like the Pools of Bethesda, this was a pool for large numbers of residents and pilgrims to use for ritual immersion.[28] The several sets of steps and landings allowed users to proceed as far as they needed down into the pool to perform their ablutions comfortably, as the water level could vary considerably throughout the year. The pool was fed directly by the Gihon Spring, and thus its waters would be considered appropriate for ritual immersion (and kept perpetually "refreshed" by the pure, living water).

Jesus not only performed miracles in connection with these pools, but as an observant Jew, he would also have used them in precisely the same way as thousands of others coming to worship in the temple, performing the necessary purifications from the ordinary pollutions that could accrue in the course of life, prior to entering into the precincts of the holy God. Archaeologists raise the question concerning how modesty, especially between sexes, might have been preserved in a public immersion pool such as this. They suggest that portable curtains or mats stretched across wooden poles could have been used to solve the problem. Several holes have been found in the steps that might have served as bases for such fixtures.[29] Another solution might have involved entering with a loincloth or tunic and removing it briefly underwater. The problem itself, however, assumes that the regulations for ritual immersion reflected in the Mishnah, which require nothing coming between the water and the skin, were already in force prior to AD 70, such that one could not acceptably immerse oneself while wearing a garment.

The unexpected discovery of this pool led to another discovery—a wide, stepped, pedestrian street leading from the pool to the Temple Mount along the valley that separates the City of David from the Western Mount (see figs. 26.13, 26.14). The earliest coins found beneath the paving stones were minted under Pontius Pilate, giving the period of AD 26–36 as the earliest possible date for the street. In the form in which it was discovered, the street with its

26. Reich and Shukron, "Pool of Siloam in Jerusalem," 244–45; Reich and Shukron, "Second Temple Period Siloam Pool," 76–77; E. Mazar et al., "Jerusalem," 5:1807.

27. Reich and Shukron, "Pool of Siloam in Jerusalem," 245; Reich and Shukron, "Second Temple Period Siloam Pool," 78.

28. Reich and Shukron, "Pool of Siloam in Jerusalem," 248–50.

29. Reich and Shukron, "Second Temple Period Siloam Pool," 80.

Figure 26.13. A portion of the early Roman stepped street leading from the Pool of Siloam to the area of the temple in the heart of the city. The flagstones are in an uncannily perfect state of preservation.

Figure 26.14. The remains of a shop situated alongside the stepped street leading to the Pool of Siloam. The raised stones between the street and the shop cover the sewer drain running beneath the length of the street.

beautiful and close-fitting flagstones may reflect the improvements authorized by Agrippa II around AD 62 (see Josephus, *Ant.* 20.219–23).[30] It seems highly probable that this street would have replaced, and thus marked the path of, an earlier street leading to the temple, likely the one taken by the blind man who would be healed when he washed in the Pool of Siloam.

30. Reich and Shukron, "Pool of Siloam in Jerusalem," 253. The drainage sewer beneath the street would be one of the last refuges of the survivors of the Roman assault on Jerusalem in AD 70 as both Josephus (*J.W.* 6.401) and the discovery of coins and intact cooking pots from the First Jewish Revolt attest. Reich and Shukron, "Second Temple Period Siloam Pool," 82–83.

The Elite Neighborhoods

Several new, elite neighborhoods grew up within the First Wall of the Second Temple period. One of these occupied the portion of Mount Zion south of the current Zion Gate in the Old City. A number of residences from the first centuries BC and AD were found in this area, some of which clearly belonged to the elite, given the evidence of plastered walls and decorative frescoes involving birds, wreaths, architectural scenes, and other such motifs.[31] According to early church tradition, Caiaphas's house was located in this area, in the vicinity of the Dormition Church, Tomb of David, and Cenacle (the traditional site of the Last Supper).[32] Indeed, the basement level of an elite Herodian-period house was found during a salvage excavation beneath one of the buildings on the campus of the Saint Sauveur Monastery. The remains of further such residences can be found on the property of the Church of Saint Peter in Gallicantu, including an early Roman-period courtyard house that sits behind a fence on the left as soon as one enters the main gate. Thick plaster can still be seen on the bases of the stubs of the remaining walls. As one descends further into the church campus, one can see the remains of a mikveh (large, but still probably intended for private use) and five cisterns north of the church on the far side of an ancient, stepped road. This likely represents the level below a large residence that was entirely canceled first by reconfiguration of the spaces in the Byzantine period and later by reappropriation of the construction materials for projects elsewhere. The stepped road was laid during the Hasmonean period to improve access from the newer neighborhood to the city, perhaps especially the Temple Mount. The remains on the south side of this road appear to represent installations for processing and storing agricultural products, while the church itself sits atop an ancient cistern, replacing any residential structure that the cistern might have served. This incidentally marks another traditional location for the house of Caiaphas, hence the dedication of the church to "Peter in Gallicantu"—a Latin phrase meaning Peter "at the crowing of the rooster" after denying Jesus in the courtyard of the high priest's house (as in Mark 14:66–72).

Far more impressive and informative remains of elite homes, however, were discovered in the modern Jewish Quarter, south of the modern David Street and the Street of the Chain. These blocks of homes would have been located not far south of the First Wall on the high ground of the western hill that sits across the Tyropoeon Valley from the southern portion of the Temple Mount. It is clear from the remains that this was a neighborhood for those

31. Broshi, "Excavations in the House of Caiaphas," 58.

32. McRay, *Archaeology and the New Testament*, 200–201.

Figure 26.15. A stone weight with the inscription "Bar Qatros," the only clue to the identity of the residents of the Burnt House.

elite who fell just short of the tier of royalty. Indeed, the houses are in close proximity both to the old Hasmonean Palace and to the palace of Herod the Great. Houses here would be slightly elevated above the Temple Mount and enjoy inspiring views of it and the Kidron Valley behind it.

In 1970, archaeologists discovered a dwelling in this area that had been destroyed by fire, its charred roof timbers and collapsed ceilings being found in a layer of soot. As a result, it is called the Burnt House. Coins from years two, three, and four of the First Jewish Revolt were found in the debris layer, locating the house's destruction precisely in the year AD 70, a casualty of the conflagration. The remains represent the bottommost level of the house, including the service wing and kitchen, workshops and other spaces of production, and storerooms of a larger mansion that continues to the east (but could not be excavated).[33] It is also devoid of the kind of artifacts and ornamentation that one finds in the living areas of the houses excavated near this one in the present-day Jewish Quarter, though those houses also had undecorated service and storage areas such as one finds in the Burnt House.[34] There is a small mikveh on this lower level, with three steps descending into the water. A variety of chalk vessels—from small cups to large jars appropriate for purifying other vessels—were also found among the remains. These attest to the residents' commitment to maintaining ritual purity.

One stone weight found in the debris reads "of Bar Qatros," suggesting that this was part of the house of a high priestly family, the House of Qatros, also known from an unflattering reference in the Babylonian Talmud (b. Pesaḥ. 57a; see fig. 26.15).[35] The purpose of this along with twenty-three other weights

33. Geva, "Stratigraphy and Architecture," 4:62.
34. Geva, "Stratigraphy and Architecture," 4:63.
35. The name also appears in the literature transliterated as "Kathros" and "Katros."

found in the excavation is unknown, but a plausible suggestion concerns the careful measuring out of tithes (weighing being viewed as the most reliable measure of calculation) that were this priestly family's due.[36] Among the finds in the house was the skeletal forearm of a young woman, a reminder of the slaughter than accompanied the torching of these neighborhoods as the Roman armies poured into the city.

Although it has since been buried under new construction, another large and luxurious residence from the Herodian period was found just two blocks west of the Burnt House. This was a courtyard house with a mikveh and a cistern, destroyed to make way for a paved street late in Herod's reign.[37] Like the other elite homes, it contained local pottery and lamps, chalk or limestone vessels, and imported fine ware (terra sigillata from a variety of provenances).[38] It contained amphorae, likely once holding wine, from Rhodes, Cos, Italy, and North Africa.[39] The residents combined a taste for the finer, costly, imported goods from around the Mediterranean with an interest in ritual purity and in the locally made goods that had become so much a marker of Jewish identity during the Hellenistic period. Part of another such Herodian-period house was uncovered across the street to the west of this house.[40]

A further network of several partially adjoining town houses that could be classified as town mansions by ancient standards was discovered a mere 200 feet away from the Burnt House during a modern construction project. These houses date from the Herodian period with evidence of earlier Hasmonean-period structures beneath and have been preserved and made available for viewing in the Wohl Archaeological Museum.[41] These were sprawling complexes with dedicated dining rooms, bathing facilities, and ritual immersion pools (mikvaoth). Given the number of mikvaoth in these mansions, it is likely that these houses were owned primarily by leading priestly families, whose members would require regular and frequent purification for the performance of their duties in the temple. The walls were plastered, sometimes sculpted to resemble masonry and to create ornate moldings, sometimes ornamented with frescoes in a manner similar to the more basic styles found in the elite homes of Pompeii (see fig. 26.16). The juxtaposition of Greek and Roman architectural styles, artistic features, and imported tableware and luxury items

36. J. Schwartz, "Bar Qatros," 315–16.

37. Geva, "Stratigraphy and Architecture," 3:1–78.

38. Geva and Hershkovitz, "Local Pottery"; Rosenthal-Hegenbottom, "Late Hellenistic and Early Roman Lamps"; Geva, "Stone Artifacts," 3:218–23.

39. Finkielsztejn, "Imported Amphoras."

40. Geva, "Stratigraphy and Architecture," 10.

41. On these residences, see further Avigad, *Discovering Jerusalem*, 95–149; Avigad, *Herodian Quarter*; Galor and Bloedhorn, *Archaeology of Jerusalem*, 88–97.

alongside mikvaoth, stone vessels for purification, and the absence of portraits of animals or human beings is a striking testimony to how far priestly families could Hellenize while also maintaining strict adherence to the regulations of the law of Moses (see figs. 26.17, 26.18).

Charring on some of the opulently frescoed walls and layers of charred beams from ceilings attest to the destruction that occurred throughout the

Author photo, courtesy of Wohl Archaeological Museum, Jerusalem

Figure 26.16. A frescoed wall in the First Pompeian style from the dining hall of the Palatial Mansion, bearing the marks of charring from the fire that destroyed the block of residences.

Author photo, courtesy of Wohl Archaeological Museum, Jerusalem

Figure 26.17. A selection of chalk vessels from the elite homes in the Upper City, attesting to their residents' care for ritual purity.

Author photo, courtesy of Wohl Archaeological Museum, Jerusalem

Figure 26.18. A selection of fine, imported terra sigillata tableware from the Herodian-period mansions, attesting to their residents' cosmopolitan tastes.

Figure 26.19. A spacious room (perhaps the main living room) in the Middle Block of the Herodian town houses, sporting an intricate mosaic with wave and labyrinth designs. Note the stone table, likely used as a service table for meals that would be enjoyed from smaller, lower tables while the diners reclined on couches (Avigad, *Herodian Quarter*, 55), and the large, finely crafted stone jars in the background.

Author photo, courtesy of Wohl Archaeological Museum, Jerusalem

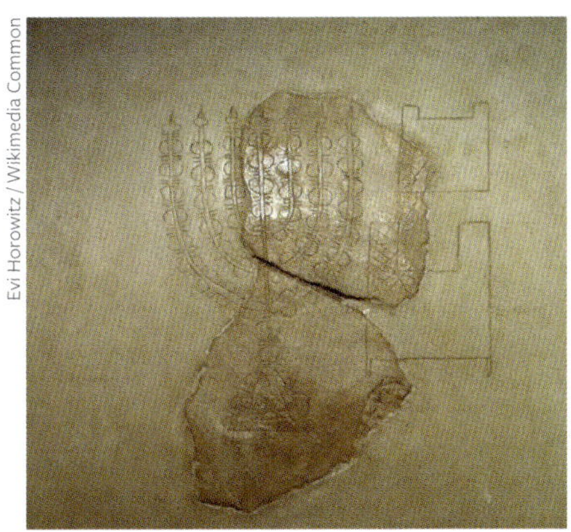
Evi Horowitz / Wikimedia Common

Figure 26.20. A graffito representing the menorah, the lampstand from the temple's holy place, carved into the plaster of an elite home. This is one of the two earliest known depictions of the menorah (Avigad, *Discovering Jerusalem*, 148).

city during the First Jewish Revolt. Coins found on the premises include issues from the third and fourth years of the revolt,[42] suggesting that this destruction was indeed caused by the Romans in the wake of the siege of AD 70, though we should remember that the Romans were not the only ones responsible for burning down buildings and supplies. Rival insurgent groups did this throughout the years of the war as well, seeking to weaken one another's position. Many of Jerusalem's residents would have felt every bit as much besieged by these insurgent groups as they would be, in the end, by the Romans.

The largest of the town houses thus far excavated is the so-called Palatial Mansion, the ground floor of which covers 5,400 square feet. Like other houses in the block, this residence was also originally multistory, to judge from the presence of the remains of staircases as well as the bottom of a fresco that begins 7 or 8 feet up one of the surviving walls.[43] The upper floor would have significantly increased the living space.[44] One entered from the street west of the mansion and descended by stairs to a vestibule adorned with a beautiful mosaic floor. Like all the mosaics in these residences, it features geometric patterns and elegant borders but avoids any representation of animals or persons (thus avoiding any possible violation of the second commandment). Cypress beams, discovered as charred remains on the floor, once supported the ceiling.

Two doorways on the left side (north) open into a large reception hall. It is here that one can see perhaps the most elegant stucco work in the block, with plaster sculpted to give the impression of masonry construction and to create decorative moldings and geometric designs on and around the ceiling of the reception hall. The walls here and in several other rooms on the main floor were further adorned with frescoes in the first, simplest Pompeian style (the imitation of marble blocks). Three doorways on the west wall of the reception hall open into three frescoed rooms that might have served as private living

42. Avigad, *Herodian Quarter*, 78–79.
43. Geva, "Stratigraphy and Architecture of Areas F-2, P and P2," 8:135.
44. Magness, *Archaeology of the Holy Land*, 143.

Author photo, courtesy of Wohl Archaeological Museum, Jerusalem

Figure 26.21. The dressing room adjacent to a bath area, decorated with a fine geometric mosaic, from the Palatial Mansion.

quarters. Another ornately frescoed room stands across the vestibule (south) from the reception hall, possibly a formal dining room. More evidence of charring can be seen blackening the frescoes here. Exiting the vestibule from the east, one steps into a large, paved, central courtyard of approximately 26 by 26 feet, which would have been open to the sky. Little of the main floor of the house on the east side of this courtyard survived beyond a small bath facility (see fig. 26.21), though the basement-level structures are present here.[45] There were no tabun ovens found in the excavated areas, suggesting strongly that some of the Palatial Mansion remains hidden and unexcavated. Pots with blackened bottoms were found in number, suggesting that there were kitchen facilities on the premises somewhere.[46]

There are eight mikvaoth in the Palatial Mansion complex (see fig. 26.23). Five of these are rather large, with an average volume of 21 cubic yards (about 4,200 gallons), while three smaller ones have an average volume of 1.7 cubic yards (about 350 gallons).[47] Most are in the lower level, while two of the

45. Avigad, *Herodian Quarter*, 58–59, 69.
46. Geva, "Stratigraphy and Architecture of Areas F-2, P and P2," 8:70–71.
47. Grossberg, "*Miqwa'ot* (Ritual Baths)," 8:245.

Author photo, courtesy of Wohl Archaeological Museum, Jerusalem

Figure 26.22. A restored bathtub with a geometric mosaic from a house adjacent to the Palatial Mansion.

Author photo, courtesy of Wohl Archaeological Museum, Jerusalem

Figure 26.23. A large, private mikveh from the Palatial Mansion. Note the preliminary foot-washing basin to the right of the modern pillar supporting the buildings above.

smaller ones are on the main floor (specifically the upper western terrace). These smaller mikvaoth may have been used for purification of hands prior to eating meat from the temple sacrifices (or perhaps even all meals) or the purification of vessels.[48] The number of mikvaoth suggests a large number of residents, likely several branches of an extended family group as well as servants and their families. One of the larger mikvaoth featured two adjacent doorways, presumably marking the path of entering and exiting the purificatory water in a manner similar to other mikvaoth that have a low dividing ridge on the steps. Following the lead of the Hasmonean high priestly family with their multiple ritual immersion pools in their palaces, these installations quickly became standard in the homes of the priestly elite.[49] It is noteworthy that the mikvaoth in these town houses do not have adjacent reservoirs, suggesting that their inhabitants followed (Sadducean?) regulations concerning ritual immersion that differed from those that would eventually be adopted in rabbinic Judaism, which presumably reflect Pharisaic opinions.[50]

While tradition has assigned other dwellings to Caiaphas, it seems more likely that a Caiaphas, who survived eighteen years as high priest (a record during the Herodian and early Roman periods), or perhaps an Annas, who served as high priest for a decade and was the patriarch of a family that produced five further high priests, would have occupied an expansive and conveniently situated home like this one.[51] It suits the stature of a high priest; it meets the requirement of a courtyard house (a detail on which all four Gospels agree; see Matt. 26:58; Mark 14:54; Luke 22:54–55; John 18:15–16); and it has the large indoor spaces sufficient for the convening of at least some part of the Sanhedrin that the accounts of the overnight trial of Jesus require.

At the edge of the excavated area, archaeologists discovered part of a peristyle (31 feet long),[52] suggesting another clear sign of Hellenistic influence—a house arranged around a courtyard surrounded on three or four sides by colonnades. The area also featured a tiled floor in the "opus sectile" style—tiles of varied geometric shapes creating intricate patterns. This was likely part of another opulent town house in the neighborhood. Excavations also uncovered pieces of columns, capitals, and other architectural fragments suggestive of larger, public buildings in the vicinity, though the identity and

48. Grossberg, "*Miqwa'ot* (Ritual Baths)," 8:247; Avigad, *Herodian Quarter*, 72.

49. Fatkin, "Invention of a Bathing Tradition," 174.

50. The water used to fill these mikvaoth would have been drawn from wells or cisterns, whereas Pharisaic-Rabbinic regulations called for mikvaoth to be filled or refreshed with water that flowed into them naturally. Levine, *Jerusalem*, 329, 392.

51. Cf. Avigad, *Discovering Jerusalem*, 120.

52. Avigad, *Herodian Quarter*, 32.

function of those buildings cannot be determined on the basis of the meager finds.[53] The Upper Market was likely located between this neighborhood and Herod's palace on the far west of the city.[54] It is possible, though by no means certain, that Herod's theater was also located in the Upper City, as the forms of entertainment presented therein would appeal more to the Hellenized elite.[55] No archaeological evidence for it has yet been found anywhere under the modern city.

A Synagogue for Diaspora Jews

A particularly important inscription, known as the "Theodotus inscription," was found in a cistern in the Lower City, dated to the first century AD prior to the First Jewish Revolt. It reads: "Theodotos, the son of Vettenos, priest and *archisynagōgos*, son of an *archisynagōgos*, grandson of an *archisynagōgos*, built the synagogue (*synagōgē*) for the reading of the Law (i.e., the Torah) and the study of the commandments, and a guesthouse and rooms and water installations for hosting those in need from abroad, it (i.e., the synagogue) having been founded by his fathers, the presbyters, and Simonides" (see fig. 26.24).[56]

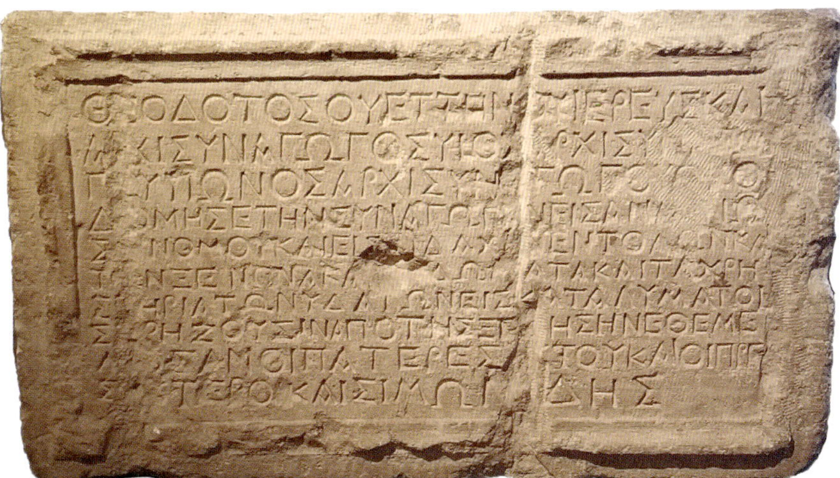

Figure 26.24. The Theodotus synagogue inscription.

53. Avigad, *Herodian Quarter*, 38.

54. Josephus, *J.W.* 2.303–5; Levine, *Jerusalem*, 334.

55. Levine, *Jerusalem*, 334. On Herod's theater, hippodrome, and amphitheater, see Josephus, *J.W.* 2.44; *Ant.* 15.268; 17.254–55.

56. Translation from Levine, *Jerusalem*, 395.

Of first importance is the fact that the inscription is written in Greek, which would have been the first language of many diaspora Jews and the common language by which Jews from the Mediterranean diaspora and Judea could converse with one another. This indicates that the synagogue catered to Jews whose primary language was Greek rather than Aramaic (thus to those who would be called Hellenists in Acts 6:1–6). The inscription also bears witness to the title of *archisynagōgos*, "ruler of the synagogue" (cf. Mark 5:22; Luke 8:49; 13:14; Acts 13:15; 18:8, 17). It is difficult to know when the title is simply honorific (being applied to benefactors of the institution), when it denotes an active role in leadership of liturgical and other activities, and when both are true simultaneously.[57] The inscription also names a variety of functions: study, gathering, and hosting. The guest rooms incorporated into this synagogue would likely be offered to diaspora Jews who had traveled to the city to participate in one of the major pilgrimage festivals (as well as at other times), suggesting symbiosis rather than competition between the synagogue and temple.[58]

Jerusalem's Necropolis

Almost all graves were to be found outside the ancient city's walls. While one might attribute this to the Jews' concern for purity, especially to avoid the ritual pollution incurred through contact with human remains, it was also standard practice in most Greco-Roman cities to locate the "necropolis"—the "city for the dead"—outside of the cities of the living. More than nine hundred rock-hewn tombs have been found within a 3-mile radius of Jerusalem.[59] Many of these are relatively simple cave-like chambers with multiple loculi (torpedo-tube-like spaces hollowed out from the rock) for depositing bodies (see fig. 26.25). A small number of tombs contained sarcophagi, which would be the one and only resting place for the deceased. It was far more common during the Herodian and early Roman periods to allow the corpse to decay in a loculus or on a raised bench inside the tomb complex and then to return after a year to gather the bones and place them in an ossuary, a limestone or chalk chest with a lid, often decorated with geometric and floral patterns. The name of the deceased whose bones were thus stored would often be scratched onto the exterior in unprofessional script (see fig. 26.26). The dimensions of ossuaries were determined by the length of the typical human femur, the longest bone in the body.

57. Magness, *Archaeology of the Holy Land*, 288.
58. Magness, *Archaeology of the Holy Land*, 290.
59. Levine, *Jerusalem*, 213.

Figure 26.25. The interior of one of the burial chambers in the complex known as the Tomb of Nicanor, an Alexandrian Jew who relocated to Jerusalem and made lavish donations to the temple, including a magnificent bronze gate. Note the square indentations at the mouth of each of the nine loculi, where a stone would be fitted to provide additional protection (beyond the stone sealing the main entrance) for the interred corpse from scavengers as well as to contain somewhat the odors of decay.

Figure 26.26. An ossuary displaying a common design of two rosettes, here flanking a roughly executed Ionic column, all framed by an inscribed meander pattern. The name of the deceased is roughly scratched in above the left rosette.
Author photo, courtesy of Terra Sancta Museum, Jerusalem

Figure 26.27. The forecourt and facade of the best preserved of the rock-cut tomb complexes that make up the so-called Tombs of the Sanhedrin, a first-century AD necropolis that sits about 1.5 miles north of the Old City wall. Note the Hellenistic elements of the facade, imitating a Greek temple with architrave decorated with acanthus leaves and other floral elements and acroteria rising from the two corners and peak.

Figure 26.28. Two tiers of loculi inside the same tomb (see fig. 26.27), the upper tier divided into pairs by the construction of three arcosolia, or benches for laying out the deceased in preparation for burial.

Ossuaries came into widespread use around 20 BC, possibly emerging as a Jewish adaptation of the Roman practice of using stone cinerary urns for the burial of the cremated remains of their dead.[60] They largely fell out of fashion after AD 70, quite likely because the Judean elite who preferred rock-cut tombs to the more ordinary pit or trench graves were decimated in the course of the First Jewish Revolt (though some continuation of the practice in Galilee after the war suggests the activity of displaced elites).[61] Over two thousand ossuaries have been recovered to date.

The tombs in the Kidron Valley were every bit as prominent and visible in Jesus's day as they remain in the twenty-first century. The move among the elite toward monumental tombs signals both the disposable wealth that a number of Judean families were able to accumulate and the degree to which they had adopted wider Hellenistic mores in regard to burial practices, as indeed in regard to many other matters, throughout the Hasmonean and Herodian periods.[62] The impetus in this direction may somewhat ironically have come from Simon ben-Mattathias and the monumental tomb complex that he erected in Modein for his parents and his glorious brothers (1 Macc. 13:27–30)—ironic, because his father and brothers had all died in a war for independence from the Hellenistic rulers of the Seleucid Empire.

One monumental tomb in the Kidron Valley is known as Absalom's Pillar, or Absalom's Monument, recalling the story of the childless son of King David (2 Sam. 18:18). In actuality, this was a freestanding monument (a *nephesh*) that was part of a larger tomb complex, all of which was carved out of the rock, from the Herodian or early Roman period (see fig. 26.29).[63] The monument stands 22 yards high. The base is a single block of stone with a volume of more than 150 cubic yards.[64] The combination of styles

Figure 26.29. The *nephesh*, or memorial monument, known as Absalom's Pillar in the Kidron Valley.

60. Levine, *Jerusalem*, 264–65.

61. Magness, *Archaeology of the Holy Land*, 239, 242.

62. Halpern-Zylberstein, "Archaeology of Hellenistic Palestine," 2:21–23; Rajak, "Jews Under Hasmonean Rule," 298.

63. Halpern-Zylberstein, "Archaeology of Hellenistic Palestine," 2:23.

64. Galor and Bloedhorn, *Archaeology of Jerusalem*, 100.

Figure 26.30. The Tomb of the Bene Ḥezir with the monumental pyramid-capped *nephesh*, the so-called Tomb of Zechariah, immediately to its south (right).

is the epitome of Hellenism. Greek influence is seen in the carved relief of Ionic columns supporting an architrave. Nabatean influence emerges in the circular decorations around the frieze of the architrave and the inverted funnel design of the top. Greek influence appears again in the carved architrave and floral scrollwork above the entrance to the burial chambers proper behind the monument, which, however, exhibit the typical local, Judean layout of loculi and use of ossuaries.

Two hundred feet south of Absalom's Pillar sits the tomb complex of another elite family, a priestly family identified as the Bene Ḥezir or "sons/descendants of Ḥezir" in a Hebrew inscription over the entrance: "This [is the] tomb and the monument (*nephesh*) of El'azar, Ḥonyah, Jo'ezer, Jehudah, Shim'on, [and] Joḥanan, sons of Joseph, the son of Obed; Joseph and El'azar, the sons of Ḥonyah, priests of [the] sons of Ḥezir" (see fig. 26.30).[65] It is possible that these were individuals of the ancient priestly clan of Ḥezir, the founder of one of the twenty-four priestly lines of the First Temple period (see 1 Chron. 24:15). Behind the rock face is a network of several burial

65. Adapted from Barag, "2000–2001 Exploration of the Tombs," 92, adding punctuation to clarify (likely) relationships.

chambers, each with multiple loculi carved into the rock. The complex may date as far back as the late second or early first century BC, though it underwent expansions (for example, an additional burial chamber with three arcosolia) as late as the early Roman period.[66]

The inscription refers to a monument, quite possibly one that once sat atop the tomb complex to the north of the tomb opening. It is unclear what form that monument cap took, whether pyramidal in the Egyptian style or perhaps a square tower decorated in the Nabatean style.[67] The freestanding monument to the south created by carving out the surrounding rock—a typical Nabatean procedure—is traditionally known as the Tomb of Zechariah, though this is likely a misnomer born of tradition as no inscriptional evidence has been found to indicate who was laid to rest here. Indeed, no actual tomb has been discovered in connection with this monument, unless it is the unfinished tomb immediately south. It seems highly unlikely, however, that a family would go through the expense of creating a monumental *nephesh* without completing any burial niches at all. Another possibility is that it was created by the Bene Ḥezir during the Herodian period as a grander replacement for their original monument, which may have been damaged or destroyed in an earthquake (perhaps the earthquake of 31 BC, which was quite severe). A stairway leading up from the courtyard of the monument into the Bene Ḥezir tombs suggests a strong connection.[68]

Several striking, monumental tombs have also been found west of the city's western wall, west of the Hinnom Valley. One of these is the Tomb of Jason, so called on the basis of a graffito on a wall calling the readers to mourn the passing of one Jason (see fig. 26.31). Drawings of warships on the walls suggest that Jason might have been a naval commander, possibly in the Egyptian navy, who died and was interred during the early part of the first century BC after relocating to Jerusalem.[69] The burial chamber contains eight loculi, one of the earliest appearances of this feature in a Jewish tomb.[70] Hellenistic influence is again immediately evident in the Doric column and the large pyramid gracing the top of the burial complex. Interestingly, the walls were also decorated with menorahs—highlighting a meaningful local connection

66. Halpern-Zylberstein, "Archaeology of Hellenistic Palestine," 2:23; Levine, *Jerusalem*, 114.

67. Barag ("2000–2001 Exploration of the Tombs," 87–92) favors the latter.

68. Barag, "2000–2001 Exploration of the Tombs," 98–99, 104; Halpern-Zylberstein, "Archaeology of Hellenistic Palestine," 2:23.

69. Halpern-Zylberstein, "Archaeology of Hellenistic Palestine," 2:21. The ships, which are admittedly crudely drawn, might also suggest that Jason was engaged in sea trade. Magness, *Archaeology of the Holy Land*, 99.

70. Magness, *Archaeology of the Holy Land*, 98.

Figure 26.31. The forecourt and facade of the Tomb of Jason. An arch in a wall of well-crafted ashlars (not pictured) provides entrance into this complex.

alongside the foreign influences and possibly pointing to the family's connection with the priesthood, which was common among the elite.[71]

A number of elite tomb complexes were dug into the rocky hills on the south side of the juncture of the Kidron and Hinnom Valleys, south of the City of David. This is the traditional location of Akeldama, the "field of blood" also known as "the potter's field" (Matt. 27:3–10), traditionally a place for burying those whose bodies were unclaimed. It was, however, clearly also a necropolis for wealthy families. A number of its eighty or so burial caves are housed within the Monastery of Saint Onuphrius (and have been significantly altered in the process of turning them into sites of veneration, as these tombs were used by Christian hermits in the Byzantine period). Others remain unaltered on the monastery's property or in the hills adjacent to it.[72] Josephus locates the tomb of Annas (Ananus), the high priest from AD 6 to 15 and father or father-in-law of several high priests who served up through

71. Magness, *Archaeology of the Holy Land*, 98–99.

72. See Avni and Greenhut, *Akeldama Tombs*, for details of excavation of three Second Temple period burial cave complexes here, two quite extensive, and the material finds associated with them; and Ritmeyer and Ritmeyer, "Akeldama," on the tomb of Annas.

AD 62, in this vicinity (Josephus, *J.W.* 5.506; cf. Luke 3:2; John 18:13–14). One particular tomb has been tentatively identified as the tomb of Annas and his family on the basis of its use of motifs associated with the temple in its decoration (see figs. 26.32, 26.33, 26.34).

Figure 26.32. The exterior of the tomb of Annas. Quarrying has removed some of the decorative facade, the room with benches (right of the tomb) of which only two arched areas remain, and the forecourt. It is likely that a monument of some kind once stood atop the tomb.

Figure 26.33. The ornate interior of the tomb of Annas, including a thirty-two-petal rosette on the ceiling, reminiscent perhaps of the decorations in the domed ceiling inside the Double Gate of the temple, and a Greek templelike facade over the now-destroyed door into the southern burial chamber (in which two of the tomb's loculi are visible).

Another cluster of burial caves can be seen about 1 mile south of the modern Zion Gate in a nature preserve called the Peace Forest. One of these burial caves contained numerous ossuaries of a family connected to one Caiaphas, believed to be the Caiaphas who served as high priest from AD 18 to 36 (Josephus, *Ant.* 18.35, 95; cf. Matt. 26:57–66; John 11:49–52). One ossuary bore the inscription Joseph bar-Qayafa, plausibly a (more authentic) variant of the

Figure 26.34. The western wall inside the tomb of Annas with three loculi at floor level. The decorative carving is believed to represent the facade of Herod's temple, which would make it the earliest extant depiction of the structure. A sealing stone would have completed the facade at the base, suggesting that this might have been the loculus that housed the body and, eventually, ossuary of Annas.

Figure 26.35. The ornate ossuary of Joseph bar-Qayafa (top) and the inscription bearing his name (left).

name that Josephus assigned to the high priest—namely, Joseph Caiaphas (see fig. 26.35).

All of these tombs attest to the practice of hewing such facilities out of the rock that the Gospels claim to have been the case also for the tomb in which Joseph of Arimathea deposited the body of Jesus in some haste before sunset on the day of the crucifixion. None of them, surprisingly, attest to the use of a round stone that could be rolled back and forth to seal or to allow access to the burial chamber (Matt. 27:60; Mark 15:46; John 20:1). The practice was, indeed, rare in the Jerusalem area, but one tomb complex—believed to have been used to inter several members of the family of Herod the Great—does have a main entrance that was once sealed with a round stone about 6 feet across and over 1 foot thick (see fig. 26.36).

Figure 26.36. The main entrance to the Herodian family tomb west of the Old City. Note the rolling stone to the left that is incorporated into the entrance.

27

JERUSALEM: THE VIA DOLOROSA

A deeply meaningful experience for many Christian pilgrims to Jerusalem is walking the path of the Via Dolorosa, the path alleged to have been taken by Jesus, beginning with his condemnation by Pilate and ending with his burial in the borrowed grave near Golgotha. It is important to bear in mind that the path of the Via Dolorosa is an invention of the Franciscan monks who served as custodians of the Holy Land beginning in the fourteenth century, not a tradition that goes back, say, to Constantine in the fourth century. It grew over time to incorporate its fourteen stations, and its route through the streets of Jerusalem's Old City was not finalized until the nineteenth century.[1]

1. See, further, Murphy-O'Connor, "Geography of Faith," 37–41, 52–53. The fourteen stations are as follows: (1) Pilate sentences Jesus to death (Matt. 27:26; Mark 15:15; Luke 23:24–25; John 19:16); (2) The cross is laid upon Jesus (John 19:16–17); (3) Jesus falls for the first time; (4) Jesus encounters his mother, Mary, on the way; (5) Simon of Cyrene is conscripted to help Jesus carry the cross (Matt. 27:32; Mark 15:21; Luke 23:26); (6) Veronica wipes the sweat and blood from Jesus's face; (7) Jesus falls a second time; (8) Jesus encounters the women of Jerusalem (Luke 23:27–31); (9) Jesus falls a third time; (10) The soldiers strip Jesus of his clothing (implied by Matt. 27:35; Mark 15:24; Luke 23:34; John 19:23–24); (11) Jesus is fixed to the cross (Matt. 27:35; Mark 15:24; Luke 23:33; John 19:18); (12) Jesus dies (Matt. 27:50; Mark 15:37; Luke 23:46; John 19:30); (13) Jesus's body is taken down from the cross (Matt. 27:57–59; Mark 15:42–46; Luke 23:50–53; John 19:31–34, 38); (14) Jesus's body is laid in the tomb (Matt. 27:60; Mark 15:46–47; Luke 23:53; John 19:40–42). As noted, some of these are grounded in the details of the passion narratives of the Gospels, with a view to harmonization. Others are reasonable inferences, but nothing more (Jesus stumbling or collapsing along the way in his weakened condition; Mary, who appears beneath the cross in John 19:25–27, also finding Jesus at some point along the way). One is based purely on a later tradition (Veronica or, in Greek,

Figure 27.1. A small portion of the massive rock scarp on which the Antonia was built, giving it a commanding position above, and view over, the entire temple compound. A few Herodian ashlars remain visible between the top of the scarp and the more recent construction of the Al-Omariya school above. (Murphy-O'Connor details significantly more Herodian masonry that has been incorporated into a number of Muslim buildings constructed against the north wall of the Haram al-Sharif ["Where Was the Antonia Fortress?," 87–88]. These are, unfortunately, not accessible for viewing.) Square niches mark places where roof beams for the north portico of the temple had been inserted. Vacant areas within the scarp and Herodian courses have been filled in with modern construction.

The Antonia or Herod's Palace?

At least a decade prior to Herod's renovation and extension of the temple complex, he dispensed with the Hellenistic-period fortress, the Baris, which stood near or adjacent to the northwest corner of the old platform. Further to the northwest, Herod constructed a far larger and more magnificent fortress, naming it the Antonia after his then-patron, Marc Antony (thus incidentally marking 31 BC as the latest date for its construction).[2] It had been built atop a high rock scarp that was then shaped and faced with ashlars to create an unscalable surface (see fig. 27.1).[3] The fortress itself rose another 60 feet above

---

Berenice) that had become so fixed a part of the passion story in popular minds that a physical location needed to be selected for its occurrence!

2. As nothing significant of the Antonia remains, we are dependent again on Josephus for a description (Josephus, *J.W.* 5.238–46). Josephus clearly exaggerates, however, when he claims the rock scarp to have been 75 feet high (Murphy-O'Connor, "Where Was the Antonia Fortress?," 88).

3. The surface of the scarp is estimated to be about 390 by 145 feet, suggestive of a sizable fortress (Benoit, "Archaeological Reconstruction," 89). Herod's engineers had cut deep into the

that. It had four square towers in its four corners. Three rose 75 feet above the scarp; the one to the southeast rose 40 feet higher than the others, making it a particularly important and strategic watchtower. A moat was dug to the north of the fortress to give it further protection. From this vantage point it had a commanding view of the temple precinct, particularly after Herod's expansion of the latter, and the growing settlement in a new suburb forming north of the Second Wall.

After Augustus removed Archelaus, Herod's heir in the regions of Samaria, Judea, and Idumea, in AD 6, the Antonia became home to one of the five infantry cohorts under the command of the Roman prefect. The Antonia was equipped with barracks, baths, and several courtyards for mustering troops. After Herod the Great had extended the temple platform to meet the Antonia, the fortress was connected to both the north and the west porticoes of the temple compound by stairways and bridges opening onto their roofs, where troops would be stationed at major festivals. Many Jews who gathered in the temple courts and looked to the northwest would no doubt have found the presence of the fortress and its occupation force intrusive. Indeed, one of the initial acts of the First Jewish Revolt of AD 66 was to break down the passageways that gave the soldiers of the Antonia access to the temple's porticoes, an act that was both practical and highly symbolic.

The Via Dolorosa begins at the approximate site of the Antonia fortress adjacent to the northwest corner of the temple platform. Visitors are shown a pavement made from large flagstones (many reaching about 3 feet squared), both in the area of the Chapel of the Condemnation and in the area of the Convent of the Sisters of Zion on the north side of the Lion's Gate Street (also named Via Dolorosa). They are told that this is the *Lithostratos*, the "Stone Pavement" (see John 19:13), on which Jesus stood when condemned by Pilate, scourged by his lackeys, and mocked by his garrison (see fig. 27.2). They are also shown a high arch spanning the road called the Ecce Homo Arch, recalling the words with which Pilate presented Jesus after the abuse he suffered by the cohort—"Look at the man!" (19:5 AT). While the Chapel of the Condemnation is in close proximity to the spot on which the Antonia stood (it certainly occupied the area south of Lion's Gate Street where the Al-Omariya school is now situated), the identification of the pavement with that of the Antonia overlooks a major development in the urban landscape of Jerusalem—Hadrian's Aelia Capitolina.

---

bedrock to make room for the expansion of the Temple Mount on its northern side, creating the cliff face of the rock on which the Antonia had been built. Bahat, "Jerusalem Down Under," 45.

Figure 27.2. A small segment of the flagstone-paved space presented to visitors as the *Lithostratos*, or "Stone Pavement," of John 19:13.

The emperor Hadrian made a tour of the eastern provinces in AD 129 and 130 with the goal of strengthening and improving these territories. Finding Jerusalem still essentially in ruins from the First Jewish Revolt, he decided that he would restore the dilapidated (and probably somewhat derelict) Jerusalem as a new, Roman colony—the Colonia Aelia Capitolina. This was in keeping with similar decisions he made to stimulate the development of the eastern provinces. While he might have thought of this as an act of general beneficence for all the people of the region, it was certainly an act of beneficence toward the Tenth Legion still stationed there and the veterans and their dependents settled there or in the vicinity. Such a large military and ex-military population deserved to live in a genuine *colonia*, with all of its civic rights and amenities, and not amid the haphazard makeovers of a former war zone. The name Aelia celebrates Hadrian's family name, Aelius. The name Capitolina connected the new colony with the Capitoline Hill at the heart of Rome and the temple to the Capitoline gods—Jupiter, Juno, and Minerva (the Latin equivalents of Zeus, Hera, and Athena)—that sat atop the hill. Like Rome, Aelia would also have a Capitolium, a temple to honor these three principal deities.

The decision to give Jerusalem an extreme makeover as a Roman city, complete with temples for the Roman gods, was not received as anything like a generous gift by the population of Judea. In AD 132, the province erupted in revolt for a second time.[4] The revolutionaries coalesced in the southern part of Judea under the firm-handed leadership of one Simeon Bar Kosiba. He was clearly a capable and charismatic leader, so much so that he was given a messianic moniker—Bar Kochba, "son of a star." By means of strategically organized guerrilla warfare involving extensive networks of tunnels through which they could appear and disappear, the revolutionaries enjoyed significant initial successes against the two resident Roman legions in the province, inflicting heavy losses on them. Hadrian sent three additional legions and his most notable general to Judea to reinforce the troops there and finally ended the revolt in a lengthy siege of Bethar, a fortified city about 5 miles southwest of Jerusalem, in AD 135 or 136. The human costs of the Second Jewish Revolt were high on the Roman side, but disastrous on the Judean side. While fighting had been largely limited to the area of Judea south of Jerusalem and Jericho, it had resulted in the destruction of hundreds of towns and villages and the decimation of the population in that region. As punishment, Hadrian banished Jews from the city limits of his new colony and renamed the province Syria Palaestina, perhaps from a desire on Hadrian's part to distance the land from the Jewish ethnos, its revolutionary heritage, and the ideology of the land that sustained revolutionary ideology.

The reshaping of Jerusalem as Aelia Capitolina was energetically resumed, resulting in a thorough reconfiguration of the northern half of Jerusalem (as the camp of the Tenth Legion occupied most of the southern part). Most relevant to the *Lithostratos* is Hadrian's new forum in the northeastern part of Jerusalem, likely functioning as the principal marketplace of Aelia. To build this forum, Hadrian's engineers had to level a large area north of the defunct Antonia fortress, which had been dismantled along with the other fortifications of the Temple Mount in the wake of the First Jewish Revolt. This leveling project included constructing barrel-vaulted and arched structures over the Struthion Pool, a reservoir of about 150 by 50 feet that had

4. Dio Cassius, *Hist. rom.* 69.12.1–2. On the Second Jewish Revolt (or Bar Kochba Revolt), see Smallwood, *Jews Under Roman Rule*, 428–66; Yadin, *Bar-Kokhba*; deSilva, *Judea Under Greek and Roman Rule*, 168–76.

Figure 27.3. One half of the Struthion Pool, bisected and covered to provide the foundations of Hadrian's commercial forum.

been open to the air in the time of Jesus (see fig. 27.3).[5] Large flagstones were then laid over top of the vaults to create the broad space of this forum, and it is this second-century AD pavement that is presented as the *Lithostratos*. The Ecce Homo Arch was related to Hadrian's project as well. It is part of a monumental triple gate, originally freestanding, that marked the western entrance into this forum. The central archway is still visible over the street, while the north pedestrian archway is now enshrined behind the altar in the Chapel of the Sisters of Saint Anne (see figs. 27.4, 27.5).

Granted, then, that no portion of the Antonia fortress is available to modern visitors, there is also good reason to doubt that Jesus's hearing before Pilate took place at the Antonia at all—and thus it is unlikely that the Via Dolorosa represents anything like the actual path that Jesus took on that epoch-making day. The question is, Where would the Roman prefect make his residence and locate his administrative offices—that is, his praetorium (cf. Matt. 27:27; Mark 15:16; John 18:28, 33; 19:9)—while in Jerusalem? For most of the year, the prefects and procurators sent by Rome to administer the subprovince of

5. Josephus (*J.W.* 5.467) recollects that Titus had to build a ramp over the pool in order to press his siege of the Antonia in AD 70.

Pierotti, *Jerusalem Explored*, plate 13

Figure 27.4. A photo of the Ecce Homo Arch from 1864, when the arch was more fully exposed to view.

Figure 27.5. The triple-arched gates of Hadrian's forums in Aelia Capitolina resembled, on a smaller scale, the well-preserved and reconstructed triumphal arch of Hadrian erected in the diaspora city of Gerasa.

Judea resided in Herod the Great's promontory palace in Caesarea Maritima, which they took over for their own use after the removal of Archelaus, Herod's heir, in AD 6. They similarly inherited, as it were, the use of Herod the Great's sprawling palace complex on the far west side of Jerusalem. This palace was nestled in the defenses of Jerusalem's citadel, which Herod had improved by building three massive towers named after people who had been particularly important to him: Phasael, his brother; Hippicus, a friend about whom very little is known; and Mariamne, a wife that Herod passionately loved but would nevertheless eventually execute (see fig. 27.6). These towers, some of which incorporated earlier fortifications, varied in their functions. One served

Figure 27.6. A model of the Herodian Palace and the Citadel reflecting Herod's improvements alongside the surviving lower half of one of his towers (the upper part, constructed from smaller blocks, belongs to a later period). Archaeologists debate whether this remaining tower should be identified as Phasael or Hippicus. If Josephus's measurements are reliable, it must be Phasael, which Josephus claims was 40 cubits (60 or so feet) across each side. At about 70 feet across, the tower is a far better match for Phasael than the narrower Hippicus (25 cubits, or about 40 feet, on each side; Netzer, *Architecture of Herod*, 127).

Figure 27.7. One of the walls built to retain the fill that provided the level and firm foundation of Herod's palace. This Herodian wall was set on the remains of a First Temple–period wall. Similar Herodian retaining walls were found within the citadel and beneath the Armenian Garden.

as a water tower for the complex; the lower portions of the other two were built for defense purposes while the upper floors contained plush living quarters. This citadel once marked the northwestern corner of the Herodian city.

Herod built his palace south of these fortifications. This was a complex consisting of two symmetrical wings that Herod named the Caesareum and Agrippaeum in honor of Augustus and Marcus Agrippa, Augustus's right-hand man, both of whom Herod counted as his personal patrons (and to whose interests he showed unflagging commitment). Josephus's description of the complex, which included hundreds of chambers, vast colonnades, a broad courtyard, and even gardens, a grove, and canals flowing with water, suggests that it covered much of the present-day Armenian Quarter.[6] Excavations under the Ottoman prison building (the Kishle) immediately south of the citadel have revealed two thick, parallel walls from the Herodian period, once filled with debris, that served as part of the foundation for the platform on which Herod's expansive palace sat (see fig. 27.7).[7] Further evidence of this complex appears along the western Ottoman wall south of the Jaffa Gate and the citadel. Several courses of Herodian

6. Josephus, *J.W.* 1.402; 5.176–81; *Ant.* 15.318. See Bahat and Broshi, "Excavations in the Armenian Garden," and Gibson, "1961–67 Excavations," 88–92, for traces of the foundations of Herod's Palace in the Armenian Quarter in the immediate vicinity of the Citadel and Kishle. Levine (*Jerusalem*, 200) estimates a complex occupying a space of about 140 by 360 yards!

7. Re'em, "First and Second Temple Period Fortifications," 137–42.

Figure 27.8. The remains of the entrance to the city constructed in conjunction with Herod's palace complex.

ashlars, a stepped approach, and the remnants of a city gate from the Herodian period suggest an entrance constructed to give access to the area south of Herod's palace (see fig. 27.8). The foundations of Herodian-period towers were found to the north and the south of the gate, as would be appropriate for the increased defenses required around an entrance.[8]

After AD 6, a Roman cohort was stationed in the citadel just as another cohort was stationed in the Antonia. Josephus gives several indications of its regular use by the prefect (or, later, the procurator) in connection with problematic episodes in the history of the period. Pontius Pilate, for example, dedicated some number of gilded shields to Tiberius and had them hung "in the palace of Herod" (Philo, *Legat.* 299), a significant investment, suggesting that he himself regarded that as his chief headquarters in Jerusalem. He also gave the leaders and people of Jerusalem a hearing at his "tribunal in the open marketplace" (Josephus, *J.W.* 2.172), which is believed to have been located directly east of and adjacent to Herod's palace complex. And when the procurator Gessius Florus would later exercise certain notorious judicial measures on the eve of the First Jewish Revolt, he did so from a tribunal erected in a presumably spacious paved area at or adjacent to the palace (Josephus, *J.W.* 2.301–2; cf. John 19:13). While the Antonia, having been constructed by Herod as a palace-fortress, was not entirely spartan, it was still significantly outdone for lavishness and spaciousness by Herod's Western Palace. There

8. Broshi and Gibson, "Excavations," 151–53. Broshi and Gibson believe this to have been a private entrance ("Excavations," 153).

is thus every reason to believe that the former palace and citadel of Herod the Great was chosen by Judea's Roman prefects and procurators as their praetorium, or headquarters, while they were resident in the city and away from Caesarea Maritima, and that this is where Jesus's accusers would have brought him for the hearing before Pilate (thus "the palace, that is, the praetorium," Mark 15:16 AT).[9]

Figure 27.9. An opening in the Hasmonean First Wall (clearly visible on the left; also on the right in the background) tentatively identified as the Gennath Gate.

A more historically accurate Via Dolorosa, therefore, would begin just south of the citadel, outside the grounds of Herod's palace, proceed north to the early first-century city wall (approximately the line of David Street in the Old City), and turn east for a stretch until reaching the Gennath Gate, located about one-third of the way from the Jaffa Gate to the temple platform. This gate also stood in close proximity to the old Hasmonean Palace, which was where Herod Antipas likely resided during his visits to Jerusalem (cf. Luke 23:6–7).[10] The execution party would then have left the city by the Gennath

9. Benoit, "Archaeological Reconstruction," 87; Murphy-O'Connor, "Geography of Faith," 34; Gibson, *Final Days of Jesus*, 91; Magness, *Archaeology of the Holy Land*, 158. Gibson (*Final Days of Jesus*, 101–3) argues strenuously that the space between the Herodian outer gate and Hasmonean inner gate at this location was the place of the prefect's and, later, procurator's "tribunal," but since the space could not be freely accessed from within the city (except by passing through the palace complex!) but only from without, this seems highly inconvenient. There would be many other places in the vicinity of the palace/praetorium for a tribunal, particularly on the east and south sides, that *could* be accessed from within the city.

10. Thirty years later we find Agrippa II living in the Hasmonean Palace on his visits to Jerusalem since his great-grandfather Herod's palace was occupied by the Roman procurator and used as the praetorium (Josephus, *Ant.* 20.189–90). Josephus indicates, incidentally, that the Hasmonean Palace had a splendid view of the temple.

Gate and proceeded north to the rocky outcropping at the edge of the quarry called Golgotha (see fig. 27.9).[11]

The Church of the Holy Sepulchre

The last five of the fourteen stations of the cross—those specifically pertinent to Jesus's crucifixion and burial—are found inside the Church of the Holy Sepulchre, the alleged site of both events. There are good reasons to believe that the endpoint of the Via Dolorosa is essentially authentic.[12]

The degree to which Hadrian transformed the landscape of Jerusalem when he founded Aelia Capitolina again becomes relevant. In addition to the commercial forum in the northeast area of his new city, he made provision for an administrative forum in the western part a little more than halfway between the north gate and the legionary camp to the south. Once again, Hadrian's plans required significant engineering. An old quarry with a number of tombs had to be filled in and buried to create a level surface of adequate size for the project (Eusebius, *Vit. Const.* 3.26). The forum became home to a grand basilica and one or more temples. It is likely that the Capitolium—the temple dedicated to Jupiter, Juno, and Minerva—was located here at the administrative heart of the city.[13] A temple to a female goddess, most likely Tyche ("Fortune"), given her appearance on coins from the period, was also erected in this forum.[14] While very little remains of Hadrian's buildings, the podium of a large structure, thought to be Hadrian's basilica, was found

11. On the Gennath Gate, see Avigad, *Discovering Jerusalem*, 66, 69; Wightman, *Walls of Jerusalem*, 128–29. Murphy-O'Connor ("Argument for the Holy Sepulchre," 83) locates the gate "at the northern edge of the Jewish Quarter between Habad Street and Jewish Quarter Street."

12. See also McRay, *Archaeology and the New Testament*, 214–17; Murphy-O'Connor, "Argument for the Holy Sepulchre." Gordon's Golgotha and tomb, the popular Protestant alternative to the Church of the Holy Sepulchre, is unlikely to be an authentic site, not least because the tomb featured there appears to have been an Iron Age tomb (eighth to seventh centuries BC) in the midst of other Iron Age tombs (including some discovered under the Church of Saint Stephen on the grounds of the École Biblique, the property adjacent to the Garden Tomb). McRay, *Archaeology and the New Testament*, 207–8.

13. Murphy-O'Connor, "Location of the Capitol"; Murphy-O'Connor, "Argument for the Holy Sepulchre," 66. Dio Cassius (*Hist. rom.* 69.12.1) asserted that it was set rather atop the Temple Mount itself, a dramatic statement concerning the triumph of Rome's gods over Judea's own, but the evidence for this is considerably weaker. It is likely, however, that a shrine to the imperial cult was provocatively built on the Temple Mount, since the fourth-century AD Bordeaux Pilgrim wrote of seeing statues of Hadrian (or, more accurately, a statue of Hadrian and another of his successor, Antoninus Pius) there (Murphy-O'Connor, "Location of the Capitol," 410–11).

14. Weksler-Bdolah, *Aelia Capitolina*, 123–25. Eusebius claims that the deity was Venus/Aphrodite (*Vit. Const.* 3.25–26).

Figure 27.10. A Hadrianic podium for a large building, possibly the basilica or a temple, found in the vicinity of the Church of the Holy Sepulchre.

in the basement of the Russian Church of Saint Alexander Nevsky (see fig. 27.10). Similarly, a portion of one of the smaller, pedestrian gates of another freestanding triple-arched gate that served as the entrance to this forum has been re-erected in the same church (see fig. 27.11).

When Macarius, the bishop of Jerusalem, received permission from Constantine at the council of Nicaea in AD 325 to construct a church to mark the site of Jesus's crucifixion, burial, and resurrection, he knew precisely where to excavate to restore access on the basis of local memory. The fact that the site he selected would require Herculean efforts at excavation (and the associated costs) speaks to the credibility that Macarius assigned to this local knowledge, for it would involve destroying Hadrian's temple complex and much of his forum. After breaking up the pavement and buildings and removing vast quantities of fill, the excavators uncovered a quarry and a complex of loculi-style tombs.[15] Local tradition seemed to have been exonerated beyond

15. The quarry appears to have extended some distance to the south, as a great deal of fill and no occupation layers until the Byzantine period were found beneath the Lutheran Church of the Redeemer (Schein, "Second Wall," 23–24). Building the Second Wall immediately east of

Figure 27.11. The reconstruction (incorporating original pieces) of the pedestrian arch in the Hadrianic triple-gate entrance to the administrative forum.

dispute, even for a skeptic like Eusebius (*Vit. Const.* 3.28).[16] Memory of the site that Christians had venerated between AD 33 and 133 had not been erased by Hadrian's radical transformation of the space.[17]

The plans for the first version of the Church of the Holy Sepulchre, built by Constantine's order and with his material support,[18] called for the

the quarry would have made good strategic sense, as the quarry served as a kind of dry moat for part of the wall's northward run (25–26).

16. Murphy-O'Connor, "Argument for the Holy Sepulchre," 60. Portions of the quarry can be seen in the Chapel of Saint Vartan and the Latin Chapel of the Finding of the Cross.

17. Murphy-O'Connor, "Argument for the Holy Sepulchre," 72.

18. Eusebius (*Vit. Const.* 2.25; 3.30–32) gives credit to Constantine, not Helena, for the construction of this particular church (against Socrates Scholasticus, *Ch. Hist.* 1.17). Murphy-O'Connor, "Argument for the Holy Sepulchre," 58.

Figure 27.12. Loculi from the rear of a first-century tomb complex still to be seen within the Church of the Holy Sepulchre in close proximity to the Edicule.

Figure 27.13. A graffito in a room beneath the Chapel of Saint Vartan in the Church of the Holy Sepulchre, dating from before AD 335, when the church was completed, commemorating a pilgrimage to the site while Hadrian's western forum was still intact. It bears the image of a ship and the inscription, "Lord, we came." Broshi ("Evidence of Earliest Christian Pilgrimage," 43) thinks it unlikely to date from an earlier period due to the brazenness of making such a claim in an active, Roman religious site prior to Constantine's legalization of Christianity. Aside from the fact that the language is sufficiently ambiguous as to allow some room for plausible deniability concerning the identity of the *dominus*, the many narratives concerning martyrdoms during the third century suggest a certain culture of brazenness among early Christians in regard to claims of allegiance to Jesus.

construction of a central rotunda around a first-century arcosolium bench.[19] This involved the cutting away and, thus, the destruction of the lion's share of the continuous tomb complex. One can, however, still see a few of the original, now-orphaned first-century burial niches in the Syrian Orthodox chapel behind the celebrated shrine (see fig. 27.12). While one cannot be certain that Jesus's body was laid on the precise slab preserved within the Edicule, it *is* certain that such slabs and loculi were available here for his temporary burial. The presence of these graves also indicates that the quarry was outside (and, thus, to the west of) the city's walls during the first half of the first century. The site, near a principal gate of the city, was perfect for the executioners' purpose—deterrence of other would-be revolutionaries.

19. Murphy-O'Connor, *Holy Land*, 56.

28

EMMAUS

Luke recounts an episode in which the resurrected Jesus walks along with two disciples to the village of Emmaus, which Luke places 7 miles (60 stadia) away from Jerusalem. Although they do not recognize him as they walk together, their eyes are opened when Jesus breaks bread with them after their arrival at their destination (Luke 24:13–35). Emmaus has been identified, however, with four different sites over the centuries. The traditional site is Emmaus-Nicopolis, but this lies 14 miles west of Jerusalem as the crow flies (about a 22-mile walk following typical paths). The hold that this identification exerted in the third and fourth centuries is seen in the adaptation of Luke's report of the distance between Jerusalem and Emmaus from "sixty stadia" (24:13) to "one hundred sixty stadia" in the fourth-century Codex Sinaiticus and a few later manuscripts so as to reconcile Luke's text with the conviction that Emmaus-Nicopolis was intended. A building formerly alleged to be an early (second or third century AD) church at Emmaus-Nicopolis (Amwas) appears to have been, in fact, merely a Roman bathhouse, incorporated into a sixth-century church, so that the tradition linking this settlement to Luke's Emmaus is not as old as is sometimes claimed.[1]

A second and more likely (or, at least, less unlikely) candidate is the Palestinian village of Qoubeibeh, which sits the required sixty stadia from Jerusalem.[2] Excavations have uncovered evidence of Roman-period habitation, and there is some evidence for a Roman-era house becoming the focal point for a

1. Meistermann, *Deux Questions*, 1:190–92.

2. Meistermann, *Deux Questions*; McRay, *Archaeology and the New Testament*, 222.

sixth-century Christian church (though it is also possible that the house was merely overbuilt by the church). Nevertheless, the connection remains tenuous.

Archaeologists have become increasingly interested in the possibility that a long-standing, ancient settlement outside the modern suburb of Motza might have been the biblical Emmaus. Excavations have revealed significant settlement of the area in the late Iron Age leading up to the Babylonian conquest but only scant evidence of occupation in the Hasmonean period (pottery fragments, an installation that could be a lime kiln). Occupation of the site increases again in the early Roman period, attested by remains of elite residences (for example, portions of walls that had been plastered and frescoed) alongside evidence of Jewish occupation (for example, two fragments of large stone jars used for purificatory rites). Excavations uncovered more significant remains of the veteran colony Vespasian planted here following the First Jewish Revolt, which Josephus locates at a site that he calls "Emmaus" (*J.W.* 7.217).[3] One significant obstacle, however, is the fact that Tel Motza sits only the equivalent of 30 stadia from the Old City of Jerusalem, meaning that Luke's distance of 60 stadia would have to represent a measurement of a round trip, which would be highly irregular. We also encounter here a disappointing reality of much archaeological work: the complete reburial of excavations for the preservation of remains when there are no plans to develop them into a protected site open to visitors.

The case of Emmaus illustrates the limitations on archaeological work and what the fruits of such work can reveal to us of the world of Jesus and his earliest followers. Significant additional excavation would be required to determine which, if any, of these four sites is actually the "biblical" Emmaus, while significant obstacles stand in the way of such further excavation. For some sites, these obstacles include limited access to excavatable areas due to modern habitation of the site or to a lack of cooperation between archaeologists and local officials because of political tensions in the region; for others, obstacles include a reluctance to disturb choice remains from a later period (e.g., Byzantine remains) in order to gamble on what might or might not be discovered beneath (though trial soundings might be undertaken). Archaeology also depends greatly on chance—whether materials have been left in place to be discovered or recycled for the building projects of later centuries, whether existing structures permit or prevent exploration, and whether sufficient documentation from antiquity and the intervening centuries permits discovery and identification of any particular site. With each passing year,

3. Greenhut and De Groot, *Salvage Excavations*, 24, 227; Thiede, *Emmaus Mystery*, 161–64, 168–69; Bar-Nathan et al., "Moẓa in the Early Centuries CE," 351–52.

however, educational institutions and other organizations fund further digs with the result of uncovering more pieces of the puzzle that is "the world of Jesus." The task of considering how these pieces supplement the picture already formed or how they force a reconsideration of the picture is one that will be perpetually ongoing.

BIBLIOGRAPHY

Adler, Yonatan. "The Ritual Baths near the Temple Mount and Extra-Purification Before Entering the Temple: A Reply to Eyal Regev." *Israel Exploration Journal* 56 (2006): 209–15.

———. "Second Temple Period Ritual Baths Adjacent to Agricultural Installations." *Journal of Jewish Studies* 59 (2008): 62–72.

Albright, William F. *The Archaeology of Palestine*. Rev. ed. Baltimore: Penguin Books, 1954.

Alexandre, Yardenna. "Karm er-Ras near Kafr Kanna." In Fiensy and Strange, *Galilee*, 2:146–57.

———. *Mary's Well, Nazareth: The Late Hellenistic to the Ottoman Periods*. Jerusalem: Israel Antiquities Authority, 2012.

———. "The Settlement History of Nazareth in the Iron Age and Early Roman Period." *'Atiqot* 98 (2020): 25–92.

Alföldy, G. "Eine bauinschrift aus dem Colosseum." *Zeitschrift für Papyrologie und Epigraphik* 109 (1995): 195–226.

Amit, David. "Discoveries from the First and Second Temple Periods near the Mamilla Pool in Jerusalem." In Geva, *Ancient Jerusalem Revealed: Archaeological Discoveries, 1998–2018*, 145–52.

Amit, David, Joseph Patrich, and Yizhar Hirschfeld. *The Aqueducts of Israel*. Portsmouth, RI: Journal of Roman Archaeology, 2002.

Anderson, Robert T. "The Elusive Samaritan Temple." *Biblical Archaeologist* 54 (1991): 104–7.

Appold, Mark. "Bethsaida and a First-Century House Church?" In Arav and Freund, *Bethsaida*, 2:373–96.

Arav, Rami. "Bethsaida—A Response to Steven Notley." *Near Eastern Archaeology* 74, no. 2 (2011): 92–100.

———. "A Response to Notley's Reply." *Near Eastern Archaeology* 74, no. 2 (2011): 103–4.

———. "Searching for Bethsaida: The Case for Et-Tell." *Biblical Archaeology Review* 46, no. 2 (2020): 40–47.

Arav, Rami, and Richard A. Freund, eds. *Bethsaida: A City by the North Shore of the Sea of Galilee*. Vol. 1, *Bethsaida Excavations Project*. Kirksville, MO: Thomas Jefferson University Press, 1995.

———, eds. *Bethsaida: A City by the North Shore of the Sea of Galilee*. Vol. 2, *Bethsaida Excavations Project*. Kirksville, MO: Truman State University Press, 1999.

———, eds. *Bethsaida: A City by the North Shore of the Sea of Galilee*. Vol. 3, *Bethsaida Excavations Project Reports and Contextual Studies*. Kirksville, MO: Truman State University Press, 2004.

Arav, Rami, and Carl E. Savage. "Bethsaida." In Fiensy and Strange, *Galilee*, 2:258–79.

Aubin, Melissa M. "Jerash." In Meyers, *Oxford Encyclopedia of Archaeology*, 3:215–19.

Aviam, Mordechai. "The Decorated Synagogue Stone from the Synagogue at Migdal." *Novum Testamentum* 55 (2013): 205–20.

———. "First Century Jewish Galilee: An Archaeological Perspective." In *Religion and Society in Roman Palestine*, edited by Douglas R. Edwards, 7–27. New York: Routledge, 2004.

———. "Galilee: The Hellenistic to Byzantine Periods." In Stern, *New Encyclopedia*, 2:450–53.

———. "The Synagogue." In Bauckham, *Magdala of Galilee*, 127–33.

———. "The Transformation from *Galil Ha-Goyim* to Jewish Galilee." In Fiensy and Strange, *Galilee*, 2:9–21.

Aviam, Mordechai, and Richard Bauckham. "Further Thoughts on the Migdal Synagogue Stone." *Novum Testamentum* 57 (2015): 113–35.

———. "The Synagogue Stone." In Bauckham, *Magdala of Galilee*, 135–59.

Aviam, Mordechai, and Peter Richardson. "Josephus' Galilee in Archaeological Perspective." In Mason, *Life of Josephus*, 177–201.

Avigad, Nahman. *Discovering Jerusalem*. Jerusalem: Shikmona, 1980; Nashville: Nelson, 1983.

———. *The Herodian Quarter in Jerusalem: Wohl Archaeological Museum*. Jerusalem: Keter, 1989.

———. "Samaria (City)." In Stern, *New Encyclopedia*, 4:1300–1310.

Avni, Gideon, and Zvi Greenhut. *The Akeldama Tombs: Three Burial Caves in the Kidron Valley, Jerusalem*. Jerusalem: Israel Antiquities Authority, 1996.

Avni, Gideon, and G. D. Stiebel, eds. *Roman Jerusalem: A New Old City*. Portsmouth, RI: Journal of Roman Archaeology, 2017.

Bahat, Dan. "The Herodian Temple." In Horbury, Davies, and Sturdy, *Cambridge History of Judaism*, 3:38–58.

———. "Jerusalem Down Under: Tunneling Along Herod's Temple Mount Wall." *Biblical Archaeology Review* 21, no. 6 (1995): 30–47.

———. *The Jerusalem Western Wall Tunnel*. Jerusalem: Israel Exploration Society, 2013.

———. "Research in the Western Wall Tunnel." In Geva, *Ancient Jerusalem Revealed: Archaeological Discoveries, 1998–2018*, 94–103.

———. "The Western Wall Tunnels." In Geva, *Ancient Jerusalem Revealed*, 177–90.

Bahat, Dan, and Magen Broshi. "Excavations in the Armenian Garden." In Yadin, *Jerusalem Revealed*, 55–56.

Barag, Dan. "New Evidence on the Foreign Policy of John Hyrcanus I." *Israel Numismatic Journal* 12 (1992–93): 1–12.

———. "The 2000–2001 Exploration of the Tombs of Benei Ḥezir and Zechariah." *Israel Exploration Journal* 53 (2003): 78–110.

Bar-Nathan, Rachel, Irina Zilberbod, Annette Landes-Nagar, Leah Di Segni, and Ithamar Taxel. "Moẓa in the Early Centuries CE: On the Identification and Nature of Roman Colonia." In Khalaily et al., *The Mega Project at Motza (Moẓa): The Neolithic and Later Occupations up to the 20th Century*, 351–79. Jerusalem: Israel Antiquities Authority, 2020.

Bartlett, John R., ed. *Archaeology and Biblical Interpretation*. New York: Routledge, 1997.

Baruch, Yuval, and Ronnie Reich. "Second Temple Period Finds from the New Excavations in the Ophel, South of the Temple Mount." In Geva, *Ancient Jerusalem Revealed: Archaeological Discoveries, 1998–2018*, 84–93.

Batey, Richard A. *Jesus and the Forgotten City: New Light on Sepphoris and the Urban World of Jesus*. Grand Rapids: Baker, 1991.

Bauckham, Richard. "Magdala as We Now Know It." In Bauckham, *Magdala of Galilee*, 1–68.

———, ed. *Magdala of Galilee: A Jewish City in the Hellenistic and Roman Period*. Waco: Baylor University Press, 2018.

Beitzel, Barry J., ed. *Lexham Geographic Commentary on the Gospels*. Bellingham, WA: Lexham, 2016.

———. "The *Via Maris* in Literary and Cartographic Sources." *Biblical Archaeologist* 54 (1991): 64–75.

Ben-Ami, Doron, and Yana Tchekhanovets. "The Givati Excavation Project 2007–2015: From the Iron Age to the Early Islamic Period." In Geva, *Ancient Jerusalem Revealed: Archaeological Discoveries, 1998–2018*, 264–72.

———. "Has the Adiabene Royal Family 'Palace' Been Found in the City of David?" In Galor and Avni, *Unearthing Jerusalem*, 231–39.

Ben-Arieh, S. "The 'Third Wall' of Jerusalem." In Yadin, *Jerusalem Revealed*, 60–62.

Ben David, Chaim. "On the Number of Synagogues and Their Location in the Holy Land." In Bonnie, Hakola, and Tervahauta, *Synagogue in Ancient Palestine*, 175–94.

Benoit, Pierre. "The Archaeological Reconstruction of the Antonia Fortress." In Yadin, *Jerusalem Revealed*, 87–89.

Berlin, Andrea M. "Between Large Forces: Palestine in the Hellenistic Period." *Biblical Archaeologist* 60 (1997): 3–51.

———. "Herod, Augustus, and the Augusteum at the Paneion." In *Eretz-Israel: Archaeological, Historical and Geographical Studies*, edited by Zeev Weiss, 31:1–11. Jerusalem: Israel Exploration Society, 2015.

———. "Jewish Life Before the Revolt: The Archaeological Evidence." *Journal for the Study of Judaism* 36 (2005): 417–70.

———. "Romanization and Anti-Romanization in Pre-Revolt Galilee." In Berlin and Overman, *First Jewish Revolt*, 57–73.

Berlin, Andrea M., and Paul J. Kosmin, eds. *The Middle Maccabees: Archaeology, History, and the Rise of the Hasmonean Kingdom*. Atlanta: SBL Press, 2021.

Berlin, Andrea M., and J. Andrew Overman, eds. *The First Jewish Revolt: Archaeology, History, and Ideology*. New York: Routledge, 2002.

Betz, Otto. "The Essenes." In Horbury, Davies, and Sturdy, *Cambridge History of Judaism*, 3:444–70.

Bloedhorn, Hanswulf, and Gil Hüttenmeister. "The Synagogue." In Horbury, Davies, and Sturdy, *Cambridge History of Judaism*, 3:267–97.

Bolen, Todd. "Magnificent Stones and Wonderful Buildings of the Temple Complex." In Beitzel, *Lexham Geographic Commentary*, 462–75.

———. "Where Did the Possessed Pigs Drown? Challenging Tradition and Respecting Textual Evidence." In Beitzel, *Lexham Geographic Commentary*, 196–218.

Bonnie, Rick, Raimo Hakola, and Ulla Tervahauta, eds. *The Synagogue in Ancient Palestine: Current Issues and Emerging Trends*. Göttingen: Vandenhoeck & Ruprecht, 2021.

Bonnie, Rick, and Julian Richard. "Building D1 at Magdala Revisited in Light of Public Fountain Architecture in the Late Hellenistic East." *Israel Exploration Journal* 62 (2012): 71–88.

Bourgel, Jonathan. "The Destruction of the Samaritan Temple by John Hyrcanus: A Reconsideration." *Journal of Biblical Literature* 135 (2016): 505–23.

Broshi, Magen. "The Archaeology of Palestine." In Horbury, Davies, and Sturdy, *Cambridge History of Judaism*, 3:1–37.

———. "Evidence of Earliest Christian Pilgrimage to the Holy Land Comes to Light in Holy Sepulchre Church." *Biblical Archaeology Review* 3, no. 4 (1977): 42–44.

———. "Excavations in the House of Caiaphas, Mount Zion." In Yadin, *Jerusalem Revealed*, 57–60.

———. "The Serpent's Pool and Herod's Monument: A Reconsideration." *Maarav* 8 (1992): 213–22.

Broshi, Magen, and Shimon Gibson. "Excavations Along the Western and Southern Walls of the Old City of Jerusalem." In Geva, *Ancient Jerusalem Revealed*, 147–55.

Browning, Iain. *Jerash and the Decapolis*. London: Chatto & Windus, 1982.

Campbell, Edward F. "Shechem: Tell Balatah." In Stern, *New Encyclopedia*, 4:1345–54.

Chancey, Mark A. "The Ethnicities of Galileans." In Fiensy and Strange, *Galilee*, 1:112–28.

———. *Greco-Roman Culture and the Galilee of Jesus*. Cambridge: Cambridge University Press, 2005.

Cohen, Shaye J. D. *Josephus in Galilee and Rome: His Vita and Development as a Historian*. Leiden: Brill, 1979.

———. "Masada: Literary Tradition, Archaeological Remains, and the Credibility of Josephus." *Journal of Jewish Studies* 33 (1982): 385–405.

———. "The Temple and the Synagogue." In Horbury, Davies, and Sturdy, *Cambridge History of Judaism*, 3:298–325.

Corbier, Mireille. "City, Territory, and Taxation." In Rich and Wallace-Hadrill, *City and Country*, 211–40.

Cotton, Hannah M. "The Date of the Fall of Masada: The Evidence of the Masada Papyri." *Zeitschrift für Papyrologie und Epigraphik* 78 (1989): 157–62.

Crossan, John Dominic, and Jonathan L. Reed. *Excavating Jesus: Beneath the Stones, Behind the Texts*. San Francisco: HarperSanFrancisco, 2001.

Crowfoot, J. W., Kathleen M. Kenyon, and E. L. Sukenik. *The Buildings at Samaria*. London: Palestine Exploration Fund, 1942.

Cumont, Franz. "Un rescript impérial sur la violation de sépulture." *Revue Historique* 163 (1930): 241–66.

Cytryn-Silverman, Katia. "Tiberias, from Its Foundation to the End of the Early Islamic Period." In Fiensy and Strange, *Galilee*, 2:186–210.

Dar, Shimon. "Samaria (Archaeological Survey of the Region)." In *The Anchor Bible Dictionary*, edited by David N. Freedman, 5:926–31. New York: Doubleday, 1992.

Dark, Ken. *Archaeology of Jesus' Nazareth*. New York: Oxford University Press, 2023.

Davies, W. D., and Louis Finkelstein, eds. *The Cambridge History of Judaism*. Vol. 2, *The Hellenistic Age*. Cambridge: Cambridge University Press, 1989.

De Luca, Stefano. "Capernaum." In Master, *Oxford Encyclopedia of the Bible and Archaeology*, 1:168–80.

De Luca, Stefano, and Anna Lena. "Magdala/Taricheae." In Fiensy and Strange, *Galilee*, 2:280–342.

deSilva, David A. *Archaeology and the Ministry of Paul*. Grand Rapids: Baker Academic, 2025.

———. *Introducing the Apocrypha: Message, Content, and Significance*. 2nd ed. Grand Rapids: Baker Academic, 2018.

———. *An Introduction to the New Testament: Context, Methods, and Ministry Formation*. 2nd ed. Downers Grove, IL: IVP Academic, 2018.

———. *The Jewish Teachers of Jesus, James, and Jude: What Earliest Christianity Learned from the Apocrypha and Pseudepigrapha*. Oxford: Oxford University Press, 2012.

———. *Judea Under Greek and Roman Rule*. New York: Oxford University Press, 2024.

De Vaux, Roland, and Magen Broshi. "Qumran, Khirbet and 'Ein Feshka." In Stern, *New Encyclopedia*, 4:1235–41.

Dušek, Jan. "The Importance of the Wadi Daliyeh Manuscripts for the History of Samaria and the Samaritans." *Religions* 11, no. 2 (2020): 1–12. https://doi.org/10.3390/rel11020063.

Edwards, Douglas R., and C. Thomas McCollough, eds. *Archaeology and the Galilee: Texts and Contexts in the Greco-Roman and Byzantine Periods*. Atlanta: Scholars Press, 1997.

Elder, Linda Bennett. "The Woman Question and Female Ascetics among Essenes." *Biblical Archaeologist* 57 (1994): 220–34.

Epstein, Claire. "Hippos (Sussita)." In Stern, *New Encyclopedia*, 2:634–36.

Eshel, Hanan. *The Dead Sea Scrolls and the Hasmonean State*. Grand Rapids: Eerdmans, 2008.

Ewald, Marie Liguori, trans. *The Homilies of Saint Jerome*. Vol. 2, *Homilies 60–96*. Washington, DC: Catholic University of America Press, 1966.

Fatkin, Danielle Steen. "Invention of a Bathing Tradition in Hasmonean Palestine." *Journal for the Study of Judaism* 50 (2019): 155–77.

Feldman, L. H. "How Much Hellenism in Jewish Palestine?" *Hebrew Union College Annual* 57 (1986): 83–111.

Fiensy, David. "The Galilean House." In Fiensy and Strange, *Galilee*, 1:216–41.

———. "The Galilean Village." In Fiensy and Strange, *Galilee*, 1:177–207.

Fiensy, David A., and James Riley Strange, eds. *Galilee in the Late Second Temple and Mishnaic Periods*. Vol. 1, *Life, Culture, and Society*. Minneapolis: Fortress, 2014.

———, eds. *Galilee in the Late Second Temple and Mishnaic Periods*. Vol. 2, *The Archaeological Records from Cities, Towns, and Villages*. Minneapolis: Fortress, 2015.

Finkielsztejn, Gerald. "Contribution of the Rhodian Eponyms Amphora Stamps to the History of the Maccabees." In Berlin and Kosmin, *Middle Maccabees*, 193–214.

———. "Imported Amphoras." In Geva, *Jewish Quarter Excavations*, 3:168–83.

Fleming, James. "The Undiscovered Gate Beneath Jerusalem's Golden Gate." *Biblical Archaeology Review* 9, no. 1 (1983): 24–37.

Foerster, Gideon, and Ehud Netzer. "Herodium." In Stern, *New Encyclopedia*, 2:618–26.

Foreman, Benjamin A. "Jesus Heals a Blind Man near Bethsaida." In Beitzel, *Lexham Geographic Commentary*, 270–77.

Freyne, Sean. "Archaeology and the Historical Jesus." In Bartlett, *Archaeology and Biblical Interpretation*, 117–44.

———. *Galilee from Alexander the Great to Hadrian*. Edinburgh: T&T Clark, 1998.

Galor, Katharina, and Gideon Avni, eds. *Unearthing Jerusalem: 150 Years of Archaeological Research in the Holy Land*. Winona Lake, IN: Eisenbrauns, 2011.

Galor, Katharina, and Hanswulf Bloedhorn. *The Archaeology of Jerusalem: From the Origins to the Ottomans*. New Haven: Yale University Press, 2013.

Geva, Hillel, ed. *Ancient Jerusalem Revealed*. Jerusalem: Israel Exploration Society; Washington, DC: Biblical Archaeological Society, 1994.

———, ed. *Ancient Jerusalem Revealed: Archaeological Discoveries, 1998–2018*. Jerusalem: Israel Exploration Society, 2019.

———. "Excavations at the Citadel of Jerusalem, 1976–1980." In Geva, *Ancient Jerusalem Revealed*, 156–67.

———. "Jerusalem, the Roman Period." In Stern, *New Encyclopedia*, 2:758–67.

———, ed. *Jewish Quarter Excavations in the Old City of Jerusalem Conducted by Nahman Avigad, 1969–1982*. Vol. 3, *Area E and Other Studies*. Jerusalem: Israel Exploration Society, 2006.

———, ed. *Jewish Quarter Excavations in the Old City of Jerusalem Conducted by Nahman Avigad, 1969–1982*. Vol. 4, *The Burnt House of Area B and Other Studies*. Jerusalem: Israel Exploration Society, 2010.

———, ed. *Jewish Quarter Excavations in the Old City of Jerusalem Conducted by Nahman Avigad, 1969–1982*. Vol. 7, *Areas Q, H, O-2 and Other Studies*. Jerusalem: Israel Exploration Society, 2017.

———, ed. *Jewish Quarter Excavations in the Old City of Jerusalem Conducted by Nahman Avigad, 1969–1982*. Vol. 8, *Architecture and Stratigraphy: The Palatial Mansion (Areas F-2, P and P-2)*. Jerusalem: Israel Exploration Society, 2021.

———. "On the 'New City' of Second Temple Period Jerusalem: The Archaeological Evidence." In Galor and Avni, *Unearthing Jerusalem*, 299–312.

———. "Stone Artifacts." In Geva, *Jewish Quarter Excavations*, 3:218–38.

———. "Stratigraphy and Architecture." In Geva, *Jewish Quarter Excavations*, 3:1–78.

———. "Stratigraphy and Architecture." In Geva, *Jewish Quarter Excavations*, 4:1–90.

———. "Stratigraphy and Architecture of Areas F-2, P and P2, the Palatial Mansion." In Geva, *Jewish Quarter Excavations*, 8:1–197.

———. "Stratigraphy and Architecture of Area Q." In Geva, *Jewish Quarter Excavations*, 7:1–51.

Geva, Hillel, and Malka Hershkovitz. "Local Pottery of the Hellenistic and Early Roman Periods." In Geva, *Jewish Quarter Excavations*, 3:94–143.

Gibson, Shimon. "The Excavations at the Bethesda Pool in Jerusalem: Preliminary Report on a Project of Stratigraphic and Structural Analysis (1999–2009)." In *Sainte-Anne de Jérusalem: La Piscine Probatique de Jésus à Saladin*, edited by F. Bouwen, 17–44. Jerusalem: Sainte-Anne, 2011.

———. *The Final Days of Jesus: The Archaeological Evidence*. San Francisco: HarperOne, 2009.

———. "The 1961–67 Excavations in the Armenian Garden, Jerusalem." *Palestine Exploration Journal* 119 (1987): 81–96.

———. "The Pool of Bethesda in Jerusalem and Jewish Purification Practices of the Second Temple Period." *Proche-Orient-Chrétien* 55 (2005): 270–93.

Goodman, Martin. *Rome and Jerusalem: The Clash of Ancient Civilizations*. New York: Vintage, 2007.

Grabbe, Lester L. *A History of the Jews and Judaism in the Second Temple Period*. Vol. 2, *The Coming of the Greeks: The Early Hellenistic Period (335–175 BCE)*. London: T&T Clark, 2008.

———. *A History of the Jews and Judaism in the Second Temple Period*. Vol. 3, *The Maccabean Revolt, Hasmonean Rule, and Herod the Great (175–4 BCE)*. London: Bloomsbury T&T Clark, 2020.

———. *A History of the Jews and Judaism in the Second Temple Period*. Vol. 4, *The Jews Under the Shadow of Rome (4 BCE–150 CE)*. London: Bloomsbury T&T Clark, 2021.

———. *An Introduction to Second Temple Judaism: History and Religion of the Jews in the Time of Nehemiah, the Maccabees, Hillel, and Jesus*. London: Bloomsbury T&T Clark, 2010.

———. *Judaism from Cyrus to Hadrian*. Vol. 1, *The Persian and Greek Periods*, 1–312. Minneapolis: Fortress, 1992.

———. *Judaism from Cyrus to Hadrian*. Vol. 2, *The Roman Period*, 313–722. Minneapolis: Fortress, 1992.

———. "Synagogues in Pre-70 Palestine: A Re-assessment." *Journal of Theological Studies* 39 (1988): 401–10.

Greenhut, Zvi. "A Domestic Quarter from the Second Temple Period on the Lower Slopes of the Central Valley (Tyropoeon)." In Galor and Avni, *Unearthing Jerusalem*, 257–93.

———. "Burial Cave of the Caiaphas Family." *Biblical Archaeology Review* 18, no. 5 (1992): 28–36.

Greenhut, Zvi, and Alan De Groot. *Salvage Excavations at Tel Moẓa: The Bronze and Iron Age Settlements and Later Occupations*. Jerusalem: Israel Antiquities Authority, 2009.

Grossberg, Asher. "Behold the Temple." *Biblical Archaeology Review* 22, no. 3 (1996): 46–51, 66.

———. "*Miqwa'ot* (Ritual Baths) in the Palatial Mansion." In Geza, *Jewish Quarter Excavations*, 8:245–58.

———. "A Miqweh with Surrounding Staircase in Area Q—a Dual-Purpose Installation for Ritual Purification and Recreation." In Geva, *Jewish Quarter Excavations*, 7:52–67.

Gurevich, David. "The Water Pools and the Pilgrimage to Jerusalem in the Late Second Temple Period." *Palestine Exploration Quarterly* 149 (2017): 103–34.

Gutman, Shmaryahu. "Gamala." In Stern, *New Encyclopedia*, 2:459–62.

Hachlili, Rachel. "Herodian Jericho." In Meyers, *Oxford Encyclopedia of Archaeology*, 3:16–18.

———. "A Second Temple Period Jewish Necropolis in Jericho." *Biblical Archaeologist* 43, no. 4 (1980): 235–40.

Halpern-Zylberstein, Marie-Christine. "The Archaeology of Hellenistic Palestine." In Davies and Finkelstein, *Cambridge History of Judaism*, 2:1–34.

Hamel, Gildas. "Poverty and Charity." In Hezser, *Oxford Handbook of Jewish Daily Life*, 308–24.

Harrison, R. "Hellenization in Syria-Palestine: The Case of Judea in the Third Century BCE." *Biblical Archaeologist* 57 (1994): 98–110.

Hartal, Moshe, and Vassilios Tzaferis. "Banias." In Stern, *New Encyclopedia*, 5:1587–93.

Hengel, M. *The "Hellenization" of Judaea in the First Century after Christ*. Translated by John Bowden. Philadelphia: Trinity Press International, 1989.

———. "The Interpenetration of Judaism and Hellenism in the Pre-Maccabean Period." In Davies and Finkelstein, *Cambridge History of Judaism*, 2:167–228.

———. *Jews, Greeks, and Barbarians*. Philadelphia: Fortress, 1980.

———. *Judaism and Hellenism*. 2 vols. Philadelphia: Fortress, 1974.

Hezser, Catherine, ed. *The Oxford Handbook of Jewish Daily Life in Roman Palestine*. New York: Oxford University Press, 2010.

Hirschfeld, Yizhar. "Excavations at 'Ein Feshka, 2001: Final Report." *Israel Exploration Journal* 54, no. 1 (2004): 37–74.

———. *Excavations at Tiberias, 1989–1994*. IAA Reports 22. Jerusalem: Israel Antiquities Authority, 2004.

Holum, Kenneth G., Robert L. Hohlfelder, Robert J. Bull, and Avner Raban. *King Herod's Dream: Caesarea on the Sea*. New York: Norton, 1988.

Horbury, William. "Women in the Synagogue." In Horbury, Davies, and Sturdy, *Cambridge History of Judaism*, 3:358–401.

Horbury, W., W. D. Davies, and J. Sturdy, eds. *The Cambridge History of Judaism*. Vol. 3, *The Early Roman Period*. Cambridge: Cambridge University Press, 1999.

Horsley, Richard A. *Archaeology, History, and Society in Galilee: The Social Context of Jesus and the Rabbis*. Valley Forge: Trinity Press International, 1996.

———. "Social Movements in Galilee." In Fiensy and Strange, *Galilee*, 1:167–74.

Ilan, Tal. "Gender Issues and Daily Life." In Hezser, *Oxford Handbook of Jewish Daily Life*, 48–70.

Isser, Stanley. "The Samaritans and Their Sects." In Horbury, Davies, and Sturdy, *Cambridge History of Judaism*, 3:569–95.

Jensen, Morten Hørning. *Herod Antipas in Galilee*. Tübingen: Mohr Siebeck, 2006.

Kasher, Aryesh. *Jews, Idumeans, and Ancient Arabs*. Tübingen: Mohr Siebeck, 1988.

Kasher, Aryesh, Uriel Rappaport, and Gideon Fuks, eds. *Greece and Rome in Eretz Israel*. Jerusalem: Israel Exploration Society, 1990.

Keddie, G. Anthony. "*Iudaea Capta* vs. Mother Zion: The Flavian Discourse on Judaeans and Its Delegitimation in 4 Ezra." *Journal for the Study of Judaism* 49 (2018): 498–550.

Killebrew, Anne. "Village and Countryside." In Hezser, *Oxford Handbook of Jewish Daily Life*, 189–209.

Kloner, Amos, and Boaz Zissu. "Jerusalem: The Necropolis of the Second Temple Period." In Stern, *New Encyclopedia*, 5:1822–25.

Kuhn, Heinz-Wolfgang. "An Introduction to the Excavations of Bethsaida (et-Tell) from a New Testament Perspective." In Arav and Freund, *Bethsaida*, 2:283–94.

Landau, Y. "A Greek Inscription Found near Hefzibah, Israel." *Israel Exploration Journal* 16 (1966): 54–70.

Lapp, Paul W., and Nancy L. Lapp, eds. *Discoveries in the Wadi ed-Daliyeh*. Cambridge: ASOR, 1974.

Leibner, Uzi. "Galilee in the Second Century BCE." In Berlin and Kosmin, *Middle Maccabees*, 123–44.

———. *Settlement and History in Hellenistic, Roman, and Byzantine Galilee: An Archaeological Survey of Eastern Galilee*. Tübingen: Mohr Siebeck, 2009.

Lena, Anna. "The Harbor." In Bauckham, *Magdala of Galilee*, 69–88.

Levine, L. I. *The Ancient Synagogue: The First Thousand Years*. New Haven: Yale University Press, 2005.

———. *Jerusalem: Portrait of the City in the Second Temple Period (538 BCE–70 CE)*. Philadelphia: Jewish Publication Society, 2002.

———. *Judaism and Hellenism in Antiquity: Conflict or Confluence?* Peabody, MA: Hendrickson, 1998.

Loffreda, Stanislao. *Recovering Capharnaum*. Jerusalem: Edizioni Custodia Terra Santa, 1993.

Loffreda, Stanislao, and Vassilios Tzaferis. "Capernaum." In Stern, *New Encyclopedia*, 1:291–96.

Luca, F. Massimo. "Kafr Kanna (The Franciscan Church)." In Fiensy and Strange, *Galilee*, 2:158–66.

Magen, Yitzhak. "The Dating of the First Phase of the Samaritan Temple on Mount Gerizim." In *Judah and the Judeans in the Fourth Century BCE*, edited by Oded Lipschitz, Gary Knoppers, and Rainer Albertz, 157–211. Winona Lake, IN: Eisenbrauns, 2009.

———. "Gerizim, Mount." In Stern, *New Encyclopedia*, 2:484–92.

———. "Gerizim, Mount." In Stern, *New Encyclopedia*, 5:1742–48.

———. *Mount Gerizim Excavations*. Vol. 2, *A Temple City*. Jerusalem: Israel Antiquities Authority, 2008.

Magness, Jodi. "Aelia Capitolina: A Review of Some Current Debates about Hadrianic Jerusalem." In Galor and Avni, *Unearthing Jerusalem*, 313–24.

———. *The Archaeology of Qumran and the Dead Sea Scrolls*. Grand Rapids: Eerdmans, 2002.

———. *The Archaeology of the Holy Land: From the Destruction of Solomon's Temple to the Muslim Conquest*. Cambridge: Cambridge University Press, 2012.

———. "The Arch of Titus at Rome and the Fate of the God of Israel." *Journal of Jewish Studies* 59 (2008): 201–17.

———. *Masada: From Jewish Revolt to Modern Myth*. Princeton: Princeton University Press, 2019.

Ma'oz, Zvi Uri. "Banias." In Stern, *New Encyclopedia*, 1:136–43.

———. "Banias, Temple of Pan." *Excavations and Surveys in Israel* 10 (1990): 59–61.

Mason, Steven, ed. *A History of the Jewish War: A.D. 66–74*. Cambridge: Cambridge University Press, 2016

———, ed. *Life of Josephus: Translation and Commentary*. Flavius Josephus: Translation and Commentary 9. Leiden: Brill, 2001.

Master, Daniel M., ed. *The Oxford Encyclopedia of the Bible and Archaeology*. 2 vols. New York: Oxford University Press, 2013.

Mattila, Sharon Lea. "Capernaum, Village of Nahum, from Hellenistic to Byzantine Time." In Fiensy and Strange, *Galilee*, 2:217–57.

Mazar, Amihai. "Beth-Shean: Tel Beth-Shean." In Stern, *New Encyclopedia*, 5:1616–22.

Mazar, Amihai, and Nehemiah Tzori. "Beth-Shean." In Stern, *New Encyclopedia*, 1:214–35.

Mazar, Benjamin. *The Mountain of the Lord*. Garden City, NY: Doubleday, 1975.

Mazar, Eilat. *The Complete Guide to the Temple Mount Excavations*. Jerusalem: Shoham Academic Research and Publications, 2002.

Mazar, Eilat, Ronny Reich, Eli Shukron, et al. "Jerusalem: Excavations Within the Ancient City." In Stern, *New Encyclopedia*, 5:1801–22.

Mazor, Gabi. "Beth-Shean: The Hellenistic to Early Islamic Periods: The Israel Antiquities Authority Excavations." In Stern, *New Encyclopedia*, 5:1623–36.

McCane, Byron R. "Simply Irresistible: Augustus, Herod, and the Empire." *Journal of Biblical Literature* 127 (2008): 725–35.

McCullough, C. Thomas. "Khirbet Qana." In Fiensy and Strange, *Galilee*, 2:127–45.

McKinny, Chris. "Southern Temple Mount Excavations." In Beitzel, *Lexham Geographic Commentary*, 442–61.

McRay, John. *Archaeology and the New Testament*. Grand Rapids: Baker, 1991.

Meistermann, Barnabé. *Deux Questions d'archéologie palestinienne*. Vol. 1, *L'église d'Amwâs, l'Emmaüs-Nicopolis*. Vol. 2, *L'église de Qoubeibeh, l'Emmaüs de S. Luc*. Jerusalem: Franciscan Fathers, 1902.

Metzger, Bruce M. *New Testament Studies (Philological, Versional, and Patristic)*. Leiden: Brill, 1980.

Meyers, Eric, ed. *The Oxford Encyclopedia of Archaeology in the Near East*. Vol. 3. Oxford: Oxford University Press, 1997.

———. "Recent Archaeology in Palestine: Achievements and Future Goals." In Horbury, Davies, and Sturdy, *Cambridge History of Judaism*, 3:59–74.

Meyers, Eric, Carol L. Meyers, and Benjamin D. Gordon. "Sepphoris. B. Residential Area of the Western Summit." In Fiensy and Strange, *Galilee*, 2:39–52.

Meyers, Eric, Ehud Netzer, and Carol L. Meyers. "Sepphoris: 'Ornament of All Galilee.'" *Biblical Archaeologist* 49 (1986): 4–19.

Miller, Stuart S. "Sepphoris, the Well Remembered City." *Biblical Archaeologist* 55 (1992): 74–83.

Murphy-O'Connor, Jerome. "The Argument for the Holy Sepulchre." *Revue Biblique* 117 (2010): 55–91.

———. "The Geography of Faith: Tracing the Via Dolorosa." *Bible Review* 12, no. 6 (1996): 32–41, 52–53.

———. *The Holy Land: An Oxford Archaeological Guide*. 5th ed. New York: Oxford University Press, 2008.

———. "The Location of the Capitol in Aelia Capitolina." *Revue Biblique* 101 (1994): 407–15.

———. "Where Was the Antonia Fortress?" *Revue Biblique* 111 (2004): 78–89.

Netzer, Ehud. *The Architecture of Herod, the Great Builder*. Grand Rapids: Baker Academic, 2008.

———. *Hasmonean and Herodian Palaces at Jericho: Final Reports of the 1973–1987 Excavations*. Vol. 1, *Stratigraphy and Architecture*. Jerusalem: Israel Exploration Society, 2001.

———. *Hasmonean and Herodian Palaces at Jericho: Final Reports of the 1973–1987 Excavations*. Vol. 2, *Stratigraphy and Architecture*. Jerusalem: Israel Exploration Society, 2004.

———. "Herodium." In Stern, *New Encyclopedia*, 5:1778–80.

———. "Jericho." In Stern, *New Encyclopedia*, 5:1798–1800.

———. *The Palaces of the Hasmoneans and Herod the Great*. Reprinted and expanded edition. Jerusalem: Israel Exploration Society, 2018.

———. "Tulul Abu El-'Alayiq." In Stern, *New Encyclopedia*, 2:682–92.

Notley, R. Steven, and Mordechai Aviam. "Et-Tell Is *Not* Bethsaida." *Near Eastern Archaeology* 70, no. 4 (2007): 220–30.

———. "Reply to Arav." *Near Eastern Archaeology* 74, no. 3 (2011): 101–3.

———. "Searching for Bethsaida: The Case for El-Araj." *Biblical Archaeology Review* 46, no. 2 (2020): 28–39.

Oakman, Douglas. "Was the Galilean Economy Oppressive or Prosperous?" In Fiensy and Strange, *Galilee*, 1:346–56.

Onn, Alexander, and Shlomit Weksler-Bdolah. "Wilson's Arch and the Giant Viaduct West of the Temple Mount during the Second Temple and Late Roman Periods in Light of Recent Excavation." In Geva, *Ancient Jerusalem Revealed: Archaeological Discoveries, 1998–2018*, 104–22.

Onn, Alexander, Shlomit Weksler-Bdolah, and Joseph Patich. "A Herodian Triclinium with Fountain on the Road Ascending to the Temple Mount from the West." In Geva, *Ancient Jerusalem Revealed: Archaeological Discoveries, 1998–2018*, 123–35.

Overman, J. Andrew. "Omrit, Horvat." In Stern, *New Encyclopedia*, 5:1987–89.

Overman, J. Andrew, Jack Olive, and Michael Nelson. "Discovering Herod's Shrine to Augustus." *Biblical Archaeology Review* 29, no. 2 (2003): 40–49, 67–68.

Parrot, André. *Samaria: The Capital of the Kingdom of Israel*. New York: Philosophical Library, 1958.

Phillips, Elaine A. "Healing by Living Water at the Pool of Siloam." In Beitzel, *Lexham Geographic Commentary*, 365–73.

———. "Peter's Declaration at Caesarea Philippi." In Beitzel, *Lexham Geographic Commentary*, 286–97.

Pierotti, Ermete. *Jerusalem Explored, Being a Description of the Ancient and Modern City*. Translated by T. G. Bonney. London: Bell & Daldy, 1864.

Purvis, James D. "The Samaritans." In Davies and Finkelstein, *Cambridge History of Judaism*, 2:591–613.

Rajak, Tessa. "The Jews Under Hasmonean Rule." In *The Cambridge Ancient History*. Vol. 9, *The Last Age of the Roman Republic, 146–43 B.C.*, edited by J. A. Crook, Andrew Lincott, and Elizabeth Rawson, 274–309. 2nd ed. Cambridge: Cambridge University Press, 1994.

———. *Josephus: The Historian and His Society*. London: Duckworth, 2002.

Rapunchuk, Mark. "The Galilee and Jesus in Recent Research." *Currents in Biblical Research* 2 (2004): 197–222.

Reed, Jonathan L. *Archaeology and the Galilean Jesus: A Re-examination of the Evidence*. Harrisburg, PA: Trinity Press International, 2000.

Re'em, Amit. "First and Second Temple Period Fortifications and Herod's Palace in the Jerusalem Kishle Compound." In Geva, *Ancient Jerusalem Revealed: Archaeological Discoveries, 1998–2018*, 136–45.

Regev, Eyal. "The Hellenization of the Hasmoneans Revisited: The Archaeological Evidence." *Advances in Anthropology* 7 (2017): 175–96.

Reich, Ronny. "Caiaphas Name Inscribed on Bone Boxes." *Biblical Archaeology Review* 18, no. 5 (1992): 38–44.

Reich, Ronny, and Eli Shukron. "The Pool of Siloam in Jerusalem of the Late Second Temple Period and Its Surroundings." In Galor and Avni, *Unearthing Jerusalem*, 241–56.

———. "The Second Temple Period Siloam Pool." In Geva, *Ancient Jerusalem Revealed: Archaeological Discoveries, 1998–2018*, 73–83.

Reich, Ronny, and Marcela Zapata-Meza. "The Domestic Miqva'ot." In Bauckham, *Magdala of Galilee*, 109–25.

———. "A Preliminary Report on the *Miqwa'ot* of Migdal." *Israel Exploration Journal* 64 (2014): 63–71.

Reif, Stefan C. "The Early Liturgy of the Synagogue." In Horbury, Davies, and Sturdy, *Cambridge History of Judaism*, 3:326–57.

Rich, John, and Andrew Wallace-Hadrill, eds. *City and Country in the Ancient World*. London: Routledge, 1992.

Richardson, Peter. *Herod: King of the Jews and Friend of the Romans*. Columbia: University of South Carolina Press, 1996.

Ritmeyer, Leen. *The Quest: Revealing the Temple Mount in Jerusalem*. Jerusalem: Carta, 2006.

Ritmeyer, Leen, and Kathleen Ritmeyer. "Akeldama: Potter's Field or High Priest's Tomb?" *Biblical Archaeology Review* 20 (1994): 23–35, 76, 78.

———. *Secrets of Jerusalem's Temple Mount*. Washington, DC: Biblical Archaeology Society, 1998.

Rocca, Samuel. *The Forts of Judaea 168 BC–AD 73*. Oxford: Osprey, 2008.

———. *Herod's Judaea: A Mediterranean State in the Classical World*. Tübingen: Mohr Siebeck, 2008.

Rosenthal-Hegenbottom, Renate. "Late Hellenistic and Early Roman Lamps and Fine Ware." In Geva, *Jewish Quarter Excavations*, 3:144–67.

Rousseau, John J., and Rami Arav. *Jesus and His World: An Archaeological and Cultural Dictionary*. Minneapolis: Fortress, 1995.

Sacchi, Paolo. *The History of the Second Temple Period*. Sheffield: Sheffield Academic, 2000.

Savage, Carl E. *Biblical Bethsaida: An Archaeological Study of the First Century*. Plymouth, UK: Lexington Books, 2011.

Schäfer, Peter. *The History of the Jews in the Greco-Roman World*. Rev. ed. London: Routledge, 2003.

Schein, Bruce E. "The Second Wall of Jerusalem." *Biblical Archaeologist* 44 (1981): 21–26.

Schiffman, Lawrence H. "Pharisaic and Sadducean Halakhah in Light of the Dead Sea Scrolls: The Case of Ṭevul Yom." *Dead Sea Discoveries* 1 (1994): 287–99.

———. *Qumran and Jerusalem: Studies in the Dead Sea Scrolls and the History of Judaism*. Grand Rapids: Eerdmans, 2010.

Schröter, Jens, and Christine Jacobi, eds. *The Jesus Handbook*. Grand Rapids: Eerdmans, 2022.

Schwartz, Daniel R. *Agrippa I: The Last King of Judea*. Tübingen: Mohr, 1990.

Schwartz, Joshua. "Bar Qatros and the Priestly Families." In Geva, *Jewish Quarter Excavations*, 4:309–19.

Segal, Arthur. "Hippos (Sussita)." In Stern, *New Encyclopedia*, 5:1782–87.

Segal, Arthur, and Michael Eisenberg. "The Spade Hits Sussita." *Biblical Archaeology Review* 32, no. 3 (2006): 40, 42–51, 78.

Segal, Peretz. "The Penalty of the Warning Inscription from the Temple of Jerusalem." *Israel Exploration Journal* 39 (1989): 79–84.

Sharon, Nadav. *Judea Under Roman Domination: The First Generation of Statelessness and Its Legacy*. Atlanta: Society of Biblical Literature, 2017.

Shroder, Jack F., Michael Bishop, Kevin J. Cornwell, and Moshe Inbar. "Catastrophic Geomorphic Processes and Bethsaida Archaeology, Israel." In Arav and Freund, *Bethsaida*, 2:115–73.

Shroder, Jack F., and Moshe Inbar. "Geologic and Geographic Background to the Bethsaida Excavations." In Arav and Freund, *Bethsaida*, 1:65–98.

Sivan, Renée, and Giora Solar. "Excavations in the Jerusalem Citadel, 1980–88." In Geva, *Ancient Jerusalem Revealed*, 168–76.

Smallwood, E. Mary. *The Jews Under Roman Rule: From Pompey to Diocletian*. Leiden: Brill, 1981.

Sporty, Lawrence D. "The Location of the Holy House of Herod's Temple: Evidence from the Pre-Destruction Period." *Biblical Archaeologist* 53 (1990): 194–204.

———. "The Location of the Holy House of Herod's Temple: Evidence from the Pre-Destruction Period." *Biblical Archaeologist* 54 (1991): 28–35.

Steinmeyer, Nathan. "Archaeologists Discover New First-Century Synagogue in Magdala, Israel." Biblical Archaeology Society, December 15, 2021. https://www.biblicalarchaeology.org/daily/new-first-century-synagogue/.

Stern, E., ed. *New Encyclopedia of Archaeological Excavations in the Holy Land.* 5 vols. Jerusalem: Israel Exploration Society/Carta, 1993–2008.

Strange, James. "Archaeology and the Pharisees." In *In Quest of the Historical Pharisees*, edited by Jacob Neusner and Bruce Chilton, 237–51. Waco: Baylor University Press, 2007.

———. "Nazareth." In Fiensy and Strange, *Galilee*, 2:167–80.

———. "Sepphoris. A. The Jewel of the Galilee." In Fiensy and Strange, *Galilee*, 2:22–38.

———. "The Sepphoris Aqueducts." In Fiensy and Strange, *Galilee*, 2:76–87.

Strange, James R., and Hershel Shanks. "Has the House Where Jesus Stayed in Capernaum Been Found?" *Biblical Archaeology Review* 8, no. 6 (1982): 26–37.

Strickert, Fred. *Philip's City: From Bethsaida to Julias.* Collegeville, MN: Liturgical Press, 2011.

———. "The Renaming of Bethsaida in Honor of Livia, a.k.a. Julia, the Daughter of Caesar, in *Jewish Antiquities* 18.27–28." In Arav and Freund, *Bethsaida*, 3:93–118.

Syon, Danny. "Gamla: City of Refuge." In Berlin and Overman, *First Jewish Revolt*, 134–53.

———. "Gamla: Portrait of a Rebellion." *Biblical Archaeology Review* 18, no. 1 (1992): 20–37.

———. "The Hasmonean Settlement in Galilee: A Numismatic Perspective." In Berlin and Kosmin, *Middle Maccabees*, 177–92.

Syon, Danny, and Zvi Yavor. "Gamala." In Stern, *New Encyclopedia*, 5:1739–42.

———. *Gamla II: The Architecture; The Shmarya Gutmann Excavations, 1976–1989.* Jerusalem: Israel Antiquities Authority, 2010.

Szanton, Nahshon. "Ritual Purification and Bathing: The Location and Function of Siloam Pool and Solomon's Pool in Second Temple Period Jerusalem." *'Atiqot* 113 (2023): 29–44.

Theissen, Gerd, and Annette Merz. *The Historical Jesus: A Comprehensive Guide.* Minneapolis: Fortress, 1998.

Thiede, Carsten Peter. "Die Wiederentdeckung vom Emmaus bei Jerusalem." *Zeitschrift für antikes Christentums* 8 (2004): 593–99.

———. *The Emmaus Mystery: Discovering Evidence for the Risen Christ.* New York: Continuum, 2005.

Tsalampouni, Ekaterini. "The Nazareth Inscription: A Controversial Piece of Palestinian Epigraphy (1930–1999)." *Tekmeria* 6 (2001): 70–122.

Tzaferis, Vassilios. "The Site: Stratigraphy and Architectural Remains." In Tzaferis et al., *Paneas I*, 15–53.

Tzaferis, Vassilios, and Bellarmino Bagatti. "Nazareth." In Stern, *New Encyclopedia*, 3:1103–6.

Tzaferis, Vassilios, Shoshanna Israeli, Miriam Avissar, Yael Gorin-Rosen, Ruth E. Jackson-Tal, and John F. Wilson, eds. *Paneas I: The Roman to the Early Islamic Periods; Excavations in Area A, B, E, F, and H.* Jerusalem: Israel Antiquities Authority, 2008.

Vermès, Geza. *The Complete Dead Sea Scrolls in English.* Rev. ed. New York: Penguin Books, 2011.

Vincent, L. -H., and A. M. Stève. *Jérusalem de l'Ancien Testament.* Vol. 1, *Planches.* Paris: Gabalda, 1954.

Von Wahlde, Urban C. "The Puzzling Pool of Bethesda." *Biblical Archaeology Review* 37, no. 5 (2011): 40–47, 65.

Vörös, Győző. *Machaerus I: History, Archaeology and Architecture of the Fortified Herodian Royal Palace and City.* Milan: Edizioni Terra Santa, 2013.

———. *Mount Machaerus: An Introduction to the Historical, Archaeological, and Pilgrim Site Overlooking the Dead Sea in the Kingdom of Jordan.* Amman, Jordan: The American Center of Research, 2024.

Wachsmann, S., "The Galilee Boat, 2,000 Years-Old Hull Recovered Intact." *Biblical Archaeology Review* 14, no. 5 (1988): 18–33.

Weber, Thomas. *Umm Qais: Gadara of the Decapolis.* Amman, Jordan: Al Kutba Publishers and German Protestant Institute for Archaeology, 1990.

Weiss, Zeev. "Sepphoris." In Stern, *New Encyclopedia*, 4:1324–28.

———. "Sepphoris." In Stern, *New Encyclopedia*, 5:2029–34.

———. "Sepphoris. C. From Galilean Town to Roman City, 100 BCE–200 CE." In Fiensy and Strange, *Galilee*, 2:53–75.

Weksler-Bdolah, Shlomit. *Aelia Capitolina—Jerusalem in the Roman Period.* Leiden: Brill, 2020.

Wightman, Gregory. *The Walls of Jerusalem: From the Canaanites to the Mamluks.* Sydney: Meditarch, 1993.

Williams, Margaret. "The Contribution of Jewish Inscriptions to the Study of Judaism." In Horbury, Davies, and Sturdy, *Cambridge History of Judaism*, 3:75–93.

Wilson, John F. *Caesarea Philippi: Banias, the Lost City of Pan.* New York: Tauris, 2004.

Wilson, John F., and Vassilios Tzaferis. "Banias Dig Reveals King's Palace." *Biblical Archaeology Review* 24, no. 1 (1998): 54–61, 85.

Wright, Paul H. "The Size and Makeup of Nazareth at the Time of Jesus." In Beitzel, *Lexham Geographic Commentary*, 30–41.

Yadin, Yigael. *Bar-Kokhba: The Rediscovery of the Legendary Hero of the Second Jewish Revolt Against Rome.* New York: Random House, 1971.

———, ed. *Jerusalem Revealed: Archaeology in the Holy City 1968–1974.* New Haven: Yale University Press; London: Israel Exploration Society, 1976.

———. *Masada: Herod's Fortress and the Zealots' Last Stand*. New York: Random House, 1966.

Yadin, Yigael, and Ehud Netzer. "Masada." In Stern, *New Encyclopedia*, 3:973–85.

Yavor, Zvi. "The Architecture and Stratigraphy of the Eastern and Western Quarters." In Syon and Yavor, *Gamla II*, 13–112.

Zapata-Meza, Marcela. "The Domestic and Mercantile Areas." In Bauckham, *Magdala of Galilee*, 89–108.

Zapata-Meza, Marcela, Andrea Garza Diaz Barriga, and Rosaura Sanz-Rincón. "The Magdala Archaeological Project (2010–2012): A Preliminary Report of the Excavations at Migdal." *'Atiqot* 90 (2018): 83–125.

NAME INDEX

SCRIPTURE AND ANCIENT WRITINGS INDEX

SELECT SUBJECT INDEX